Malcolm Tent Takes a Holiday

Stan Griffin

This book is a work of fiction. Names, characters, places, and incidents are products of the author's imagination or are used fictitiously. Any resemblance to actual events or locales or persons, living or dead, is entirely coincidental.

Copyright © 2008 by Stan Griffin
All rights reserved, including the right to reproduce this book or any portions thereof in any form whatsoever.

Cover art by Stan Griffin
Photographs © Stan Griffin

ISBN 978-0-6152-0349-2

This story is dedicated to anyone who's ever chuckled at one of my letters or e-mails.

Thank you. Appreciate the smile.

I

Somewhere in Nowheresville, the morning was gradually transforming from a state of non-existence to one of undeniable presence, and eventually progressing to just after breakfast time. Malcolm Tent sat in his small blue one bedroom apartment wasting electricity on his portable television and stolen stereo system. On the phone was the only woman he knew who'd even give him the time of day. Young Malcolm wasn't big on optimism or warmth or energy or random acts of salutations. His life was one of pure chance and danger. Smiles and "Howdy doos" were for the idiots, the ninnies, and pinheads of the world. If he was to wink at a stranger or say "Hello" to a neighbor that didn't say "Hello" first, he'd be perceived as weak and vulnerable. People would take advantage of his natural friendliness. That wasn't his style. He lived on the edge, always on the lookout for trouble.

99.9% of his soul was dedicated to blood and guts, greasy carburetors, and spitting on the sidewalk. But this morning was different. As it happened, Malcolm was expressing an unusual level of vulnerability and sensitivity over the telephone to his future girlfriend. He trusted her with his emotions, his insecurities, and his unpredictable fits of romance. She was always there for him and he needed her then like never before. He listened as she provided concrete insights to the sensibilities of modern society and comforted him with her experiential world views.

Softly, seductively, she explained, "At the tone the time will be 7, 47, and 50 seconds... MEEEP."

"So what're you doing later?" Malcolm inquired, boldly.

"At the tone the time will be 7, 48, exactly...MEEEP," she joked.

"You like Chinese food?" he asked as he scratched his unshaven chin. He was like that. Out of the blue, he'd reach up to his face and scratch his chin. Macho meant nothing if it didn't mean Malcolm.

Nervously, she told him, "At the tone the time will be 7, 48, and 10 seconds... MEEEP."

"I realize you can't talk now. I mean, I know you're at work and all, but maybe..." she was putty in his hands. His subtle indecision gave her a false sense of dominance. It wouldn't last. As soon as he had her undivided attention he'd unleash his animalistic side and make her beg for his touch. He had the sex appeal of lip balm and he knew how to apply it.

"At the tone the time will be 7, 48, and 20 seconds... MEEEP," she continued with a subtle confidence that only Malcolm could detect.

"Maybe after you get off work we can get together. Maybe?" he asked as he moved in for the kill.

Her voice quivered, "At the tone the time will be 7, 48, and 30 seconds... MEEEP."

"I really admire what you do. You're different. Most women don't have the time to chat, but you... You're the greatest and I'm so..." He was about to give her that classic mixture of obscure flattery and self deprecation that gets a girl to feel good about herself in a strange new way, then feel sorry enough for the lame dude on the other end to say, "Don't say those mean things about yourself after saying all those nice things about me, because if you're no good then those weird compliments don't mean anything and just once I'd like to hear an honest compliment, even if it's weird, so don't put yourself down. You idiot." But! Before he could finish the sentence, his conversation was interrupted with impeccable timing by an obnoxious clicking sound. "Click click."

"At the tone the time will be 7, 48, and 40 seconds... MEEEP," she said, pretending not to notice the interruption.

He was all messed up. His timing was off. He had to let the moment slip through his fingers. "Hey, listen, I gotta go now. There's someone on the other line, but I do want to see you sometime. I'll call you later. Bye! Luv yuh," he said in a gooey kind of insincere tone as he feverishly pressed the receiver to activate the call waiting service and accidentally dropped the phone.

"Hello?" he said as he picked up the fire engine red telephone from his green shag carpet.

"Yo, Malc, what're you doin' over there?" asked Armadillo Cleef.

"Hey man, I just got off the phone with Veronica Marvel," replied Malcolm. "Damn! I was about to get a date with her!"

"Rookie hooker?" asked the callous Armadillo.

"No, just a friend," Malcolm said, pathetically.

Armadillo was silent for a moment then he asked cautiously, hiding his smile, "So you're not taking her out?"

"Not yet. I don't want to pressure her. When the time is right, I'll know it," Malcolm smirked at his clever pun then grimaced and felt like vomiting. "I'm love sick, Armadillo!"

Armadillo scoffed, "Liar! You were probably tapped into some sleazy five dollar a minute mondo phone sex hotline. You can catch diseases that way."

Malcolm looked at the phone and yelled, "No, you can't! ...And I've never had to pay for it my life!"

"Your whole life or just the boring part!" Armadillo laughed, "Ha, ha! Ha!"

Malcolm felt dejected and low, he'd been mocked before, and come dangerously close to contracting phone sex hotline diseases, but to hear the word 'boring' outside of his daily horoscope recording was more than enough. Too much, perhaps. He wanted to reach his hands into the phone and choke Armadillo. Even if that was physically possible, the bill would be pretty steep and he imagined the headlines would read something like, "Malcolm Tent, charged with reaching out and strangling someone was indicted today in federal court on three counts of tax evasion." He slammed the phone down and belched. He was alone, he didn't care anymore. It was best that no one talk to him for at least forty days and forty nights. Sulk. Big sulk!

The phone rang again, Malc leered at it cautiously. Then the damn thing rang again! Its persistence was astonishing. Malcolm lifted the handset and spoke into the end with the microphone, "Duh, yello."

The sound of a familiar voice emitted from the end with the speaker, "Yeah, so the reason I called was to see if you got my fifty bucks yet."

"Look, Armadillo, when I get it, you'll get it. Until then, get off my back."

"So I should call you later?"

"No!" Malcolm shouted, "I'll call you!"

"Need that money tomorrow or I'm gonna send my goons after you," said Armadillo with an air of uncertainty.

Malc laughed, "You mean your two little brothers? They're like twelve years old, aren't they?"

3

"Well, yeah, but they know some of the dirtiest tricks in the world and you're gonna find your shoe laces tied together when you least expect it, Bud."

"You don't scare me," sneered Malcolm as he hung up the phone and checked his shoelaces.

Through the window of Malcolm's apartment peered four strange eyes. The eyes could have belonged to maybe half a spider, but they didn't, they were in the heads of Armadillo's younger brothers, Slurp and Gurgle Cleef. They saw their adversary, their victim. They'd seen his vulnerable side. He was weak, and stupid. They ducked down and began plotting.

Again the horrible bell on the telephone was electronically activated. Malcolm picked it up and yelled into the receiver, "What do ya want?"

Armadillo responded quietly, "The Vengeful Yuppies are playing at Club Pokey tonight. You want to check 'em out?"

Malcolm shook his head with disgust, "Armadillo, I'd like to, but I just spent my last fifty bucks on an ear wax removal system so I'm not only broke, but I've got more important things to do. Leave me alone."

Armadillo was silent just long enough to be irritating, then spoke to compound the aggravation, "Okay, so what about checkin' out the Stare Masters at Murph's instead?"

"I'm broke! I have no cash whatsoever, you imbecile."

A heavy sigh pushed its way across the phone lines. Armadillo was disappointed, but persistent. "No prob, dude, Lenny's at the door and he owes me money. We're in!" A hint of enthusiasm trailed the update. "Hey! I'll spot you fifty bucks."

"Man, I am not in the mood. I'm sick of clubbin' every night. It's always the same anyway. We go out, you get the babes, I get tanked, you spend the night with some arbitrary goddess, and I spend the night hugging a porcelain god." Depression was lurking in the shadows of Malcolm's shady mind and blues songs echoed in its recesses. "Some other time, all right?"

"Suit yourself, sputnik," said Armadillo and he hung up the phone. Just like that. Totally cold, "Suit yourself, sputnik. Click!"

Malcolm wondered how people could hang up the phone without saying "goodbye". Technically, one person could wait indefinitely for the other person to officially end the conversation. The psychological term for the goodbye thing is 'closure'. That's ending a relationship, conversation, or a purely physical relationship with all parties understanding that the episode is complete. Without closure someone could wind up starving to death, literally die, just waiting for that one simple little insignificant word. "Death by non-closure" was how the coroner's report generally appeared, or "Too stupid to live," as Darwin would say. Often these tragedies went unreported. There must have been millions of apartments all over the world with dead people just sitting in them, holding phones to their ears, plates full of soggy nachos right there, just out of arms reach. Makes ya kinda weepy.

It wouldn't have mattered to Armadillo. He had one of those "if you die, you die" attitudes towards Malcolm. Not that he was unkind to Malcolm. On the contrary, he was actually very decent. Most people ignored him completely. At least Armadillo was thoughtful enough to pester the guy from time to time. He always fronted the cash and he was always willing to cook nachos. Generally their conversations ended with Malcolm feeling like dirt, but that's better than nothing, ain't it?

After a few minutes of contemplating the sensation of starving to death waiting for a goodbye, Malcolm hung up the phone. The silence gave him an opportunity to think about his solitude, his self worth, his good qualities, and his failures. He took a good hard look at his life and couldn't remember where he kept the cyanide. Another failure. Normally, he'd continue that type of self destructive meditation for hours, but this day was different. It was a Tuesday with a special tingle. Rather than wallowing in the tides of depression, he decided to do something challenging and new.

We'll get back to absolute depression versus tingling Tuesdays in a minute. You may well wonder, "Who the hell is Malcolm Tent?" and also ask yourself, "Doesn't he know he can get his name changed?" To answer the first question, Malcolm was just an average everyday guy who wanted nothing more from life than to meet a nice girl and become independently wealthy before arriving at that terrifying age of thirty (when all the fun stops). Either that, or spend the rest of his life running around in the streets naked, clapping his hands over his head, and making airplane noises. Rich and happy or nude and nutty, Malcolm could go either way.

His life history was pretty straight forward. He was born, he did stuff, and he finally made it to the point where he was at the time. Just like you and me. There were stories that Malcolm was abandoned in the Siberian outback and raised by timber wolves until he was old enough to sell religious pamphlets door to door. Most of those stories and related tragedies were unfounded and exaggerated strictly for marketing purposes. Any timber wolf would be happy to testify to the truth, that Malcolm was a lying noodlehead who couldn't make a nickel selling his version of religion. Nevertheless, it was the kind of story that made Malcolm feel important and for some reason he thought that it had the potential to impress women. He told that damn story to every woman he met. He put it in singles ads. One evening, in a drunken stupor, he came dangerously close to having the story tattooed on his back. If he thought the tattoo artist knew how to spell "Siberia" he probably would have gone through with it. Malcolm Tent was a very lonely, very dim-witted guy.

Soon he would meet a girl, a terrific girl, the kind of girl that a guy only meets once in a lifetime, but not before his life was cast into an inexorable state of cataclysmic worthlessness. Actually, he'd meet several women, but only one that he could truly love. His love life was going to reach its pinnacle, but he wasn't ready for the world of true romance. Malcolm Tent thought love meant never having to say, "How much?"

He was spending his twenty-seventh year of life as a warehouse worker. His plan was to continue doing hard physical labor until he was accepted into any Ivy League campus that would take him. The warehouse job would be a temporary position until he could save up enough money to pay for all the college application fees. Every time he saved up an amount of any significance, he'd encounter some kind of dire financial responsibility that would soak up his life savings. They could have been car problems, legal problems, medical problems, or helping Nigerian royalty flee oppression. Sure, he had problems. If he didn't have enough problems, he'd just create a few more. There was no way he could ever quite manage to pay the application fees to any of the more prestigious Ivy League institutions. Little did he know that if he had managed to pay the fees, he would have been disqualified from any financial assistance programs for being too wealthy.

It's probably better that Malcolm wasn't able to get into college when you consider how poorly campuses (campi) are run all across the country. You figure that millions of intelligent people attend the nation's colleges daily and the campus administrators aren't smart enough to figure out a way to make money from the collective youth, innocence, integrity, or devotion of their students. Getting into college should be more like getting a job than meeting the egotistical standards of some random brain-dead group of ivory tower self important pseudo intellectuals. Face it, colleges ask questions like; "What was your high school GPA? What are your extracurricular interests? What are your favorite hobbies?" and they expect the prospective student to believe that any of those answers are more important than the real question which is never asked, "How much tuition can you fork out?" How many businesses operate on the pretense that they'll make money from grants? Organizations just give money to companies? And their employees will pay the company to be employed? That wasn't Malcolm's understanding of the business world's complex mechanisms. Or course, Venture Capital was a subject that Malcolm knew nothing about. And he knew less about the sacrifices made by the employees of start-up companies, who might as well have been paying to be employed.

Damn it! As far as Malcolm was concerned, all college administrators should have been dethroned, feathered, and sent off to burger flipping factories permanently. Then they'd be replaced with administrators who knew how to make money. Really! College applications would say, "How can you make money for us quickly?" That's the only question that needs to be asked. Colleges would employ students rather than bill them as clients. Students, in turn, would work their butts off to make the colleges flourish. VC's would offer millions of dollars and expect ridiculous turnarounds on projects that were about as profitable as barking spiders. Can you imagine the change in world order? Any student, rich or poor, black or white, male or female, fauna or flora, would be able to get an education. Businesses would be a hell of a lot more involved with supporting colleges if they knew that they could pay for recruiting rights and bring in fresh, hard working, knowledgeable employees straight from the graduation ceremonies. College athletes have been doing it for decades.

Corporate America should be scratching its pointy head and saying, "Let's think of a good recruiting ad for our brand new and insanely lucrative Capitalists' Allied School of Hard Knocks and Institute of Technology. And somebody better order some fresh doughnuts, more tequila, and more cocktail napkins! We need convince ourselves that we have a business plan!"

Platonic purists would rightfully object, "Hey! I'm useless but intelligent," then continue, "What about art? What about philosophy? What about things that don't make money? What about my tenure?" Tenure... burp. Art, philosophy, social sciences, psychology and similar academia don't make money directly, but any boss who's ever found herself in a tight position doubtlessly discovered that she could extricate herself using a fresh idea, an artistic approach, a philosophical approach, or a psychological angle. That stuff plays into the whole "insanely lucrative" scheme and can't be ignored. Without it we'd become a society devoted to instant gratification, dependent on overpriced foreign oil and underpaid foreign labor and ingenuity.

Then again, Malcolm Tent didn't really care about any of that. All he knew was that he couldn't get into college and was pretty bitter about the consequential limitations. He really wanted to turn every college campus into a city park or a vineyard, but his hopes of leveling all the self proclaimed "Institutes of Higher Learning" never materialized. That was okay, he had many more impossible dreams to chase. As a young failure with no redeeming qualities and basically so boring that nobody cared about him, he was an untapped well of worthless potential.

Regarding Malcolm's intriguing qualities, the average reader of the average checkout-stand celebrity news rag probably would not care the slightest bit about him. However, it may interest that person to know that Malcolm Tent was actually the illegitimate offspring of Queen Elizabeth XII and several horny space aliens. At any moment he could sprout a giant blue dragon's head from between his legs and wipe out the first born male of every family that has a last name beginning with 'M'. Keep reading. It could happen any minute now.

The philosophical gravity of the whole money/college/news rag thing left Malcolm feeling mentally and physically poopy. The time was right to improve his life. It was time to dive into a cerebrally stimulating novel, or get off his butt and get in shape. "Gotta get in shape. Today's the day!" Right. Maybe tomorrow's the day, today just doesn't feel like the perfect day. Malcolm had been feeding himself that line for months. Need the exercise, tomorrow. Hey, tomorrow would be too late. Malcolm was thinking "today". If there was one thing he wanted be, it was to be a "today" kinda dude. He put down his bag of orange cheese doodles, raised his fist straight up to the heavens and proclaimed unabashedly, "I think I'll go for a jog. Today!"

Now, the problem with those kinds of obsessive compulsive decisions was that they usually ended with Malcolm getting hurt. He had not exercised in many moons. For one thing, he wasn't sure if he could recall how he was supposed to exercise. He seriously couldn't remember how to ride a bicycle. He remembered how to fall off a bike, but that wasn't the kind of workout he was looking for. The other thing, the more obvious and relevant obstacle to exercise was that he was a lazy dude. Jogging? Jogging. Ugh! The word itself is stupid. Jog, Jogging, Jog-ged. Lift right leg, fall forward, lower right leg. Lift left leg, fall forward, lower left leg. Repeat seven million times. Finding the motivation to jog was difficult if one weighed the physical requirements, and basically impossible when the sheer stupidity of the task was considered. Yeah, yeah, yeah, it's not all that bad. It's a good way take your mind off your problems and improve your cardiovascular system. Nevertheless, the act of jogging is hard and stupid and dangerous. Let's just be glad they passed a helmet law for it.

Naturally no self-respecting jogger in the world was going to set foot in the streets unless he or she was souped-up in red and purple and orange glowing vinyl polyester running attire. Back in the Sixties people dressed down to jog. They knew they were going to get sweaty, possibly muddy, doubtlessly look like escaped mental patients, so they wore boring old heavy cotton clothes that would cover their bodies and keep them warm despite their unavoidable perspiration. The clothes were called "sweats," not jogging suits, not warm-up outfits, not bun hugging social rump duds, just "sweats." The name's not pretty, but neither are most joggers. The deal was that a jogger had to be willing to look terrible for two or three hours a week, so that he or she could look swell and feel perky the rest of the week. Good trade off? You betcha!

In his ratty old grey sweats, Malcolm Tent jogged. His journey began in the most pleasant part of Nowheresville in a small community which bordered on the east side of Greatness. The streets of Nowheresville were filled with charming and delightful little episodes of suburbia. The lone jogger carried himself quietly through the gentle winds. The sound of fallen mulberry leaves crackled occasionally beneath his feet as he dodged toys left out by children the day before. Refreshing mists of sprinkler spray cooled his face as he passed the homes of well manicured lush green lawns. Eager husbands stumbled clumsily down their driveways carrying a final bite of breakfast or coffee which they juggled as they opened the doors to their $30,000 automobiles. Staunch young business women marched out to their practical cars forgetting to turn off their clock radios as they sped off into the urban jungle. Delinquent teenagers rolled into their driveways guzzling shots of mouthwash before going inside to recite their well rehearsed excuses. Cautious milkmen received warm welcomes from gleaming housewives as they delivered their goods, wondering if they'd get a tip. Nowheresville was much like Yourtown, except for the name, and the people, and probably the chief industry, and of course, Yourtown didn't have Malcolm Tent jogging tirelessly through its streets.

Observing the cheerful smiles of the milkmen as they stepped out of the houses of gleaming women, Malcolm contemplated the implications of a career change. What kind of training would he need? He knew not what went on inside them there houses, but with all that gleaming and smiling, he knew the benefits would be great. It didn't matter, he wouldn't pursue a career in the milk delivery business and he knew it. He was a quitter, he was a failure. He'd never amount to anything. Besides, they don't bottle milk anymore, at least not in Nowheresville. He was confused, frustrated, and he had indigestion. He kicked a rock, shook his fist a stray cat, tripped, fell, skinned his knee, and bled real bad.

Bleeding and writhing in sweat and self pity, Malcolm was about to the leave the suburbs and pass through a bad area. The Nowheresville suburbs had all the greenery and character of a Norman Rockwell painting, but the bad area was a lifeless domain of unlandscaped tenements that gave off evil vibes. Bullet holes peppered dingy grey walls and the rusting abandoned cars in front of them. Red and blue graffiti covered everything that couldn't move after dark. Derelict humans lay in the gutters waiting for death to carry them away. Naked children played in the mailboxes and frightened away the mail carriers. It certainly was not a Norman Rockwell painting. It was actually just a very convincing anti-drug billboard, but it still made Malcolm feel uncomfortable. He always shivered and yearned for sedatives as he passed it.

Surviving another exposure to the terrifying anti-drug campaign, Malcolm decided to sit down at a park bench and take a breather. For some reason the park always attracted some very pretty women who happened to look quite nice in their jogging suits and bun hugging social rump duds. While Malcolm wasn't particularly good at taking advantage of opportunities to strike up conversations with those women, once he got started he operated with sheer artistry. Among the talents of the higher primates is what's known as practical gibberish. Any moron can belch out a boisterous, "Hey, baby! You got a nice butt! Let's get together and make sparks, make the sparks fly, ah, I wanna jump your bones!" Sometimes introductions like that led to long meaningful relationships, but the school of practical gibberish insisted that the only way for a guy to successfully initiate a serious relationship was through spontaneous, clever, non-intimidating, and fluid, or at least liquid, conversation.

Malcolm had special skills in that area. At any given moment, he could choose a pick-up line from his vast repertoire of seductive gibberish and cause any woman to melt. For instance, "Helloo, it's a blutiful dray far da joggingooferduh, Mmmuhg. I'm sorrluy, me me me me me. Oooo," was usually effective. If that didn't work he'd just run away and hope that the girl would chase after him to help. On such a groovy Tuesday, depriving the park of all the beautiful women didn't seem fair to all the other guys, so Malcolm just sat back and watched people go by. From the park bench, he had a nice view of a lake and some trees, no mountain goats, no snakes, and no pretzel vendors. Sound appealing? Malcolm liked it.

He sat, and sat, didn't advance his life much, but on that bright and shiny morning he just didn't care. An exceptionally attractive woman in black and red running gear jogged past him. He thought of incorporating some of his profound practical gibberish, but hesitated when he noticed that the young woman appeared to be too upset to be easily seduced. Tossing aside the trappings of practical gibberish, he thought it would be nice to offer the woman some assistance, or at least lend her an ear. Seemed fair, he wasn't using his ears. He started a practical non-gibberal conversation.

"Hey, baby!" he said in a gravelly voice.

She gave him a hostile leer and he pointed to a small child in diapers sitting beside the bench attempting to light a cigarette.

She noticed the infant and shouted, "Hey, baby!"

Malcolm felt a warm feeling all over. The small child tossed the cigarette into a burning bush, slipped on a pair of dark glasses, and toddled away.

There was something special about that girl. Something very different, but very attractive in her personality. Malcolm had given up on spontaneous sexual encounters years ago. He'd pretty much given up on sex altogether. At best he figured he'd die tragically young and lots of cute girls would attend his funeral and toss undergarments into his coffin, but that was about as optimistic as he got. Sex wasn't as important as pleasant conversation. Face it, sex can't last forever. If it did, people would have all kinds of sores and wouldn't walk normal. Think of the drop in world productivity... But back to Malcolm's jogging gal, okay, she was physically attractive, but he would have gladly sacrificed a lifetime of physical intimacy for a half an hour of scintillating conversation.

She looked over at Malcolm and said, "Are we crazy or what?"

He'd been spoken to. He was petrified. What kind of a crack was that? People often commented about his behavior, but how'd she catch on so quickly?

"The doctors say I've been listening to too much rock and roll lately."

She smiled, "I mean it's too hot to be jogging."

"Oh," he replied with a smile.

"I'm Sharon," she said.

"I'm Malcolm," he said and set a new duration record for a conversation with an attractive woman.

"Here, have a seat," he offered.

He knew she had a seat. He meant that she could sit down on the bench next to him and he patted the bench to clarify his outburst. The world was too vulnerable to misinterpretation. At least the girl understood what he was getting at. She did sit down beside him. It was the moment he'd been waiting for all his life. She was very natural, unpretentious, healthy, and damn good looking.

He observed her. "Excuse me. I know this is going to sound, well, like a come on, but you are by far the most beautiful woman I have ever met. Please, just humor me and meet for dinner at the Tres Bona Cantina 'y Grillo tonight at seven. I know the owner, we'll have the best table in the house," is what Malcolm thought of saying. But he actually said only, "Hey."

The young woman looked over at him and said, "Hey," back.

"If I could just take you in my arms, you'd feel the passion of my heart pounding through my chest, beating from the depths of my soul. I'd give you all my love, my life, my Tom Jones albums. Just kiss me, kiss me, kiss me," went through Malcolm's mind as the word, "Hey" passed over his tongue.

"Hey," she said in response.

"You are a vision of beauty, a goddess who has fallen from the heavens to put light into the eyes of the blind, to put feeling into those who never wanted to feel again, to put a special tingle in my tippy toes," he thought as he said again, "Hey."

"This place could use a good pretzel vendor," thought the young woman as she said, "Hey," once more.

Malcolm began thinking, "I'm driving down to my big new beachfront mansion in La Jolla tomorrow. I know we've only just met, but I want you to come with me and raise a family..."

"Oh, shut up," she thought.

Malcolm's deep and imaginative thought process was interrupted when a brash young punk walked behind the bench and said to the girl, "Hey, Nice butt!" while he thought, "Duhhhhh."

Little idiot. He kept walking. Sharon looked at Malcolm, then at the idiot. Much to Malcolm's surprise, she got up and followed the dinky twerp. Those stupid, offensive, obtrusive pick-up lines really worked. Malcolm's world was shattered. He'd spent most of his life trying to be respectful and sensitive and somewhat considerate to women, but women didn't like that. Women wanted to be told what to do and treated like dirt. It was a serious problem for Malcolm. How could he compete in the world of men who were far more experienced at typecasting women and hurting their feelings and reading sports magazines? It never occurred to him. It would have been easier for Malcolm to accept a minor apocalypse or gravity boots. Imagine what it would feel like to get the bottom of a box of Cracker Jacks and not find a toy. That's how Malcolm felt at that nearly pivotal moment in his life. Gut wrenching anguish and heart felt loss of innocence.

If he'd known that the young woman would eventually follow the punk to a dark secluded area in the park and pepper spray him on all the soft tissue she could get to, he might have felt differently about his new approach to gal wranglin'. Since he wasn't aware of that, he set out to change his ways. Seducing women by making them feel like insignificant objects didn't make sense, but he had to try it, even if it meant corrupting all his values and morals. He'd start first thing the next morning. He had a jog to finish, but he couldn't clear his mind of the thought that Sharon went away with that young schmuck.

His dreams of breaking that psychological barrier of having a long mutually gratifying conversation with a beautiful woman had been lifted to the surface that separates dreams from reality, and then smashed like so many shards of jelly jars. With nothing left to hope for that day, he lifted his right leg, fell forward, lowered his right leg, lifted his left leg, fell forward, lowered his left leg, and repeated. He wasn't as enthusiastic as he was when he started, but as long as he kept that sequence going through his little mind, he could stop worrying about his impending social metamorphosis. After a few thousand repetitions, his mind was at ease, but his body was nearing rebellious levels.

II

So, Malcolm was jogging along, just jogging, minding his own business. He happened to be passing through his friend's neighborhood, so he decided to stop by Armadillo's love pad (and grill).

Outside Armadillo's unassuming abode, two youngsters played, as youngsters do. They were cheerfully throwing an old shoe to a big brown and white happy lovable doggy. The perky pup would retrieve the well worn shoe and playfully encourage the boys to throw it again. Is it still wonderful to be young? Who cares? The whole innocent scene was wrapped up in good clean fun.

The two kids happened to be Armadillo's younger brothers, Gurgle and Slurp. At ten and twelve years old, they'd probably caused more destruction than most World War II veterans, but it was generally all in fun and no one was ever seriously injured. Actually, no one was ever killed... at least no one who wasn't asking for it. The older of the two, Gurgle, was an outspoken, underhanded, bubble gum spitting bully. His most notable schemes included delivering 500 pepperoni pizzas to the Pentagon using Saddam Hussein's stolen credit card number, subletting the Empire State Building to the California System of Correction for the Criminally Insane at a rate of one handful of beads every month, and changing the name of Gila Vista to Nowheresville. He was growing up to become one of the most diabolical nuisances of the century. His younger brother, Slurp, was an evil henchchild. In his signature white bandanna, he would do anything his older brother requested. Sneaking turtles in between hamburger buns, hooking up police sirens to play "We're Off to See the Wizard", taunting monks, nothing was beyond his realm of fair game. He was good at it too. A wizard with electricity, he could rewire a cash register to give incorrect totals, he knew how to send power surges to escalators so they'd jerk forward then stop, he could even program a VCR. If only he'd used his brilliance for good instead of evil, the world would have been in perfect harmony.

As Malcolm approached the doorsteps of Armadillo Cleef's small house, the puppy became much more aggressive. The kids started playing a little rougher and before you knew it, the shoe they were playing with was swallowed by the motley mutt. The sudden disappearance of the pull toy created a fair amount of anxiety for everyone involved as they weren't exactly sure how to proceed with their merriment. Fortunately, Gurgle's ingenuity kicked in and the mongrel began jumping up and down with great enthusiasm as Gurgle pretended to throw a non-existent shoe half way around the world. Slurp did his best to encourage the canine to return the non-existent shoe as soon as possible. The slobbering bouncing beast became more and more excited, but at the same time more frustrated by its inability to locate the elusive footwear.

Thoughtless as it may have been, Malcolm interrupted the game and asked, "Armadillo home?"

Gurgle dropped the imaginary shoe and stared at Malcolm, "Dat's not his name. We like it if you was to call him Arthur."

Coldness crept into Slurp's dark brown eyes as he focused on Malcolm.

"Whatever," said Malcolm as he knocked on Armadillo's front door.

The two youngsters looked at one another, smiled, and pointed at Malcolm's feet. "Shoe, Catnip, Shoe! See the shoe? Get the shoe, boy. Get the shoe, Catnip!" shouted Gurgle as Slurp began to dance and leap around Malcolm.

Again, Malcolm knocked on the door, with spirit. The domesticated wolf, hardly larger than a trash can or a rowboat, became very interested in the commotion. Clumsily, it approached Malcolm and began sniffing his shoes. Malcolm took a couple steps back and the canine followed, still sniffing, as the two imps encouraged it to fetch the shoes. He took one more step back and the dog lowered a paw on his left foot, causing him to lose his balance and fall backwards. When he fell, his legs went into the air and the hound lunged, taking one of Malcolm's feet in his mouth. Quickly, perhaps too quickly, Malcolm jerked his shoe away from the menace, stood up again and jumped back. He looked at the rip in his new tennis shoes and asked himself, "Is that blood?"

Catnip had a new playmate.

Slurp patted Malcolm on the back, leaned his face towards Catnip, and told the dog directly, "Shoe!"

The puppy wagged its tail and Malcolm suddenly took up speed jogging. After breaking the three minute mile, a series of backyard fences, and possibly his right arm, Malcolm finally succumbed to the dog. The monstrosity managed to tear off his first shoe without taking too much flesh with it. Considering that his life was in imminent danger, he had no problem sacrificing his remaining shoe to the back of a passing garbage truck. The truck sped off to a dumpsite unaware of the violent evil hound that aggressively pursued it.

Safe from the dog, alone in a stranger's front yard, Malcolm got the feeling that he was going to have another rotten day. Cross-eyed and shoeless, he began limping back to his apartment. On that bright and shiny morning, the street and sidewalks had become warm to the touch. After walking several miles on the warm streets and blazing hot sidewalks, his feet had become somewhat tender. No, not tender, his feet had become large blisters at the ends of his legs. The soft grass in front of his apartment complex offered a slight relief to his suffering. The apartment complex also had a small pond in front that decorated the otherwise drab and lifeless building. While the pond was definitely cool and refreshing, it was not as deep as it looked, and contained much more algae than the average pond watcher would expect. Malcolm really regretted diving into it.

As he sat on the grassy edge of the pond with his feet dangling in the water, green and brown muck dripping from his bruised chin, he observed a commotion that had become fairly common between some of his neighbors and the local police. A patrol car rolled slowly into the parking lot. The two policemen inside were joking about something. As soon as they parked their car, three energetic young women ran out across the parking lot wearing the standard issue stretchy nylon shorts and loose fitting brightly colored bouncy T-shirts. The police got out of their vehicle, holstered their batons, and waited for the girls to meet them at the car.

"Hi, guys!" said a blonde girl. "We'd like to register a complaint."

The first cop, Nat, rolled his eyes and folded his arms has he leaned backed against the car. The other officer, Bart, responded to the young lady, "What's the story today?"

The blonde batted her eyelashes and grinned, "We want you to arrest them."

"And lock 'em up and shoot 'em," interjected a brunette.

Nat looked at the blonde and asked bluntly, "How do you feel about being identified by your hair color?"

Smiling from embarrassment, the blonde twirled her hair and said, "I like it."

"Okay, Blondie," continued Nat, "We got a call that somebody's making way too much noise and dancing around naked on their balcony. You know anything about that?"

All three girls giggled. Jessica, the blonde, tossed her hair back and asked Bart, "Did you get the other call? We've been calling emergency 411 all morning long and they keep giving us our own phone number and that number's always busy. It's a good thing our lives weren't in serious danger."

Helen, the brunette, jumped in, "But our lives were in danger! First of all, we want you to arrest the person who called you. They're in violation of penal code section 8 which says - No person shall knowingly be oversensitive to loud music and screaming, or else they must have the right to remain silent."

She wasn't sure if that sounded stupid enough to be cute, so she threw in, "Do you think I look fat?"

The cops looked at each other and smiled and nodded. "Fun girls" is what they thought. Still recovering from a cow tipping incident that went horribly wrong, Nat wanted to make sure none of the girls were cleverly disguised men. He needed to hear the new girl speak. He asked the redhead, Tamara, "What do you have to say about all this?"

Tammy was contemplating the impact of recent Midwest floods on grain prices, but responded as well as she could, "I say freedom of speech means that you don't have to wear clothes on the balcony if you don't want to!"

Fun girls in any book. Nat tilted his hat back, snickered, and said, "The Supreme Court is still waiting to decide on that one."

Bart winked at Nat. Then he winked at Tamara. Then he blinked a few times at a passing seagull because he wasn't real sure what the winks meant at that point.

"Look girls, we've got a complaint and we need to make sure everything's okay before we leave here. How's it gonna look if we write in our report - Still waiting for that Supreme Court Freedom of Speech decision?" Bart asked with a serious expression.

"You didn't answer me," insisted Helen, "Do you think I look fat or not?"

She put her hands on her hips and made a cute pose. The cops chuckled and thought about sex.

"No, ma'am. You look marvelous," said Bart as he waggled his head.

Helen blushed and stuck out her tongue for some reason. Not to be out done by Helen's tongue, Tamara began to unbutton her blouse. When she got about half way down, Jessie interrupted, as Tammy expected. "Tammy!" she yelled, "You can't undress in public until the Supreme Court says it's okay. Okay?"

The cops were more than a little irritated with Jessie, but knew she was right. Nat put his hand on Jessie's shoulder, "So, do you think you can keep the music down and keep your clothes on for a while or do we need to take the three of you downtown?"

The ladies all would have complied right away if the officer hadn't thrown in that feigned threat. Looking around for more trouble to stir up, Jessica noticed Malcolm walking gingerly through the parking lot. "We'll turn the music down if you arrest that guy!" she said as she pointed to Malcolm. "He won't play with us."

Malcolm looked over at the crowd cautiously. Bart and Nat put their hands on their service revolvers and motioned for Malcolm to join them. The pavement was still very hot as Malcolm approached the unpredictable herd of people.

Bart gave him a hostile leer and asked, "What do you think you're up to?"

"I just got back from the park," Malcolm explained innocently.

"These young ladies tell us you've been snubbing them," Bart said.

Snubbing. To snub, snub, snubbing, snub-bed. Illegal snubbing. "I can explain that," Malcolm guessed. He wasn't exactly sure what the definition of snubbing was, but he knew it was either intentionally ignoring another person or some kind of crazy new late night activity and he would have remembered that.

Bart winked at Tammy, pulled out his baton, and slapped it in his palm, "Aren't snubbing 'em maliciously, are you?"

"Think we should call in for backup?" asked Nat.

Bart sneered, "Naw, I think we can take care of this punk ourselves. Get out the shotgun."

Malicious snubbing was definitely illegal in Florida, but the California laws weren't as clearly defined and Malcolm was at the mercy of those two knuckle-headed kamikaze cops. The girls had huddled together and were thoroughly amused by the macho demonstration of the cops and the victimization of simple Malcolm.

Malcolm smiled at the girls and explained to the cops, "I don't think I've done anything to bother them. I hardly even know 'em, and if I knew 'em better, I know I wouldn't bother 'em."

Helen stepped in, "How come you never come over?"

"You never asked!" objected the young goofball.

Tamara chimed in with Helen, "Oh! We ask all the time, you just ignore us!"

Nat drew his gun.

Malcolm watched Nat and felt a renewed sense of concern. "You never asked me over," he said and paused, "Unless you're talking about the times you yell invitations through the walls."

"What do you think I'm talking about?" asked the angry vixen.

Malcolm thought about it for a minute, "But that's always at, like, two in the morning and you're usually just yelling 'Hi neighbor', and 'Won't you be my neighbor', and something about marrying the boy next door. How am I supposed to respond to that?"

Bart stepped in and solemnly said, "You might try being just a little more considerate."

By that time, the girls were on the verge of hysteria. They jumped between Malcolm and the cops. "Please, fellas, don't arrest him. He didn't mean any harm. He doesn't know the law," said Helen.

Hesitantly, the two cops backed away.

"Ignorance of the law is no excuse for breaking it," said Bart as he holstered his weapon. "We're gonna let you off easy this time, but we're watching you and if you screw up and bother these girls again we'll be on you like sugar on a doughnut."

"Like a bad cold," added Nat.

"Thanks," said Malcolm.

"Don't thank us," said Bart, "thank your neighbors."

Feeling confident that they'd impressed three very attractive chicks and kept at least one confused kid out of jail, the cops were ready to move on. They nodded their heads at each other and walked back to their car. Hands on their sidearms, they looked over their shoulders every few steps to make sure Malcolm didn't try anything stupid.

When they turned their backs again he put his elbow in his ear, but they totally missed it. Suckers!

"Thanks, guys!" shouted Jessie to the police, "Come back tonight! We'll be partying!"

The cops waved and shouted, "Arriba!" as they drove off with their red and blue lights flashing.

Surrounded by three good looking fun girls, Malcolm had almost forgotten that he had been used as a pawn in their little game of deception. He liked it. Actually, he was going to suggest that they all go out and deceive some more uniformed authority figures, but Jessica interrupted him, "Sorry, Malcolm. I hope the cops didn't scare you too much."

He shook his head and pointed his finger at the girls, "Cops didn't bother me, but I was afraid you all went stupid on me. Don't ever do that again."

The girls laughed.

Tammy smiled and explained, "Just your standard use of sexual suggestivity coupled with cerebral submission directed at potentially threatening adversaries to dispel the comical physical dominance ploy. It's coming back into fashion y'know."

Malcolm stood his ground, "It just bugs me... Do it again and I'll scuff your sneakers."

Noticing his sudden hostility they quickly began twirling their hair and giggling.

"I said stop it!" insisted Malcolm.

"We can do anything we want!" said Tammy.

Helen joined in, "Yeah! This is, um, America y'know. We live here too!"

"That makes us Americans," said Jessie. "Do you think I'm fat?"

Malcolm was disgusted, "Fat American fun girls! It's more than I can take. I'm outta here."

"See ya, Malcolm. Come by tonight! We're having a party!"

"You're always having a party," he responded, "Besides, I gotta work late."

"We'll have you arrested!" shouted Tammy.

Malcolm blew them a kiss and waved good-bye and shook his fist. It was true that they were always having parties. As much as Malcolm liked them, they were all pretty wild. The few occasions that he attempted to start up relationships with any of them, he was expected to go bungee jumping or tiger hunting or ice biking. He didn't think he could survive their outdoor activities, much less their anything that went on in their beds. He hadn't given up on them completely, but he was pretty sure that they'd just remain friends.

Malcolm's apartment building was filled with a variety of well meaning obnoxious neighbors and was constructed with very thin walls. Tammy, Jessie, and Helen lived on one side of his studio. The ski models; Jared, Biff, and Sherman lived on the other side. There was a coquettish rivalry going on between the boys and girls, and it got pretty loud at times. Unfortunately for Malcolm, they carried on their teasing rituals directly through his walls. Once in a while he was required to translate the muffled insults, but generally the verbal attacks passed clearly from one wall, through his living room, and through the next wall without much distortion. If they weren't arguing, they were partying. They partied all night long. A group of disrespectful punk rock brats lived below Malcolm and blared music all day. An old *old* deaf couple lived above him and cranked evangelical broadcasts over the television all day. Maybe they didn't know that the television volume was shaking the building, or maybe they were just hoping that they might regain their hearing one day and didn't want to miss anything. At any rate, the people above and below him cranked the volume all day long and the people on each side of him partied all night. Strangely, the combination of noise created a kind of melodic cacophony that was really quite enjoyable, in a stupid artistic twisted way.

Not all the other tenants in the building were as tolerant as Malcolm, and usually they'd call the landlord's answering machine or the police when the noise levels began to shatter windows. The police had a great time when they came out because the girls next door to Malcolm loved to tease them, and the cops had a legitimate excuse to talk to some hotties. Getting bad guys off the street and helping good people get back on their feet was rewarding, but spending half an hour getting the girls next door to stop singing and yelling "whoop, whoop," was always a treat. The punk rockers would protest to the police and call them fascists, but they eventually caved in and put on some nice classical music at a reasonable volume. When Jared, Biff, and Sherman were confronted by the cops, they admitted they were ignorant and apologized repeatedly and hid in their rooms for the rest of the night. The old couple never answered the doorbell. Malcolm was generally harassed because he was there.

Worn out by the long painful jog and the brief dose of police brutality, Malcolm just wanted to go back to his apartment and sleep. But duty called and he had to get ready for work. He got undressed to take a shower and all of a sudden there was a knock on the door. His door did things like that. Through the peephole of the door he peeped. It was young Tawnette. Healthy, voluptuous, and dumb, she was the kind of girl that mothers called, "healthy, voluptuous, and dumb." Malcolm wrapped himself in a towel and opened the door.

"Hi, I'm returning your bicycle pump," said the bubbly young Tawnette.

Malcolm attempted to lick his eyebrows and smiled, "I'll see your pump and raise you two pumps."

Tawnette felt a tingling sensation throughout her body and said with short breaths, "Okay."

For a guy who didn't have much interaction with women, he was having great day. He stared at her and tried to think, but his brain was so small! He thought, "Healthy, voluptuous, dumb girl standing outside my door, I'm wearing nothing but a towel, this is a perfect opportunity to take a chance with her. I've got one thing on my little mind. I'm goin' for it!" He opened his mouth and asked, "Could I maybe ride a bicycle with you to the beach someday?" He knew he shouldn't have been so bold, but the moment was right...

"Nope," she said as she patted his towel and skipped away.

The senselessness, the sheer stupidity of the whole encounter was annoying. But that's just it, that's the way all Malcolm's conversations worked. See pretty girl, say something stupid, remain embarrassed.

The possibility of chance romance was dashed against the rocks again like so many tired clichés. Every day was the same; doom, desolation, and finitude. It was existential, but pre-destined for misery.

The standard cure for such a depressing situation was to eat soup and corn chips. That's about the only sustenance he had in his apartment and it was conducive to his, um... mushy flaky mood. You ever get like that? When the whole world is plotting against you, and every friend you ever had has abandoned you and you don't want to do anything except rewind that last conversation with the girl at the door and try again! So, when you get like that just have some soup and corn chips. Much better than anything you could imagine... So! After taking a cold shower, Malcolm fixed himself a lunch of canned vegetable soup and wiggly corn chips. Talk about turnin' the world around.

Having gone through the transformation from mushy and flaky to hot and wiggly, he was ready to watch television until it was time to go to work. If that sounds crazy, it is. Don't try it at home. It was eleven o'clock on that bright and shiny morning. The daily soap operas were confiscating the national networks. The music channels were spewing out pay for airplay two minute videos comprised of two hundred blurred glimpses of breasts and butts and grody musicians cashing in on teenage libidinal frustration. The television commercials in young Malcolm's era were geared towards making the average viewer self conscious of his or her weight, various body odors, nutritional ignorance, and healthy appetite. Of course, the appetite could only be controlled through the consumption of fat ridden, breath tainting, junk food that were advertised in 30 second segments of two hundred blurred glimpses of breasts and butts and an occasional grody musician.

For about half an hour, Malc sat in front of his television flicking the channels from dramatic vignette to dramatic vignette. While none of the daytime soaps had any actual plots, they all had dozens of deep meaningful subplots. Simpleminded Malcolm could hardly follow the complexities of any single show, so he had fun creating stories from bits and pieces of all the shows. His creations used characters and story lines that crossed network boundaries and time slots. For instance, on one channel, the dead twin of the mayor's daughter suddenly reappeared as a burglar in the house of the family that was being extorted by a group of political lobbyists; another channel was wrapped up in the affair going on between Myrna and Jeff who had previous been married to the other's lover. The average newborn reached puberty in six months, while no one over thirty ever aged. It was true cerebral fodder. If that wasn't enough to create an interesting story, Malcolm could always spice up his daily collage of drama with one of the captivating sagas created by the music channels.

So that morning Malcolm pieced together his own story from the various television programs. By the time the identical triplets found out that one of them was a killer that made love to an alcoholic maid who was actually their rich cousin, Nectarine, who didn't realize she was rich with the amnesia and all, it was too late. The doctor's receptionist had already performed the brain surgery and fallen into the lake. If it wasn't for the magic guitar and a strange letter written in blood and chocolate by an unknown woman with the same handwriting as Doctor Candy Stripe, the whole town could have been destroyed by stampeding donkeys carrying loads of coconuts back to Brazil.

That's when the doorbell rang.

Malc sneered and dashed to the door. Another incendiary bag of fecal matter had been left in the hall on his doorstep. No courier in sight. A million questions raced through Malcolm's head (sort of like racing through molasses); "Who did this?", "Why'd they do it to me?", "Don't I need to sign something?", "Zounds!" He wasn't about to suffocate the flames using his body as a mortal fire extinguisher, again. Nor was he going to call the fire department. Firefighters had a warped sense of humor. Historically, Malcolm's spur of the moment decisions caused him all sorts of unexpected problems. This situation required further uninterrupted deliberation. Malc shut the door and went back to soap opera roulette.

As he meditated quietly, the smoke alarms and fire alarms and screaming neighbors and sirens rattled the building. How was a person supposed to concentrate or make *any* rational decision in an environment like that? The door on his apartment was quickly devoured by the flames. Within seconds his entire ceiling was immersed in a sea of red and orange waves. The heat was so intense that Malcolm's velvet bullfighter poster burst into flames before the fire hit the living room wall. Malcolm winced, pouted, and shrugged his shoulders.

His attempts to produce a well thought-out decision had failed. He had to make a quick decision instead. He quickly decided to get nervous. He began tapping his finger on the mottled green coffee table in front of him, nervously. There was too much going on to follow the soaps so he turned off the television. One less distraction was all he needed to make that critical choice for a course of action. He jumped to his feet and dashed to the kitchen. Just as he suspected, the fan over the stove hadn't been turned on. "What a dope," Malcolm thought, self-consciously. The switch on the fan seemed to be out of order, and Malc knew it was the worst possible time for an exhaust fan to go out. It was time for another deliberate action. He looked into the gaping facade of flames as it consumed his kitchen and knew what had to be done. Reaching inwards for that rare strength that can only be found in times of catastrophic disasters and yellow traffic lights, Malcolm picked up the phone to call building maintenance. It was unfathomable, but Malcolm quickly discovered that the phone wasn't working either.

No kitchen fan, no telephone, apartment in flames, and a burnt bag of poop right outside his apartment door. Some people might have credited the phenomenon to coincidence, vandalism, or even an apocalypse, but Malcolm was absolutely convinced that this tragedy was created by a conspiracy between the phone company, the electric company, building maintenance, and possibly the Soviet Union (allegedly defunct). Naturally, he wasn't going stay in an apartment complex that was involved in such a diabolical underhanded scheme, so he threw his important belongings into a duffel bag and ran out the front door through an opening in the flames.

The apartment hallway was filled with smoke. It became so thick that Malcolm had to drop to his hands and knees to get clean air. All his instincts told him to look for a missing contact lens, but he didn't. He remembered that the best way to extinguish flames was by rolling around, so he started to roll. Of course, he wasn't on fire, but he still wanted to put the fire out. He rolled all over the place. He even threw in one or two somersaults. Those were the kinds of life saving acrobatics he'd seen in so many of the old police shows. He loved 'em! Neato-like! Then! With that flash, it occurred to him that someone might be making a television show of this disaster. Possibly his fearless escape was part of some multi-million dollar action thriller. Damn. Why did he always think of those things at the last minute? He tucked in his shirt and started smiling as he rolled around.

With the threat of public scrutiny looming over his head, the whole "me first, look out for number one" philosophy was blown out the door. He couldn't very well just walk out of a burning building without saving somebody. Imagine the embarrassment. So began his quest for fire victims, preferably innocent victims that were physically or mentally incapable of saving themselves. He thought, "If I was an innocent helpless victim who looked good on camera being saved, where would I be found?" He didn't have a clue. He was about to throw himself into the flames as some kind of noble sacrificial marketing gesture when he heard a faint cry. It was so meek and distant that Malcolm thought it might have been one of those damn cats that kept him awake so many nights. But the cries became louder and seemed to be coming from a child, no, no, yes, no, children! Helpless children! What luck! He'd look fantastic on film saving helpless children from a raging fire! He'd never been happier.

As quickly as his new found happiness was born, it was replaced by the severity of the situation. The flames began to burn through the ceiling. He knew those kids needed help fast. If he didn't find them soon, the whole gaggle would be lost. He followed their faint calls. Crawling and rolling down the hall, Malcolm was getting closer to the children, but the heat was becoming more and more intense. Through the smoke, Malcolm saw the distinctive silhouettes of several small bodies standing at the end of the hall. He jumped to his feet and ran towards them. All he could see as he turned the corner was the stairwell door closing slowly in front of him. The kids must have freed themselves and found the way out on their own. He'd be a hero another day, it was time to save himself.

As he stepped into the stairwell he looked down over the stair railing and saw a huddle of youngsters run out of the stairwell onto the second floor. They must not have known how to get out of the building, or perhaps a stray collie was hurt and they wanted Malcolm to follow them. At least they were off the fourth floor. He ran down the stairs and entered the second floor. The children were already at the other end the hall screaming in front of the opposite stairwell entrance. Malcolm yelled at them and they looked back at him, but none of them stopped. He ran down the hall to rescue them, but they managed to get to the stairwell at the other end of the building and went out safely. Malcolm was relieved, but as he entered the stairwell, he heard the door above him close. Nutty kids must have become confused from all the commotion.

He went up to the third floor and just as he went in, he saw the kids go out through the door at the opposite end of the hall. They were quick little helpless children! Well, the chase went on for about twenty minutes. Malcolm got to the stairwell just in time to see the kids exit the stairwell on the wrong floor and he would enter the floor just in time to see the children go into the opposite stairwell. Finally he stumbled in a stairwell, fell down a couple flights of stairs, and just lay in pain on his back on the landing looking up.

Motionless and bruised, he was assessing his injuries, when he noticed the heads of several small children peek over the railing. Not just three heads, but six heads. They weren't frightened little heads, they were giggling little heads. The heads vanished for a moment, then a short parade of screaming laughing children bounced down the stairs, leaped over Malcolm, and ran out of the burning building. Malcolm tried to grab their skinny little ankles but the kids were too slippery. You know the type.

Covered with black soot, blood, contusions, and humiliation, Malcolm dragged himself out the door. Once outside, he saw six more children running out of the opposite side of the building. The whole troop met on the other side of the complex and collectively collapsed in laughter. The little marsupials were just hiding in the stairwells and utility closets appearing and vanishing as necessary to keep their savior in pursuit. Kids these days are so clever. Malcolm made it out of the building with barely a moment to spare. He had survived the smoke inhalation, the scorching heat, the flaming jaws of death and escaped with no broken bones. The embarrassment was still pretty tough to overcome. A final kid ran out of the building laughing and pointing a video camera at the collapsed Malcolm. Yeah, very embarrassing!

Outside, in the parking lot, the firemen were chatting with the girls next door. The girls pointed at Malcolm and shouted something about him snubbing out hot fires and not warming up to them. The firemen took out their axes and began marching towards him. Rather than hassle with a long drawn out explanation of his understanding of flame snubbing, he ran across the street. The firemen stopped and turned towards the fire. They looked at the building and then at the girls, and went back to the girls.

From the other side of the street, Malcolm stood on the sidewalk watching the grey smoke and orange fire pirouette through the light blue sky. It was actually kind of pretty. Perhaps a career in arson would suit young Malcolm. He rubbed his chin and coughed. Too much tragedy in pyromania. Besides, he already had a job. It wasn't the best job in the world, but it got him through the day. The building gradually became a cathedral of flames that devoured everything inside it. All of Malcolm's prized personal possessions from a Kareem Abdul-Jabbar autograph to a picture of his grade school sweetheart were lost. The stolen stereo and flickering television could be replaced, but the memorabilia of a lifetime was gone forever. He'd forget about them by the end of the day, but he still didn't like to losing his stuff. Of course, Malcolm could have paid an extra five dollars a month and got a fireproof safe and renter's insurance. Every other tenant in the building opted for the additional expense, but he figured he didn't need it. The flames began to die down as the structure started to become more and more of a skeleton, leaving behind nothing more than black ashes and pipes and fireproof safes.

III

Most people would have stayed at the fire scene and searched through the embers for their belongings, but Malcolm knew he'd lose his job if he didn't get to work. His employer was so cold that even the old, "My home just went up in flames taking everything I own and almost killed me" excuse wasn't good enough. Considering that Malc was three months behind in his rent and his apartment had been robbed two days prior to his evacuation, he wasn't too upset about abandoning the old homestead. In fact, he was looking for some kind of motivation to get moving again. He still needed shelter.

At a time of life threatening emergency, he wanted to turn to his friends, relatives, government agencies, horoscopes, or talking dogs for assistance. He couldn't. His family moved to Wisconsin and took all his friends and talking dogs with them. Sure, he could have gone to Wisconsin and moved in with them, but they'd just move on to Hoboken or Miami ...And they'd keep moving as long as he followed them. His family was very religious and the dogs had told them that Malcolm was the anti-Christ. His friends had seen him drink and play basketball, so they were certain there was something strange and evil about him and they avoided him at all costs. Government agencies might have been a better option if Malcolm didn't despise them so much. He loathed handouts and truly believed that welfare programs were the first steps towards communism. Besides, the homeless shelters wouldn't take people that had jobs and the shelter for battered women expected him to pass some kind of embarrassing, possibly discriminatory physical examination.

By ruling out government organizations for assistance, he had only his horoscope for advice. He knew good fortune was smiling on him when he found an unopened newspaper lying in the ash filled gutter at the end of the street where his apartment once stood. The cryptic daily astrological message that usually promised him wealth and romance, or warned of danger and intense negativity simply read, "Seriously Capricorn, horoscopes aren't real. I've never seen them work unless the person just needs an extra push for confidence and you should really be able to get that from any friend, relative, government agency, or even a talking dog. I quit." Somewhere in Nowheresville a newspaper company was looking for a new astrology writer.

At this point, he could have tried the simple remedies like cyanide, arsenic, or square dancing, but Malcolm didn't have the stomach for such cop outs. He'd attempt to live just one more day. At least things couldn't get worse. Malcolm was reminded of the ancient conversation between the famous Greeks, Euripides and Eupaypherdes, where the playwright told the toga salesman that they could probably save the entire Roman civilization if they just stopped partying and tried doing some real work once in a while. That was a message for hope. That tiny bit of optimism was all it took. He suddenly remembered Armadillo. A friend indeed. Even if Armadillo wouldn't take him in, his car was sitting in front of Armadillo's house. He could sleep in his car for a while. Everything was gonna be great. Zippity doo dah, zippety, eh?

He'd drop by Armadillo's Love Pad and Grill after work and crash there until he could afford to move into a new and improved apartment complex. Things were going so well, he'd probably meet a hot chicky-baby that evening and score, big time. And he had a little money saved up! He was hoping to use it as a dowry, but if worse came to worse he could always use some of it for food. Four hundred dollars went a long ways in those days.

The twenty bucks he had in his pocket would probably last him through the week. If things weren't already too good to be true, a bus was coming his way that would take him directly through the E. Camous Memorial Business Park where he worked. Malcolm got on the bus and left the driving to a total stranger. It was okay, everything was okay.

Hot Diggity Dog Delivery Service and Grill was the name of his employer. The job didn't pay well, it wasn't prestigious, he busted his butt every day, but at least the hours were bad and as long as nobody else would take on the challenge of such an abysmal career, Malcolm had work. It was a small operation, consisting of about twenty people with exciting and diverse backgrounds. While no one was particularly happy with their occupation, they all knew that they were stuck with it. They believed they were stuck, anyway, and spent most of their days groveling and complaining and wallowing in self pity. They all knew that the capitalist dream was demonstrated by people with capital.

It was just an average work day to his co-workers. No one knew about the tragedies Malcolm had endured that morning. Then again, no one would have cared and Malcolm preferred to keep his personal life personal. He entered the rolling bay doors at the loading dock and was immediately met by the warm wit of Bert.

"How's it hangin' there, cabbage head?" Bert asked as he examined the mold growing on the underside of his coffee mug and scraped at it with his fingernail.

"Bert! Why you picking at that cup?" replied Malcolm, "Did you misplace your nose again?"

Bert shook his head, stuck his finger in his nose, and walked away. Bert was in his early thirties and was very comfortable with his incredible ability to put people off with his irritating behavior. The two of them had developed an adversarial relationship six months earlier when Malcolm was promoted to Warehouse God after only three months of employment while Bert had been with the company since it started. Malcolm received the promotion as a result of hard work and smart thinking and small bribes, while Bert felt that he deserved anything he wanted simply because of his seniority. Since that time, Bert never missed an opportunity to take a jab at young Malcolm. It was kind of fun for Malcolm because none of Bert's insults reflected much intelligence and Malcolm could usually throw them back at Bert without much trouble. Bert was the kind of guy that yelled "Third base!" every five minutes because he laughed hard when he first heard the Abbott and Costello "Who's on First?" sketch.

Still, that crack about "cabbage head" was totally out of the blue and Malcolm couldn't think of a clever retort. It was especially painful for Malcolm because, unbeknownst to Bert, Malcolm's parents truly were cabbage heads. Sometimes the most innocent comment can be so cruel. Why can't people think before they speak?

Malcolm tried to recover from his sudden emotional upheaval with a cup of coffee from the break room, but to get to the coffee he had to walk past Devlette. Her job was primarily in customer service, but she made sales calls occasionally in her spare time. She was good looking, fairly bright, outgoing, and constantly making passes at Malcolm. As desperate for love as Malcolm was, he knew better than to mess with Devlette. On several mornings he'd seen her come to work in a taxi wearing a red sequined halter top, a short black leather skirt, and high heeled shoes with mirrors on the toes. Not that that's all bad, but he suspected that she worked as a hooker when she needed extra money and she probably wouldn't have denied it. In the height of sexually transmitted incurable deadly diseases, Malcolm wasn't about to risk his life for a one night stand, but he was tempted, every morning.

She was at her desk shuffling papers when he went to the coffee room. "Hi Malcolm. Need some Java?" she asked.

"What's that supposed to mean?" he responded knowing full well that there was some kind of disgusting degenerate innuendo in her question. "That's so sick."

Devlette grinned, "Come on, Malcolm. I just said 'Hi'. You've got to give me a little slack. You'd think I was trying to jump you. I know you're not interested in me romantically, so today I just wanted to be a friend. I've got to start somewhere if we're ever going to have a Platonic relationship. Sometimes you're so judgmental, almost prejudiced." She lowered her eyes in shame.

For the second time that morning, Malcolm was nearly moved to tears. He hated prejudice in any form. He wasn't sure that the accusation was justified, but he was clearly in the wrong, "I'm sorry, Dev. I've been having kind of a bad day. My apartment burned down and Bert called me a cabbage head. I'm not a bad person. Really."

A warm seductive smile slowly grew as she looked up at Malcolm with her big brown innocent eyes, "I know you're not. I'm sure you're very good. I'm sure you're one of the best. Maybe I can do something for you. Have you ever had it with chocolate syrup?"

Malcolm, still overwhelmed with guilt, looked up at Devlette, "What?"

"With your coffee, would you like some chocolate syrup? I can get you some chocolate syrup and pour it all over. You really should try it. You can try it on mine first to see if you like it... Then you can really enjoy your coffee. I know you'll feel better afterwards."

"Well, thanks, but no thanks. I just want sugar this morning," Malcolm confessed.

Devlette became flushed, "God! What the hell kind of a perverse thing is that? How do you use sugar, you madman!"

"I just pour it on top of the coffee," Malcolm further confided.

Devlette smiled and licked her lips, "One of these days we'll try that together."

"Okay. Sorry about that prejudice thing. I'll try to be less defensive from now on." Malcolm knew she could be a pal if he'd just let her. He continued his morning ritual.

Devlette laughed quietly and went back to shuffling paper and stapling things that didn't belong together.

As Malcolm left the office, Barney strut past him and slammed his hand on Devlette's desktop. "Think a grown man could fit under that desk, young thing?"

Devlette looked at her fingernails, "Grown men fit just fine. Bring me a grown man and I'll give you a show," she said and shook her head at Barney.

Barney didn't want a show. He was seriously making a pass at her, again. He'd been turned down by virtually every woman that ever entered the building. He'd even been turned down by a few men. Technically, Barney was a certified steaming horndog.

"Look, Bimbo, you can't talk to me like that! I'm better than half the guy's you date. In fact, I'm better than any man you ever known!" Barney looked around to make sure no one was watching his outburst.

Sensing an unusual level of hostility in Barney's behavior, Devlette had to, once again, put him in his place. She felt a certain moral obligation to deal with him harshly. She looked up at him slowly, emotionlessly, with a naturally sultry expression. When their eyes met, she stood up and kept Barney's focus on her eyes, all hypnotic like. Then she put her nose as close to his as she could without touching and said softly, "At your best, you'll never come close to being half as good as my worst date. On your best day you couldn't come close to being half a man. You... are a bug. You are an insignificant insect. If you ever use that tone with me again I'll tear off your legs and squish you."

Barney's little brain was overloading. He had to back down or attack her and he was afraid to do either, so he just stood there.

Devlette stood up straight and said calmly, "Now fly away little bug, fly away." She stepped back and squirted him with a perfume atomizer and coughed. "Insecticide," she said waving the mist out of the air.

Barney jumped back, whined, called her a biscuit, and ran out of the office to the bathroom. He passed Malcolm coming out the bathroom, "That Devlette wouldn't know a good man if he came up and bit her on the ass. She's probably afraid of men. Probably never touched a man. Probably wants to be a nun."

Astonished by the candid admission of the certified horndog, Malcolm thought, "Gee, I guess I did misjudge her. She's a nice girl after all." He pondered his feelings towards Devlette as he went into the coffee room. No, Devlette was a floozy. She was a nice floozy, but Malcolm wasn't going to get involved with her. He liked her though. Great smile and she had lots of funny stories about men she'd kidnapped.

For every horny dirty minded Devlette, there are at least two women that carry an equal amount of purity and chastity. It's some kind of government regulated ratio. At HDDDSG, those two pure souls would be Nora and Marie. Together they formed a team of anti-sexual titans. In their eyes, all men wanted only one thing, and they'd heard one too many gory details of exactly those animals got their thrills. The conversations between Nora and Marie were limited to flower arranging and exactly how they'd deal with any male human that tried any funny business with them. They were pretty nice, but they really did need some good lovin'. They might have seriously considered getting good lovin' if they didn't believe that it would lead to drug abuse and sloppy grooming. Both of their husbands disagreed with their opinions and secretly harbored warm intimate feelings towards drug addicts with dirty duds who could make peek-a-boo bouquets in a pinch.

Anyway, Malcolm had a lot of fun teasing them, and they tolerated his antics only after he'd convinced them that he couldn't cause them any problems since the terrible disfiguring helicopter blade accident he experienced in the war. Regardless of Malc's alleged physical limitations, they figured he might have been working as an agent for the other male humans in the shop. They carefully weighed every word he said, constantly searching for sexual overtures or suggestions. They wouldn't find any. He just liked to make them laugh.

So, when he found Nora in the break room, he started in, "Nora, I'm flying to New York tonight and I need some new bat wings. If you could get a hold of a good wingsmith for me, I'd sure appreciate it."

"What?" asked Nora.

Malcolm held back a smile, "Need some new wings. My old ones are all torn up and the feathers have been scratching me like you wouldn't believe," he explained.

"You said 'wings'?" she asked, still bewildered at finding no salacious reference.

"I know, I know, they're hard to think of as wings when you see 'em all folded behind my back, but those babies have some pretty good mileage on 'em. I used 'em at Kittyhawk!"

Just then Marie walked in.

"Malcolm says he needs some new wings," Nora announced.

"What?" Marie asked without much interest.

"Wings! He's going to New York," Nora said.

"Oh? And just what are you going to do in New York?" asked Marie, full of suspicion.

"Well, I've got a little nest egg saved up and after being cooped up around here for so long I thought it might be nice to spread my wings a little, fly up to New York City, cop a perch on top of the Empire State Building for a while," he said looking up at the ceiling.

"Nora! He's doing it again! He's teasing you!" Marie said as she looked at Malcolm and double checked, "Aren't you?"

"Yes, I am," he admitted.

Marie smiled, "He's an awful man!"

Nora shook her head, "Sometimes I wonder about you, Malcolm Tent. Wings. It doesn't make any sense. It's not even funny. Where do you get this stuff?"

Marie put her hands on her hips and began clucking like a chicken. Nora laughed and joined in. Having accomplished his good deed for the day by providing pleasure to two women at one time without any physical contact, Malcolm walked away. Barney, the horndog, walked in, noticed the strange behavior of the women, and began taking his clothes off, primarily to ruin the moment.

"You're a couple of crazy birds," he said, "but we need the eggs."

Before he could get his shoes off, he was assaulted with pepper spray, hog tied, gagged, and stuffed in a cupboard. Nora and Marie left the coffee room satisfied that another useless perverted male had been subdued and silenced.

Coffee in hand, Malcolm went to the back of the shop and stumbled on an electrical cord. Blistering hot coffee on shirt, he sat down at his makeshift desk and contemplated his status in the big scheme of life and world history. Not bad at all, he thought. He had everything a warehouse warrior could need; warehouse, forklift, and a box cutter. He was a happy warrior. His work area was his kingdom.

"Maynard? Maynard!" Malcolm shouted, "Bring me a box or a roll of packing tape or something."

Maynard wasn't anywhere in sight, but Malcolm really liked yelling at Maynard more when Maynard wasn't around. "Maynard! Bring me more coffee and shine my shoes, you nincompoop!"

Maynard was in earshot, hiding behind a forklift. He often hid behind the forklifts or up in the pallet racks, especially when his boss was hollering at him.

"Swab the deck, ye scurvy dog!" Malcolm yelled.

Maynard snickered to himself. Malcolm threw his hands up in the air, yet they remained on his wrists, and he used them next to pick up the telephone and call one his drivers who hadn't come into work yet. The driver he was calling had been late every day for the last three weeks. Malcolm was in charge of calling him and reminding him to get his butt on the road. Generally, the guy just needed to be awakened, and a crank call usually did the trick.

"Uh ullo, uh" grumbled the voice on the other end of the phone.

Malcolm giggled, "Good day, sir. This is Irving from the church. We'll be in your neighborhood this morning and we were wondering if we could count on you for a donation?"

"Uh, no man, I mean brother... father. I'd like to, but I'm broke. I just spent the last of my paycheck on groceries."

"Well, we need to take something," said Malcolm.

"What?" inquired the groggy driver.

Speaking in monotone, Malcolm said, "Someone will be by this morning to pick up your soul."

After a short silence, the driver replied, "...Satan?"

Malcolm hung up the phone and went back to managing his inferiors. "Maynard! I want to see your truck loaded and moving in five minutes or I'll make your life a living hell! Now get to it!"

Maynard peered out from behind the forklift and waited for Malcolm to leave. After a few minutes of rustling papers and throwing darts, Malcolm noticed that Maynard still wasn't anywhere in sight. "Maynard! You flea bitten, good for nothing, sorry excuse for a furball! Get your rear end out here right now!"

Nothing.

Slamming his fist on his desk, Malcolm exclaimed, "If I have to wake you up, you'll be spending your dying days scrubbing the parking lot!"

As clever as he was lazy, Maynard threw a screwdriver across the warehouse.

"Maynard!" shouted Malcolm, "you're in a lot of trouble!" He ran to the area of the warehouse where the screwdriver landed.

Capitalizing on his clever diversion, Maynard made a dash to his truck, popped open the hood and waited for Malcolm to return. As Malcolm stomped back to his desk, Maynard smudged his hands with motor oil and appeared from the front of the truck.

"Where the hell have you been?" shouted Malcolm.

Maynard shrugged his shoulders, "I just been checkin' the oil on my vehicle. Weren't you gonna get us some more 10-40 oil?"

"Yeah, I think I might have a can or two back in the cabinet. Have a look, and if you find any, you might try opening it with this," Malcolm tossed the screwdriver to Maynard. Maynard smiled and Malcolm shook his head.

"You loaded?" asked Malc.

Working up his best stupid expression, Maynard explained, "No, boss. I got nothin' to deliver this morning. I do got one pick up at, um, um, Archue, then..."

"Then your going to Zuntite to see about that hayseed load that got bumped from the turnip shipment," Malcolm demanded.

"Ah, but... What about my allergies!"

"Don't you back talk me, young man," said Malcolm as his face turned bright red, "I get enough of that from your mother."

Maynard lowered his head and began pouting.

Malcolm scowled, "Get along now and don't be late for dinner. We're having rich people."

Maynard's eyes lit up as he skipped off to his truck and drove away. Malcolm returned to his menial tasks. He thought about pouring coffee on the rest of his shirt to hide the stain, but he noticed that the stain looked like Underdog so he decided to keep it. The daily buzz was starting up again as people returned from their lunch breaks.

Some of the work that went on around the Hot Diggity Dog Delivery Service and Grill involved automatic mail processing. They had machines that could label brochures, fold letters, and put postage on mail. They even had machines that could stuff an envelope, seal it, stamp it, and then repeat the process hundreds of thousands of times without stopping. At least that was a primary selling feature of the automatic inserter. Reality was that it could, but it didn't. Throwing all that paper together, it would barely stuff two hundred letters without jamming; sending springs and suction cups and unwanted mail all over the place. Most people couldn't care less about such a contraption. Most people would say, "So that's how all that garbage gets handled. Huh," then go on back to biting their fingernails. Not Malcolm, he stopped short of biting his fingernails and watched the machine do its thing. Fingernail biting can be exciting, but fascination with mechanical labor saving devices has marveled mankind for centuries.

Descartes thought animals were automata. Malcolm thought that automata would make good animals. Just before Malcolm fell into any deep philosophical meditations on the metaphysics of mailing machines, a vision of beauty walked through the door. Malcolm figured could he still maintain the metaphysical connection if the woman turned out to be a true goddess. It was the girl from the park, but she wasn't wearing her jogging duds. She was wearing some kind of turtle neck, jumpsuit, sweater combination that Malcolm had never seen in his life. She was making a fashion statement and it said, "I know my clothes, buster!" Her arms were full of newsletters for the Nowheresville Museum of Modern Art and Grill. Malcolm didn't care. She had big blue eyes, a smile that could have seduced a small country, and a body that made Malcolm say "gosh" and "golly".

Malcolm had to muster up all his courage to initiate a conversation. He needed to think of something to say that wasn't a tired old line that she'd heard a hundred times before. Comments on eyes, smiles, and bodies are all tired and old. Comments on chins, earlobes, and belt buckles are fresh and exciting. Malcolm was starting to obsess because she seemed to have it all. Then he put the brakes on. There wasn't a woman on the planet who had it all. Anyone that good looking should be modeling mascara, lipstick, lingerie, or sloppy hamburgers. That kind of babe can get any guy she wants; rich, good looking, abusive... any guy she wants. Nature dictated that she must possess terribly evil psychological problems. What if she didn't? Despite his stupidity, daring, and bumbling failures, Malcolm had great taste in women. He knew the cards were stacked against him, but he had to say something.

His practical gibberish approach wasn't going to be the best angle for a young sophisticated conscious woman. He leaned in towards her. "Hey, baby, what's your funky love sign? Huh? I could go for you in a beeeg way," he said softly with his best French accent.

She looked at him and smiled cautiously, "Hi. I need to have these mailed out by next Tuesday."

Malcolm searched uselessly for some kind of sublime affirmation or acknowledgement in her response. There was nothing but the obvious. He tilted his head, like a curious dog, "Would you mind terribly if I lick your ear lobes?" Used a British accent that time.

She laughed, "Can you lick 'em fast enough to get my brochures mailed out by Tuesday?"

She didn't insult him, she didn't slap him, or give him a shot to the midsection. Malcolm didn't know what to do. She was being nice to him. Gorgeous and nice? The woman was obviously confused or drugged. He had to act quickly before she regained her senses. "I met you in the park this morning. Didn't I? We were talking until that guy made a, uh, a compliment about your figure."

It took her a moment. She remembered but didn't feel it was necessary to explain the physical pain she inflicted on her admirer in the park, "Oh, yeah. Sorry I didn't recognize you. It's been a very long day."

It occurred to Malcolm that her apartment complex might have also burned down that morning. He really needed to be more considerate, yet deceptive enough for her to respect him. The situation called for something new, something devious, something so despicable that even the sweetest, kindest nun in the world would have spit on him. He pulled out a family picture that came with his wallet.

"This is... was my girlfriend," he said as he tried to wipe a tear from his eye, "I, uh, I lost her in a pillow fight. I still love her. That's our son. He joined the orphanage. They were all I had, aside from my broken heart. I guess I'll never fall in love again with a woman who loves children as much as I do."

She looked at the photograph and laughed, "She was pretty. Your son's adorable. And you look much younger in person. You look blonder with greener eyes. You look totally different! That is so neat."

Malcolm gave up, "I'm sorry. It's not my picture. I mean, it's my picture, but it's not a picture of me. I thought it might impress you because it's so... pathetic. Don't hate me. That's my motto. Don't hate me because I'm pathetic."

She put her finger on the picture, "So you didn't really lose her in a pillow fight?"

"Oh, I don't know. It all happened so fast. All I remember was the screaming and feathers. When I woke up, the cops were swarming all over, and she was... I can't talk about it anymore," he feigned a sob, "She loved her bubble baths."

At that point he was starting to snicker, "Hey, what's your name again? And, how can I help you?"

She bowed her head and explained with a big smile, "My name's still Sharon, and I'm kinda flattered, and you are so sweet."

...Sweet? Guys hate sweet. Malcolm felt his face turn red and stomach turn over.

She paused and shook her head for a moment, "Look, I'd like to stay and talk, but I have to get back to work."

Damn. Malcolm was in love. The girl was great. If you were looking for a friend, there she was. If you were looking for a lover, you'd have to get past Malcolm. But, let's forget about you for a minute. Malcolm took the material from her and set it with all the other incoming junk that would eventually litter the mailboxes of thousands of people all over the country. He picked up a sample from her mailing, looked into her eyes, and drifted off to that neurotic mental haven where unconfident guys spend most of their waking hours.

Malcolm's idiot trance was broken when she spoke, "Well, I do have to get going. You should already have the mailing labels. It was nice to see you again."

As she walked away, Malcolm knew it would be the last time he'd ever see her. Somehow that was okay. He could accept it. She was too good for him and she deserved better, and he deserved worse. She was now part of Malcolm's long series of missed opportunities and failed first attempts. Giving up too soon was probably his greatest weakness, but he convinced himself a long time ago that if a woman says she's not interested, she's probably telling the truth. Sharon hadn't actually said she wasn't interested, but she implied it by being so perfect. He accepted it.

Wait a minute. Malcolm didn't accept it at all. It was an opportunity of a lifetime. She was the girl of his dreams. She practically begged him to lick her ear lobes! He wasn't about to let her slip away. After dropping Sharon's mailing material on the floor and slipping on spot of oil and falling on his face and jamming his elbow, he ran straight out to the parking lot and tripped over the curb. She was nowhere in sight. He looked into the sky, and she wasn't there either. She was sitting at a bus stop, but Malcolm didn't notice her. Smiling to herself, she knew he was looking for her, and he was a nice guy, but she really wasn't interested. Malcolm went back inside dejected, depressed, bloody elbow, sore nose, grease on his shoe, and as often happened at the worst possible times, his fly was open. He'd had better days.

The missed chance of romance and his failure to discuss marital options was depressing, but it was also exhilarating because he knew that there was a woman out there somewhere who was perfect and didn't get nauseous in his presence. Suddenly it was quite a red letter day for young Malcolm. He spent most of the afternoon daydreaming about her captivating eyes, her warm smile, her subtle perfume, and the way she didn't jab him in the spleen with a blunt object. His depression slowly subsided. He even forgot that his apartment had burned down.

IV

Visions of beauty can only last so long without becoming obsessions. Instead of obsessing, Malcolm went back to watching the mailing equipment cause ulcers for the low wage employees. The basic concept of the inserter was to... yes, insert mail into envelopes. It grabbed folded pieces of paper from a hopper and dropped them on a conveyer belt. As the conveyer belt moved, the stack of folded letters would get progressively larger. The more stations on the conveyer belt the more mail that could be stuffed into the envelope. It's true! The inserter had a stuffing station that seated the envelope and opened it. Once it was open, the stack of letters would get pushed into it, then the flap of the stuffed envelope would pass through a moistening mechanism and the flap would be closed. Finally, the sealed envelope would pass through a postage meter and get thrown onto another conveyor belt to be sorted or placed in a tray or lost or something.

Even more exciting, those malicious machines jammed if the paper didn't fall correctly, or if the envelope didn't open just right, or if the sealing mechanism got paper in it, or if the operator cursed at it. It was an unpredictable chaotic bliss and Malcolm loved it.

When the machine started moving, Malcolm strolled over to its side and watched it stuff away. It would stuff, it would jam, the operator would curse and it would jam again. The perpetual cycle saved millions of hours processing something that nobody wanted. Junk mail. Tons of junk mail rolled off the end of that machine on its way to the post office and eventually into the innocent mail boxes of millions of homes all over the world. It was just a good thing that there were machines to do it because nobody liked doing it by hand. The history of it? Oh, well, people used to label envelopes by hand using a long strip of mailing labels and a funky pair of scissors that had a pot of glue stuck on it. Those people were called "dickers". Not all dickers were happy with their work, but when automatic labelers came along, most of the dickers were unemployed. It made them angry and they cursed and the machines jammed, so they all laughed really hard. That was the happy ending to the tale of the displaced dickers... Since then the world has never been the same and the story would only get more pathetic if not for Malcolm's menacing curiosity in the whole process.

The inserter continued to rattle, whine, stuff, fold, spindle, and mutilate mail. The operator, R. Lee McGruter, who happened to be the president's son-in-law, was becoming more frustrated by the minute. The floor around the inserter was ankle deep in red and white envelopes. The trash cans were overflowing with smashed letters. Even the bucket specially designated for oily rags was spilling over with paper.

The aggravation on R. Lee's face was obvious to any fool, and a stream of obscenities that flowed sporadically from his mouth gave Malcolm the idea that perhaps some pleasant conversation would help the disgruntled machine operator.

"Workin' hard," dumb pause, "or hardly workin'?" Malcolm asked as he pointed his finger like a cowboy and winked.

R. Lee threw a pair of needle nose pliers in the direction of Malcolm's voice and impaled a five gallon can of yellow paint. Fortunately, Malcolm was looking at the floor when the pliers whizzed by his head and didn't notice their deadly trajectory.

Malcolm continued with his pleasant conversation, "I think we should try making artificial wood with this stuff."

R. Lee ignored him.

Malcolm thought about all the possibilities of artificial papier-mâché trees, artificial forests, artificial national reserves. He was thinking about artificial forest fires when he smelled authentic smoke coming from the oily rag bucket.

"So R. Lee, hate to interrupt, but what do you know about spontaneous combustion?" he asked.

R. Lee perked up, "Spontaneous human combustion?"

"No, just spontaneous combustion," said Malcolm as the smell of burning rags became stronger.

"One time, there was this guy in England who was just sitting there watching television, eating crumpets and kidney pies and the next thing you know... Poof! He just went up in smoke," R. Lee was an expert.

Malcolm shook his head, "I think we can safely blame space aliens for that, but there's a lot of smoke..."

"Smoke! That's all there is! You watch some of your more seasoned spontaneous human combusters and you'll see some real pyro-talent. They gotta be good! Some are so good, they'll burn up all the oxygen in a room in less than 3 seconds. They can actually put fires out! Lot of fire stations are hiring spontaneous human combusters lately. I hear the pay's good, but... "

As the smoke from the rag bucket began making it difficult to breath, R. Lee had trouble finishing his story. "Holy guacamole!" he shouted.

"Holy smokes," corrected Malcolm.

"We gotta get outta here."

"Or at least get a fire extinguisher," said Malcolm calmly.

R. Lee ran out the door. Malcolm grabbed a fire extinguisher from the other side of the shop, but by the time he returned, the fire was out of control and spreading towards a cache of propane tanks. The neighboring business was a chemical research facility that specialized in testing the efficiency of all the new laundry detergents and caustic defoliants. If the flames came too close to the adjoining wall, the entire building would be blown clean out of the business park. Yes, it would! If that wasn't bad enough, Nora and Marie were dragging Barney violently towards the inferno. There wasn't a horndog alive that could match the sheer physical strength of two furious scorned women. They were so committed they would have sacrificed their own lives in martyrdom if they thought they could put an end to just one overly promiscuous soul.

As a person who hated to see others hurt, especially by fire, Malcolm had to take action to prevent a pervert tragedy. He ran towards the fuming women and stood in their path with his fire extinguisher pointing at their feet, "Come on, now. Nobody wants to get hurt here. Put the horndog down."

Nora looked at Marie, then at Malcolm, "Get out of the way, Malcolm! This awful man's going to get a taste of hell on earth."

Marie was more animated, "We're taking him to a weenie roast!"

To clarify the obvious, Nora added, "And he's the weenie!"

The reference made Malcolm shiver, "No, no, I've got a better idea. Let's make him live with himself. What could be worse?"

Nora scratched her head and Marie loosened her grip on Barney. Barney fell to the ground and pulled his pants up. Malcolm expelled a sigh of relief. Astonished by the mercy of the women and the humanity of Malcolm, Barney thought about what it would be like to live with himself for any length of time and began walking towards the fire. Annoying as he was, there was no sense in letting a person burn himself to death. Malcolm would have felt responsible,

"Barney," he yelled over the crackling blaze, "I'm sorry! I think you have some options here. Just take a few minutes to think about this. You can always kill yourself, but this might be the only chance you have to turn your life around and make up for all the terrible things you've done to women over the years. Think of what you'd be missing out on."

The potential sentimentality of the moment was wasted when Devlette ran past the group and Barney ran after her screaming something about a personal fire hose. Nora and Marie picked up a couple of flaming sticks and followed Barney in hot pursuit. The whole parade of smoke and bad puns made Malcolm sick. He stumbled to the door and gagged profusely.

Looking back into the smoke, he saw the silhouettes of two temporary workers still diligently plugging away at their five dollar an hour jobs. He ran back in, grabbed their arms, and quickly escorted them out of the building. Responding to their protests, he assured them that they were still entitled to their full ten minute break period and they could smoke their cigarettes outside.

As they reached the door, an explosion threw all three of them to the ground. Within minutes the building was engulfed in flames. Fire trucks circled the building and their hoses were spread out as they arrived. Malcolm recognized some of the fire fighters from earlier that day. They recognized him and started chasing after him, waving their axes, and shouting first aid tips. A maze of old pallets served as a temporary hiding place for Malcolm and gave him a chance to think. He began to wonder if perhaps he was gifted with some sort of supernatural fire powers. He studied the appearance of each of his hands, then pointed to a fire hose and raised his finger. The fire hose suddenly became taught. He raised his hand and his boss saw him (the fire hose didn't do anything).

"Tent! R. Lee says you started this whole thing!" said mean old Mr. Norton.

"Well, actually I think it was spontaneous combustion," explained Malcolm.

"Spontaneous human combustion?" asked Norton.

Malcolm was in trouble, "Yeah, that's what it was. There was this strange English guy who came into the shop while no one was looking and said if we didn't stop sending him junk mail he was going to burst into flames. I told him that he had to live with junk mail and he turned red and ignited."

Mean old Mr. Norton sneered, "How stupid do you think I am? If he was a professional he would have put the fire out!"

"He could have been a rookie," lied Malcolm, like a rookie.

"I've listened to all I can take. You're as dumb as you look, fart face," he really said that, "You're fired! I want you out of my sight before I tear you limb from limb."

Well, Mr. Norton was mean, but at six foot three and about 98 pounds, he wasn't particularly threatening. Malcolm stood up and grabbed his former employer by his shirt collar, "I quit. You can't fire me. I mean, I can't fire you. No, me, you can't fire me! I'll quit!"

Norton quivered, Malcolm thought about what he'd just said until he was sure he got it right, "And another thing, you can shove and take, just shove this job... You can take this job and shove it. Damn it!"

Norton smiled, "You can't even quit right."

Malcolm pushed Norton away and stepped on his own shoe and fell backwards into a pile of trash bags. His ex-boss steadied himself and walked away. If Malcolm had nothing else, he had no dignity either. After burning down his place of work and failing to come up with a good insult for a ninety eight pound mean old man, he was lying in a pile of trash that didn't even qualify as good junk mail. Plus he twisted his knee after he tripped on shoe, and it really really hurt. That made him sulk.

Man-made clouds of thick black smoke barreled upwards as the fire fighters attempted to douse the intense flames. The mixture of chemicals and wood was a tenacious combination that Nowheresville's best couldn't overpower. There was nothing they could do to save the structure. At best they'd minimize the toxic fumes that were spewing into the wind. Malcolm couldn't help but feel guilty about the tragedy. It would be months before the insurance money would kick in and that would only take place after a lengthy criminal investigation to determine who was at fault. In the mean time, the residents of Nowheresville would have to get their junk mail from Elsewhere.

V

Miraculously, no one was killed or even physically injured at the Hot Diggity Dog Delivery Service and Grill disaster. But some scars aren't so visible. Some tragedies result in much deeper emotional turmoil. There was one unspeakable loss in the HDDDSG firestorm. One person lost his job. Malcolm Tent had joined the most loathsome ranks in the world, the unemployed. He'd been working since he was ten. In a period of less than seventeen years he'd gone from paper boy to hamburger cook to grocery clerk to paper boy to exotic dancer to Warehouse God. But that kind of success doesn't come cheap. Over the years, Malcolm had slowly developed into the callous capitalist he'd learned to despise in his pre-teen years.

In less than four hours of one day, he'd become a societal leech, a carrion of the, uh, diligent worker's tax contributions. He was a remora on the corporate sharks, he was a knocker on the door of, the door of, well, he wasn't quite a knocker, but he wasn't where he wanted to be in life. He was unemployed and homeless. Unemployed was one thing. Homeless is okay. But homeless and unemployed was below the level of the leech, the carrion, the remora, and even worse than the knocker. He was really bumming out, that's what Malcolm Tent was doing.

For the first time in his life he had to face the fact that anyone can get fired, or get laid off, or have to quit and he didn't want to admit that. He was all for higher education, but learning that anyone can find himself alone on the street wasn't at the top of his training schedule. Then again, nobody living on the street was realizing his or her dreams in life. The vast majority of homeless people in Nowheresville had mental illness, or drug problems, or both. They were physically sick or had been kicked out of their homes by abusive spouses, or lost their jobs and couldn't pay rent or mortgages. If someone had leukemia or heart failure, we hope they're getting medical treatment. If someone's schizophrenic or addicted or bankrupt, we don't think twice about them ending up on the street. But Malcolm wasn't thinking about any of them either. He was being selfish.

Malcolm tried to deny his circumstances. Somehow he had to convince himself that he wasn't homeless and unemployed. Technically, sure, his home and warehouse went up in flames and he didn't have a clue as to where to start rebuilding, but how long could it last? With all the opportunities in the world, who needs talent? Let's explore skills sets a little. Observe any civil construction task. You're driving down the street; you pass a construction site, nine times out of ten you'll see four guys standing next to one guy pushing a broom around in no particular direction. There's no question about the quality of the talent of the people standing next to a guy pushing a broom in no particular direction. If the homeless population was ever asked to change a light bulb, that would be a real dilemma, but to stand around as back up for a guy pushing a broom in no particular direction, let's assume the homeless could handle it. Malcolm knew that the homeless could handle it, and if he had to, he too would devote his life to standing around watching a guy pushing a broom in no particular direction. Then again, with all the technological advances that had taken place over the last few decades, it would only be a matter of time before somebody came up with a machine that could stand around watching a guy push a broom in no particular direction, and once more, Malcolm Tent would be unemployed.

He wandered aimlessly through the streets. Nowhere to go, no shelter, no friends he could trust... He was okay with that. Let's not forget that every aimless journey starts with a single step. He could rough it for a night or two until something came along. He sat at a bus stop and watched water running along the gutter down a storm drain. A black man was wandering down the street, panhandling. The panhandler looked healthy enough to get a job. He was the reason the country was in such bad shape. People perfectly capable or contributing to society were feeding off the goodwill of others until the goodwill was sucked away. It disgusted Malcolm to look at the man.

The beggar passed him and asked for a handout, "Say, buddy, can you spare some change?"

Without looking at the man, Malcolm replied, "Change yourself."

Always ready with a comeback, the man said, "Yeah, thanks, I'll change myself. Guess I'll be white." He shook his head, "Or maybe I'll jus' skip the white thing and change to rich directly. I guess maybe I'll just be anybody but me."

Malcolm watched him while the one way conversation continued.

"Well, I could become an ambassador to some oil producing country. Wonder if OPEC needs anybody to help 'em figure out what to do wit all that oil." He scratched his head, "Hey, buddy, what'd North Sea Sweet Crude close at today? I might need to sell off some of my commodities. I need to change something anyway." The man laughed to himself and continued on his street search for excess money.

Malcolm wasn't the type of guy who went around trying to instigate trouble, but that guy was way out of line with his Sweet Crude crack. "Hey," he said boldly, "you do need to change. It's people like you that have turned this city into a sewer."

The beggar stopped and turned around to get a good look at bold Malcolm. He stepped slowly towards him. "Yeah, that's right," he exclaimed. "People *like me* love turning these wonderful cities into sewers. Every Tuesday night my people get together to figure out better ways to mess up the system. Not you, though, eh? You're part of the system that keeps everything running smooth. If everybody was like you, world would be perfect."

Malcolm started to agree with him, but didn't feel like pushing the issue. The guy could have been some kind of maniacal gun packing drug dealer. The bum stood for a second waiting for Malcolm to respond. He got no response and muttered as he walked away, "Rising from the wake of burgeoning sewage, the soul surfer shows the world how to ride it out. World don't want to know." He looked back at Malcolm and smiled, "You hear?"

Malcolm didn't reply and the vagrant vanished into an alleyway. Malcolm looked over his shoulder and the beggar was gone. "Yeah, right!" he thought, quietly, to himself, "Dude reads too much beach graffiti."

Unbeknownst to Malcolm, the vagrant was followed into the alley by Armadillo's younger brothers, Slurp and Gurgle.

"Hey", said Slurp to the unemployed gentleman, "You probably don't like that guy much, do ya?"

The bum looked at them and clasped his hand around the few coins he had collected that morning. "I don't got nuthin' 'gainst nobody. I just mind my own business and I got nuthin' for you to take," he said as he crouched down and huddled into a ball.

Gurgle set a twenty dollar bill in front of the bum and asked, "How would you like to have some fun with that guy you were just talking to?" His eyes met the bum's distrusting expression. "Nothing dangerous, just fun! I'm talking about a scam. A legal scam."

The bum snatched up the twenty and smiled, "I ain't never tried a legal scam."

Slurp and Gurgle smiled. A short conversation ensued.

Back on the bus stop bench, Malcolm was passing time. Other people passed on the sidewalk. Malcolm sat and watched them and thought of the burgeoning sewage, thought of the people that looked ahead and walked without making eye contact, thought of the little groups of little men that walked ahead and looked at purses, wallets, and watches, thought of the smoke that spewed from city buses, thought of bags of instant food that were steadily being pumped into the masses. The beggar was right, the sewers were exploding and everyone was quite content to wallow in the wake. It didn't matter to Malcolm either. He had managed to hit a new low. If the earth opened up and swallowed all of mankind into its unforgiving craw then shut again tightly, Malcolm would have considered it a happy ending.

In the thirty minutes that followed, the earth didn't open up, mankind thrived ahead, and Malcolm continued on with his miserable bright and shiny evening. He wasn't sure if he was perpetuating the day, or if the day was perpetuating him. He decided that he'd let the day perpetuate him for a while and casually strolled around the downtown area of the city.

It was a campus community filled with big dreams and little minds. The free spirit of other people's youth irritated Malcolm. They either thought that they were justified in oppressing because they were financially empowered to do so or they had been oppressed so long that they felt retribution was fair recourse. They may not have consciously oppressed their neighbors, but they oppressed them anyway. He saw them all as arrogant offspring who would much rather get away with murder than pump life into the world. Not one of them knew why they were doing what they were doing, and that was pathetic. They might have had great thoughts or great parties or thought they were having revolutionary romance, but they couldn't have known how lucky they were to be in college. Most of them would learn on their own, but a lot of them would continue to do things because they were told to live a certain kind of life with no questions asked. Malcolm too would eventually learn that he had to make life, then live it, but that was Malcolm's future, and his immediate world was enveloped by uncaring insensitive brats. The college kids were terrible, the bums were terrible, the average American was terrible. Malcolm needed a blues song and he needed one fast.

His frustration with American youth was compounded as he overheard a conversation between several young idealistic intellectuals taking place near the bus stop bench. Let's listen in.

"You know, Chad, I think your views about television really are sexist," said Chip, an average collegiate renaissance man with an orange baseball cap and big green plaid shorts.

Chad, who was wrapped in rich kid grunge duds, bristled and barked, "Nuh, uh! I just said that women are constantly portrayed as, like, physical objects and I don't think it's right. Not all women are gorgeous models with perfect figures."

"Yeah, but by saying that television commercials should be censored, you're saying that women can't distinguish between truth and fiction. That implies that women are stupid!"

"Now that is sexist!" shouted Chad.

"Nuh, uh," said Chip with equal conviction and vigor.

"Uh huh! You're saying that I'm saying that all women are stupid just because I'm a guy. If I wanted to say something like that, you'd be all over me."

Talk about annoying. Those people were serious. There happened to be a young female college student in the intellectual circle at the time, and as luck would have it, she was gorgeous with a perfect figure. She allowed her male counterparts to continue arguing like idiots for a few minutes. She assumed that they were both trying to impress her with what they believed to be contemporary philosophies on how women should want to be treated and how rough life was for the modern woman. Since neither one of the guys was particularly good looking and neither one had a nice car, she was willing to let them battle it out to the death if necessary. At least that would leave one less imbecile she'd have to turn down for a date. Unfortunately for her, she coughed and the two guys were forced to acknowledge her presence and consequently forced to acknowledge that she might have an opinion, even though she was a woman. Naturally, they never let on that her opinion would be inferior due to her femininity.

"Oh, so, Amy," said Chip, looking at her feet, "What do you think about the way women are treated in the media?"

"They're actresses, they get paid to work, right?" she replied.

Chad joined in, "The money's not the point. We're talking about women degrading other women by the millions. Selling out their Sisterhood."

Not having an official sisterhood membership card, Amy wasn't sure if she should address the selling out thing, but she definitely had an opinion, "Yes, I think it's criminal what they're doing to women today."

Chip and Chad were secretly happy.

Amy continued, "They've been providing women with the means to gain self confidence through appearance far too long!"

Chip and Chad were secretly confused.

Amy went on, "Just because a man can succeed in business by putting on a suit and tie to look good and perform brainless tasks is no justification for women to try and look good for the same reason."

Chip and Chad sensed a certain amount of facetiousness.

"Anyone who takes a television commercial that seriously can't be too bright. It's just a thirty second shot at getting into somebody's wallet. Money is the only point! Anyway, I suspect that if market surveys indicated that men purchased the same products that women purchased today, they'd still be marketed the same way except they'd use men for models instead of women."

"So men would be acting all sexy and covered in make-up," said Chad, ironically.

"They would if they bought make-up," Amy explained.

"All I'm saying is women are forced to wear it and act stupidly," said Chip, stupidly.

"But I want to look good," demanded Amy.

"Yeah but you don't have to," Chad observed.

"I don't? What a relief! Finally," she sighed, "Hey, either of you need an old razor or mascara? Or shampoo? I used to prefer to try to look good. But now I'll trade all my stuff for your orange cap and those baggy shorts. Oh, is it cool with you dudes if I fart?"

Woo! The conversation had come to a point where nothing else needed to be said. The whole man versus woman thing had been settled again. The guys stood there scratching their heads with no clear direction in life. Amy took her books and went off to the library where she could continue to prepare herself intellectually for a business world that was dominated by idiots of all genders.

Nice butt, thought Chip and Chad as she walked away. With no icky girls around, the two abrasive intellectuals were free to talk about more meaningful topics of much greater gravity.

"Why'd you say that? Idiot," asked Chad.

"Idiot."

"At this very moment the universe is expanding at an astounding rate!" said Chad.

Chip tried to appear thoughtful, "Then again, it could be collapsing as we speak."

"Damn!" thought Malcolm, "I better pick up my dry cleaning."

He knew of course that his dry cleaning wouldn't be ready because he had no dry cleaning. He knew the universe wouldn't implode completely for a couple weeks. He also knew that paranoid young people would continue to thrive on their own fear and the fears of others. Businesses would survive off the fear of competition and promote fear to market their goods and services. A stray mongrel was kicking back against a wall watching various human cultures disintegrate.

Malcolm said to himself, "It's a doggie dog world in a collapsing universe, and here I am with no dry cleaning to speak of."

He contemplated the wealth of societal sustenance wasting itself away and flowing into oblivion. It angered him to think that there were areas of the world that were once bursting with life but were quickly becoming vast deserts from lack of water because civil engineering contractors convinced a third world government to pay for a dam or reroute a river. He thought of the endless reserves of food, goodwill, brilliance, and skills that his country was hoarding and wouldn't share with anyone.

As he began to shrivel up into a misanthropic lump of useless flesh and bone, a stranger tapped him on the shoulder. Malcolm was not in the mood to acknowledge the existence of another being, so he ignored the stranger. The stranger shook Malcolm's shoulder and Malcolm contracted his body letting out an unintelligible gasp.

The stranger spoke, "Malcolm?"

Wallowing in hatred and spite, it was difficult for young Malc to accept the voice. The fact that some strange person actually knew his name meant that he would have to postpone his social retreat until the stranger had been acknowledged, given suitable recognition, and sent on his way with the increased awareness that good old Malcolm was a hopeless loser. Malcolm looked up and smiled. It was the beggar he ran into earlier. He stopped smiling. "What do you want?"

"Do you remember me?" the beggar asked shyly.

"Are you the guy who invented sweat scented deodorant?"

The beggar smiled, "No, man, I was talking to you earlier..."

"Oh yeah, you're the black guy who thinks that you got to be white to succeed. I got news for you buddy, the world stinks for everybody. You just think you found somebody to blame. Well, this white guy can't do anything for you, and if you think..."

The beggar interrupted Malcolm's little soliloquy, "No, no, I'm sorry about that outburst earlier. Ya see, I've got a family I'm trying to feed. I've got a beautiful wife, two beautiful children... Actually, Malcolm, I've got three children. Two of 'em are beautiful, then there's you."

Malcolm rolled his eyes in reply.

The transient continued to ramble, "About twenty five years ago I met a beautiful night club dancer in Des Moines. We dated a few times, one thing led to another, and about nine months later, you came along. Now, I don't need to tell you that a young black man and a young white girl didn't have a snowball's chance in Hell of giving a kid a decent life twenty five years ago. Alice, that was your mother's name, she had to put you up for adoption. She made me promise her that I'd follow you for the rest of your life. I had some friends working for the county and they were able to tell me where I could find you. For a long time it was easy to follow you. At least up until a few years ago when I lost track of you 'cause you left your adopted parents. I just figured you were out of the picture and I got problems of my own so I thought that was the end of it. I gave up on you son, I never expected to see you again. When I saw you earlier, I didn't recognize you, you know? ...Thought you was one of those college punks dressin' down to be cool. By the time I realized who you were, you were gone. It ain't easy to find a person around here. Anyway..."

"Hang on, Pop," said Malcolm, "I hate to ruin your story, but let's just get a few things straightened out here. I've never been to Des Moines, my parents lived in Long Beach all their lives, I'm the spitting image of my dad, and if none of that's enough, there seems to be a slight difference in our racial backgrounds."

The beggar looked himself over, "Your mother was very strong."

"You're black!" Malcolm yelled, trying not to offend anybody.

"Your mother was white, and my father was white, but my mother was black, you see? The mother's skin color always matches the baby's. How else could you be white? Come on now, I know you're smarter than that."

"Yeah, well, I have nothing against African Americans. I've met good and bad people from all backgrounds. For all I know, your race and role could just be some literary vehicle for a higher moral message to society. But I thought that brown eyes and dark hair were dominant traits, and I've got green eyes and blond hair. I mean, you couldn't be my father. Look, I'm sorry, I'm sure you'd make a nice father, and all that, but you're not my father, and I don't have any spare change, and if you don't mind, I'm trying to give up on the whole human race."

The beggar was used to being rejected and wasn't about to let some kid get away without having a little fun. "Don't you talk like that to me young man, I'm your father. Your poor mother must be rolling in her grave right now. All that talk about dominant genes and dark hair and blond hair... Man, all that stuff sounds like something from Adolph Hitler to me. Now, I didn't raise no Nazi racist, and all I can say is I hope that's not the path you've chosen, but if it is, well, it's your life. Hope your luck turns around. Take care. I'm glad I got to see you one last time." The bum stood up and began walking away, then stopped and turned around. "Son, I have to give you something before I go."

Malcolm's big innocent eyes watched the beggar reach deep into his pocket and pull out... his hand. Then they watched him reach into his other pocket and pull out... his other hand. Somewhat confused and disappointed, the homeless man thought about his attempt at generosity for a moment, then punched Malcolm in the shoulder.

"Ow!" whined Malcolm.

The bum held back a smile, "That was a magical charley horse."

Rubbing his shoulder, Malcolm asked, "What's so magic about it, jerk?"

Feigning astonishment, the beggar explained, "Now, now, every time you think of that pain in your arm, you're gonna know the pain you given me over the years. You remember the first time you took your adopted father's car without his permission?"

Malcolm replied cautiously, "Yeah..."

"And the first time you smoked that cigarette," the bum added, "And the time you snuck that shot of hard liquor?"

"But how did you know?" Malcolm asked.

"Didn't feel too good afterwards, did you?" the street master asked.

Shaking his head for no good reason, Malcolm started to object to the generality of the questions, but the bum interrupted, "I was there. I put that pain in your head and your heart. Just like I put that pain in your shoulder. I want you to think about that, son. You do right by your father or you'll feel the magical pain again. Every time!"

Perhaps it wasn't the most ingenious barrel of baloney ever to roll through the streets of Nowheresville, but it was enough to confuse Malcolm into believing that it must hold some truth.

The old man turned his back to Malcolm and smiled as he said, "Son, I wanted you to have the best of everything, but you let me down. I can't do anything for you until you stop hurting yourself. If you can't even do that, I'm gonna have to give up on you." Without looking back he walked slowly down the sidewalk.

The thought of a father giving up on his son was the epitome of Malcolm's nickel philosophy on the degradation of the American society, but that beggar was obviously playing games with him. The bum wandered slowly away, glancing back once or twice to see if Malcolm's attention was following him. There was nothing Malcolm could do for the poor guy that he couldn't do for himself. He was physically capable and he was sharp. He had more going for him than most corporate executives. Malcolm felt no compulsion to chase after him or offer him so much as a good word. With the vagrant out of the picture, Malcolm was free to return to loathing and hating mankind.

Less than a minute after diving into a deep social repulsion, Malcolm's meditation was broken by the sounds of happy children. He'd completely forgotten about children, but he wanted to include them in his hate session, so he took a quick glance towards the impish voices. As the old man wandered into the passing crowd, two children ran up to Malcolm and showed him some brightly colored drawings. One of the pictures displayed a house and a red sun and a dog and two kids and a mommy and a daddy. The other was a brilliant aquamarine seascape stretched out under a mauve sunset created by long delicate brush strokes playfully blending form and color. The foreground depicted a sandy rock-peppered beach meeting the waves with two young lovers strolling hand in hand along the shore. Seabirds raced along the water's edge and you could practically smell the salty sea air and feel the sun's warmth.

"Realism," thought Malcolm, "Ha!" When he was a kid he certainly didn't have time to dabble with oil painting and artistic creativity. He was busy listening to his predecessors complain about their torturous childhood toils of wandering forty miles through the snow, crossing endless expanses of sand dunes in bare feet carrying their four siblings in one arm just to get an ice cube for their drunken uncle's martini or to pick up some blisters for their bed ridden moms. Then again, Malcolm's childhood wasn't so bad, as he recalled. He had toys, television, eight track tapes, records, two butlers, box seats at the L.A. Coliseum, a private jet, a picture of Raquel Welch in rockin' cave duds, and a chemistry set. His memory may have been fooling him a little bit. He was certain about the Raquel Welch picture, but the other stuff may have belonged to the neighbor's kid. No, the chemistry set was Malcolm's. He vaguely remembered using it to make gunpowder, melt toys dolls, and accidentally burn down his parent's garage. If he had another father, he certainly would have remembered him. There was no way. No possible way that the strange African American soul surfing man was his real birth father.

Alone in hard times, he wandered the dusty inner city streets. Following no direction, the city seemed to guide him from street corner to street corner. He walked for hours eventually winding up in a silent urban retreat. The day had slipped into darkness sooner than he expected. The sidewalks were empty and the few cars that passed through the streets moved quickly, their drivers focusing only on the road in front of them. It seemed like a good place for him to hang out for a while with no distractions, no annoying urbanites, and no possibility of running into anyone he knew. Although he hated seeing homeless people curled up on the sidewalk, he couldn't deny that he was exhausted and needed to get some sleep. He sat on the sidewalk and propped himself against a wall. Everything was quiet when an old man approached him and shook him until he woke up.

The old guy was wearing nice clothes, a white cardigan sweater and blue polyester pants. Snazzy duds.

"Excuse me," the man said hesitantly. "You don't appear to be dying of any incurable malady, and your clothes can't be more than a year old. Are you absolutely sure you're in the right place?"

The guy seemed nice enough, but the last thing Malcolm needed was to be harassed because he wasn't dying soon enough. "What do you mean, 'Am I in the right place?' I was hoping to get a penthouse suite at the Amalgamated Inn, but somebody stole my reservation. Leave me alone."

The gentleman appeared hurt. "I'm sorry. It's just that most people I meet in this area have nothing left to live for. It's a pretty rough part of town, you know? If you can walk, I'd like to suggest that you find somewhere else to rest. Did you know that two people, homeless people, were killed here just last week, and another died of pneumonia."

Malcolm didn't need advice from a benevolent old man with nothing better to do than save dying bums. "I'll manage," he said curtly.

"I really do think you should move along before midnight," the old man said nicely, but firmly.

"Listen, I can take care of myself. Maybe *you* oughta move along."

The elderly fellow sensed Malcolm's naiveté. He'd seen it before and had been called into the morgue to try and identify the consequences of such foolishness, "Maybe the police can persuade you."

"Hey, I'm just mindin' my own business. Why don't you do the same?"

The kindly man shook his head, "I don't know what else to do. I've asked you politely to move on," he pulled out a gun. "Now I really must insist."

Malcolm was hardly ever threatened at gunpoint. He didn't like it, not much anyway. He stood up quickly and stepped back.

The old man was scared, but determined, "I'll give you to the count of ten."

Malcolm took a step backwards.

"Run!"

And Malcolm ran for three blocks before he looked back and saw that the man was still standing there. When the menacing philanthropist saw that Malcolm was committed to moving on, he slowly turned around and walked the other direction.

It wasn't so much the gun that bothered Malcolm, it was the look of kindness in the man's eyes. Of course the gun didn't help, but the guy seemed so rational, deliberate, even wise.

As Malcolm walked along the street he found a cop sitting in a patrol car and told him about the incident. The officer wasn't interested until Malcolm described the age of his assailant.

The cop laughed, "You shoulda thanked him! He wasn't gonna hurt you, he probably saved your life. Do you know how many people die on the street around here from violence? A kid like you wouldn't make it through the night. Get outta here before I shoot you myself."

Feeling very agreeable, Malcolm kept walking. He'd been threatened by a cop and a nice old man in less than fifteen minutes. His outlook on life was changing a little. Maybe he really was naive. Maybe people that were expected to be good, were actually evil, and if that was true, then it followed that evil looking people must be good. Just down the street, he saw someone sitting on a motorcycle outside a third rate strip bar who was obviously willing to do damage to any living creature. There was something about the guy that seemed off. It was probably a combination of the tattoo of Manson on his forehead or the rabbit foot keychain (which happened to have the entire rabbit attached to it).

Curious Malcolm walked up to him and explained his dilemma.

The street denizen looked at him and shook his head, Malcolm's head, and said, "Heh, that old guy's something else. If you were sick or bleeding to death, he'd take you to a doctor's. If you were hungry he'd give you food. But if you got two good feet, he'll get you movin'." The mean looking fellow smiled malevolently and said, "Now I'm gonna have to shoot you 'cause you're too stupid."

He grabbed Malcolm's shirt and drew a gun from his belt.

Thinking quickly Malcolm stuck his finger into the barrel of the gun. The hoodlum balked, classic balk. Then Malcolm, still new to street life, tickled the maniac's chin. The blood thirsty gun toting "kill you where you stand" madman giggled and had to drop the gun to cover his mouth. When the gun hit the street, it went off and shot the murderous rogue in his leg. Good had triumphed over evil and Malcolm felt somehow relieved that some of his instilled values were fatefully rewarded.

Malcolm ran and ran and ran. See Malcolm run. He stopped, looked behind him, and ran some more. Gripping, isn't it?

Blackness was crashing down on Nowheresville and the night life began to materialize. The city streets were generally either filled with deadly stillness or wild crowds. Malcolm found the deadly stillness of the business district's vacancy on a Tuesday night. He rested in a quiet stoop and watched the night slowly take control of his destiny. He knew that anyone who crossed his path that evening would have to be on drugs or lost or crazy. A light rain passed over the city that night. It wasn't enough to wash the dirt from street. On the contrary, it only managed to bring the dirt back to the surface. Malcolm was dampened by the rain and he had no way to get dry, but he eventually found shelter from the rain beneath a corrugated metal loading ramp. Exhausted and covered in misery, he fell asleep.

He woke up a few hours later, the memories of a violent dream still fresh in his head. He dreamt that legions of armies carrying broadswords were attacking families without men. There were guns and grenades, and Malcolm lost his legs somehow. He remembered the face of a woman as she held a gun to his head and pulled the trigger. Nobody likes those dreams. The memory was palpable. Waking up could have been worse.

Throughout the rest of the night, he barely shut his eyes at all and after several hours of introspection, the morning sun began to cast light on the city. He had survived the night, but the day ahead of him seemed to offer just as many threats. No job and no place to stay, if he could at least get back to his car, he'd have a safe place to sleep and possibly a way to get around. He set off to check on his car. It would probably take him all day to get there, but he wasn't in any hurry.

As he walked in the general direction of Armadillo's home he found an old portable radio. It was sitting on the sidewalk at the end of an alley. To his surprise, it worked, but as he attempted to tune into his favorite station, the tuner knob broke. Fortunately, it broke on a station. Unfortunately, it stopped on a top ten country music station. Worse yet, the country station was playing a song,

> "Oh... My dog up and left me,
> then my gal say'd good-bye,
> I'm so dern sad and lonely,
> I could curl up, and die"

It wasn't much, but music kept Malcolm going. Music truly was his only friend. The singer was performing solo, without background instruments and that really hit home for Malcolm. He too was on his own, completely alone.

*"Well my house caught on fire,
and the judge called my bluff,
I fell down in the shower,
enough is enough."*

Malcolm didn't usually listen to country music, but in those words, those deep magnificent meaningful lyrics, he felt for the first time that he had some distant companionship in his miserable existence. The Human Condition was politely shared by ten maybe twenty other wretched illiterate souls listening to the same station.

*"I been wanderin' the ghettos,
and the small backwoods towns,
and I don't see no grinnin',
just them long lonesome frowns."*

The gravity of the brutal, base, unfeeling fist that Life uses to pound the wind out of every human and knock all hope from the frail psyche was honestly conveyed in those words. There could be only one solution, one final way out, but Malcolm sensed for the first time in years that he would not take that path alone. Somewhere a bucolic angel cast out sympathy to the unwanted, the tired and the poor.

*"Well my story's all done now,
I'm through killin' time,
but my limo is waitin',
I get paid by the rhyme."*

Some stinking rich cheesy paste faced squeaky clean bigoted yodeling mama's boy knew exactly how Malcolm was feeling, and making millions off it. And Malcolm, well, Malcolm was alone again, but at least there were dozens or maybe five other people in the world with broken radios who knew exactly how Malcolm felt.

*"So I hope I have touched ya,
with the sound on my voice,
but don't feel that it's over,
cuz we all have a choice."*

He was alone. He knew it. He took that old broken radio and threw it at a big green dumpster. He missed and it landed on the asphalt, and broke a little more. So he picked it up and threw it again, and missed again. So he just yelled at it and stomped away. Bad radio. Bad.

After Malcolm was about fifty feet away from the giant trash receptacle, a strange human head began to rise above the edge to watch him go. As the first head leveled off, the distinctive white bandanna of young Slurp Cleef poked up with a sinister grin. Armadillo's younger brothers climbed out of the dumpster and picked up their radio. Gurgle took the speaker and the receiver out of the plastic case and put it in his pocket. Slurp sang a couple more lyrics about Malcolm into a miniature microphone using his best country twang. They patted each on the back and both fell over laughing.

VI

It was a little early in the day for Malcolm to feel abject depression, but Malcolm didn't care about the time. He was at the end of his rope again. He needed to turn his life around, or at least find a longer rope, so he set out to make some fundamental changes in his own little world. He decided to get out of the Nowheresville, Man. Get away from it all. The irritating song on the radio somehow inspired him. He wanted to visit the country, the rural backroads. Maybe find a quiet lake and do some fishin'. Umm humm! That was it. Malcolm Tent was officially on Holiday.

He decided he could get his car later that night if he felt like it. At that moment he just needed some fresh air, a little honest exercise, and then some serious relaxation. That's all he needed to clear his mind and refresh his soul. He'd been wrapped up in the material trappings that capture and constrain the inhabitants of the civilized world far too long. A day with nature was the best thing he could do for himself.

It took him a while to get to the edge of Nowheresville and the walk was invigorating. His body was beginning to heal and flush the urban toxins out of his system. It made him feel warm... no, it made him feel groovy... no, no. It made him feel like a natural ma'an. It also made him pretty hungry. Unfortunately, there weren't any wheat germ, or tofu, or carob stores outside of the city as far as Malcolm could tell. There was, however, by miraculous coincidence, a gourmet chili dog shack right there in spitting distance. He ordered up a few rounds of Parisian style Sheeli Doogs with a side order of French sauerkraut and consumed them like a passionate pig (as any culinary aficionado will explain, is the only way to chow down on a chili dog).

He supped, he burped, he continued aimlessly in his crusade for healthy pursuits. Somewhere outside the Nowheresville was the Holy Touloume Reservoir. If Malcolm could just make it to that oasis of serenity, he'd be safe and free to fish. The lake was only two hundred yards from the chili dog shack, so he was pretty confident he could make it. There were still obstacles to overcome before he could abandon himself in the timeless tradition of so many smelly fishermen that had fished before him. First of all, he didn't have a fishing pole. Second, he didn't know how to fish. Finally, if he ever caught a fish, he had no idea what he would do with it. Those were some tough challenges for the serious fisherman to overcome, but Malcolm, being neither a fisherman, nor serious, and not really all that tough, was ready to cope with any obstacles. He simply dismissed them (copius dismissius). The act of dangling a line in the water while surrounded by peace and quiet would provide him the therapy he yearned for.

A brief search for fishing gear led him to a broken kite sitting next to a trash can. He took one of the cross braces from the kite, unraveled a little string, and made his own custom trademarked Malcolm Tent fishin' pole. The remaining kite parts were left behind outside the trash can just in case some other innovative camper needed to build an igloo or something.

With his string and pole in hand, he marched straight to a nice shady old oak tree overlooking the lake, sat down at the trunk of the tree, dropped the line in the water (about three inches deep), leaned back and dozed off. Talk about stress maintenance.

About four hours later, he was awakened as something tugged at his pole. It jerked the pole clear out of his hands. He opened his eyes expecting to see an angry marlin or an uncanned tuna fish staring right at him. What did he see? A 250 pound cop!

"Hey, buddy. There's no fishing in the Holy Touloume Reservoir."

Malcolm looked around for a no fishing sign or any sign of intelligent life, but saw none.

The police officer continued, "You got a license?"

"No," Malcolm explained in a groggy voice, "but I wasn't planning to catch anything."

"Oh. You just decided to go fishing, but you weren't going to catch any fish."

Understanding that the guy probably learned those kinds of trick questions in cop school, Malcolm nodded, gulped, and said, "Yes, sir. I really really wasn't going to catch anything."

Raising an eyebrow, the officer asked, "Yeah? Did the fish know that?"

The fish in the reservoir listened closely as Malcolm replied, "No! Look, this isn't even a fishing pole. No reel! There's no hook, no bait! "

"Hey, I'm not a fish, so don't try that line on me."

Malcolm shook his head.

"I suppose if you were holding a gun to my head, you'd tell me you didn't plan to shoot," said the officer.

Malcolm started to argue, but couldn't get a word in.

"That's it. You're under arrest."

"For what!" demanded Malcolm.

"Fishing in a no fishing zone, fishing without a license, and resisting arrest."

"I wasn't resisting arrest!"

"A second ago you were holding a gun to my head," the cop said vengefully.

Argue. That's what Malcolm could not do. He was cuffed, taunted, and taken downtown.

It must have been a slow day at the police station. Malcolm cooperated completely as he went through the motions; searching, booking, fingerprints, pictures, autographs, begging for mercy, lengthy monosyllabic conversations, the usual stuff. None of that prevented him from getting thrown into the drunk tank accidentally. Drunk tanks aren't so bad, when you think about it. Most bars are like drunk tanks except that bars have intoxicated people of all genders and jail cells just have men. Women's drunk tanks might be a completely different story and Malcolm made a mental note to get thrown into one of those at some point in his life. After sitting in the holding cell for four or five hours watching young drunks vomit and old drunks tell epic depressing stories, the booking sergeant called Malcolm to the desk to go over the charges. The cell door was opened and Malcolm felt the stale air of freedom.

As the booking sergeant read over the charges to Malcolm an expression of confusion fell across his face. He looked at Malcolm apologetically then looked around the station for any kind of explanation. A few patrolmen were watching him with amusement from across the room. The sergeant excused himself and struck up a conversation with some of the grinning officers. They were pointing and making fishing pole gestures and they all seemed to be having a good laugh. Cop work never looked so fun as when the booking officer pretended to choke the arresting officer. The sergeant returned and tried to explain the whole kooky mix up.

"Alright, Mister Tent, apparently there's been some kind of unusual misunderstanding. It seems that a couple of your friends have put a good one over on everyone here," said the officer.

Without crumbling into a state of uncontrollable agony by pointing out the obvious, Malcolm asked, "What friends?"

The sergeant looked serious, "The Cleef brothers. They worked it out with Occiffer Grizeldi. They said that you wouldn't mind a little harmless harassment this afternoon. And frankly, Grizeldi just brought you in to irritate me." He paused thoughtfully, "So if you're even thinking about bringing charges of false arrest against the Nowheresville Police Department, I've got news for you, punk. These are all very serious crimes and we could easily bring you up on charges. You could be doing some hard time in county jail for your disrespect of the law. You were in violation of 8479.38 of the Fish and Game Code, I122C.K of the Health and Sanitation Code, and OOOG.12 of the Civil Code."

"If only I'd had my secret decoder ring I could have got away with it," replied Malcolm.

The booking sergeant was frustrated with the whole scene, but, "I'll tell you what I'm gonna do. If you leave right now, we won't press charges, and if you watch your step and keep your nose clean, we'll let this whole thing slide. Consider this your lucky day."

It would have been much easier for Malcolm to consider it his lucky day if he had been hit by a truck.

"The problem is, sir, I don't have a car and I need to get back home," Malcolm said as he remembered that he had no home.

"We'll get you home all right. Grizeldi will be happy to take you anywhere you want to go. And you might want to have a word with the Cleef brothers about their pranks. We don't have time for this kind of thing down at Nowheresville Central," said the officer in an apologetic vindictive way.

As the booking sergeant went over to Grizeldi, Malcolm thought about how he could pay back Slurp and Gurgle Cleef. Knowing that the two bipedal rodents, Slurp and Gurgle, were far too cunning to ever fall into Malcolm's cleverest traps, his options were limited to name calling and obscene gestures. He watched the conversation between the Sarge and Grizeldi. Grizeldi was waving his arms around and the Sarge was pointing at all the desks in the office. Both of them had their hands on their revolvers. Finally, the booking sergeant pulled some breath mints out of his pocket and offered one to Grizeldi. With tears in his eyes, Grizeldi forced a smiled, took a mint, and soon they were both laughing at the whole zany situation.

The sergeant returned to Malcolm. "Grizeldi will meet you out in the lobby as soon as he finishes his paper work, Mister Tent."

Feeling a little unjustly treated, Malcolm wasn't quite ready to go. "Can I have a breath mint?" he asked politely.

The sergeant put his hand on his revolver, "No way."

Malcolm squinted at him and backed away towards the front of the building.

The lobby was filled with cheap pine benches and plastic palm trees, and sunflower seeds were all over the floor. It was painted in a dingy yellow earth tone and all its walls had anti-drug posters and paintings of old TV cops shows hanging on them. Malcolm sat on a bench in the lobby of the police station waiting for his ride. There were a few other people in the lobby looking very uncomfortable, very nervous. Depression began its gradual uncompromising descent into Malcolm's mind ...but it was interrupted. Yay! An attractive young woman entered the station. She had long blond hair that flowed down over her shoulders, the way long hair does. Malcolm tried not to think about sex as she walked by, but let's face it, guys are pigs and she was absolutely hot. As she crossed the lobby to the front desk, Malcolm sensed an energy that was vivacious and frustrated, perky, yet troubling.

"I need to post bail for someone," she told the desk clerk.

The desk clerk, a civil servant, continued to do whatever it was she thought she was doing. Without looking up at the young women, she spit out the word, "Name?" She said it like, "Hello" and "How can I help you" had never come out of her mouth in her entire miserable life.

"Jimmy Shwirl," said the young woman, Matilda.

The grumpy public employee looked at Matilda with a blank expression on her face. Those expressions… What do they mean? Are they trying to say that they didn't understand the words they just heard? Is the blank face supposed to indicate that they've done everything they plan to do and won't even honor their counterpart with another word? Maybe the blank expression is a physical reaction of someone who's very close to passing a large volume of gas.

Matilda didn't have time to figure out the cause of the blank expression. She had to deal with the stressful task of bailing out her stupid boyfriend.

"The name Jimmy Shwirl should be on a piece of paper and on the computer next to you. Since you can get to that information more quickly than anyone else in the world, I'd really appreciate it if you could find his name and tell me what you know about Jimmy Shwirl's bail," she said all feisty like!

That was a tone that the American civil servant, paid by American taxes, could understand. She was capable of responding not because she needed to save face and assist one of her clients, but because she was comfortable believing that she really did have the worst job in Nowheresville. Having affirmed her position as an abused employee, she had nothing better to do than work. She put both hands on the computer keyboard and stared at the screen. "What was the name?"

With an angry smile, Matilda repeated in an even tone, "Yes. It's Jimmy Shwirl, S, H, W, I, R, L."

"I have a James Shwirl," said the idiot clerk, a little more congenially.

"That's his code name," replied Matilda.

The clerk was on a roll. "He was brought in today at 10:30 a.m. and bail was set by Judge Arump."

"How much?"

"The Honorable Arump has set bail at $15,000," said the clerk.

Matilda couldn't believe what she heard, she wasn't exactly in love with the moron she was bailing out and even if she was, she didn't have $15,000. "$15,000?" she asked, suddenly at the mercy of the clerk.

"Judge Arump has set bail at $15,000. You can pay 10% of that amount by cashier's check and we'll let him out," said the important government worker as she began plugging away at a calculator.

Matilda fumbled through her purse.

"That's $150," said the clerk, hesitantly.

Matilda pulled out $1500 in cash and set it on the counter.

The clerk, somewhat feverishly, punched buttons on her calculator. "That's $1500," said the clerk more confidently.

Matilda pointed to the cash and the clerk looked at it like it was a can opener.

"You need to pay the cashier," she said and pointed to a barred window that said "Cashier" above it. "And bring me the receipt when you're done."

Patiently, Matilda collected the money and walked over to the cashier's window. There was no one at the window. There was a bell, the bell was rung, the ring was heard, and the front desk clerk magically reappeared behind the cashier's window and stared at Matilda with a blank expression.

Matilda initiated the conversation with the clerk's alter ego, "I'm posting bail for James Shwirl."

The clerk took out a pad and pencil and spoke as she wrote, "Jaaamesss Shhhhwirrrll. James Shwirl. I'll be back in one second." She locked her cash drawers, went back to the counter where she was previously, did a little more work, returned to the cashier's window, unlocked her cash drawers, and spake, "The bail is $15,000. You can pay $1500 by cash."

Matilda set $1500 on the cashier's counter.

The astute clerk responded quickly, "And you'll be paying in cash?"

Matilda rolled her eyes. The cashier took the money and counted it three times, out loud. She was really good at counting. Matilda didn't say anything.

"Fifteen hundred dollars," the clerk said as she wrote out a receipt. She gave Matilda the receipt, locked the cash drawer, and sat quietly behind the cashier's window.

Matilda looked at the cashier, looked at the front desk, looked at the cashier and sighed. She took the receipt to the front desk, rang the bell, the ring was heard, and the cashier was transformed back into an annoying blank faced front desk clerk. Once again, Matilda was required to explain her presence and clarify the name of the person she was bailing out.

The clerk recognized Matilda and decided it would be acceptable to start up a little pleasant conversation, "We're so understaffed here with all the cutbacks."

Matilda placed the bail receipt on the counter and pushed it towards the clerk and consoled her, "That's what happens when you get too efficient."

The clerk looked at Matilda with her blank expression then took the receipt and wandered away through a rear door into oblivion. Matilda watched the door for a minute, then looked around the lobby and took a seat on the bench next to Malcolm.

Without saying a word, Malcolm began to take inventory of her qualities, like a sexist bastard. Her perfume was subtle, yet captivating. Her hair fell down around her shoulders like nobody's business. Her skin, her body, everything about her was peachy and creamy. Then she turned and looked at Malcolm and took his breath away. She had perfect soft blue eyes that reminded him of clear mountain sky. She gave him a pleasant smile that was both seductive and innocent. For the second time in his life, he had found the perfect woman.

Still he didn't say anything. He tried to think of something clever, but every time he opened his mouth with a witty opening line, all that came out was, "Hey". It was some like kind of syndrome. After a minute or two of trying to untangle his tongue, he got up from the bench and stood in front of her. She calmly looked up at him, her eyes sparkling with curiosity.

He knelt down on one knee, held out his hand and said, "I know we've never even met, but you are the most dazzling woman I've ever seen all day long. Will you marry me? I mean that. I promise I'll take care of you, rub your feet, eat your cooking, just don't say no. Please, please, please."

She smiled and began to say something, when out of nowhere her boyfriend appeared. He was the typical Cro-Magnon type with all the decency of a wild boar, but he was a good looking guy with that rough animalistic charm that seems to attract so many of the human women. Grumble.

He walked past Malcolm, who was still waiting for an answer, and said to Matilda, "Let's go."

She looked at the boyfriend, then at Malcolm, and said, "Okay." Then she got up and followed her boyfriend out the door.

Malcolm was ecstatic. Finally, he got up the nerve to not only ask a girl out, but actually ask her for a lifetime commitment and she agreed. She wasn't even on drugs. The possibility that she may have been responding to her boyfriend's command didn't enter his head. The fact that she was gone didn't faze him. He met a beautiful girl, he asked her to marry him, she said "okay", and that's all that mattered. What an excellent day! If he could have remembered how to do the Calaveras Shuffle he would have cut a rug right then and there. That's how happy he was.

After wiping the tears from his eyes and getting up from his knees, he looked around the precinct for his fiancée. He didn't even know her name, which made it difficult to shout out in anguish, but he tried anyway, "Girrrrl! Honeeeey!" He got no answer. He could have gone on for any length of time, but he knew no one would care. She was probably some kind of hallucination anyway.

His ruminations on spit-in-the-wind romance were quickly dispelled when the arresting officer came out to take him home.

"You see that guy?" asked officer Grizeldi.

Malcolm didn't remember seeing any guy.

"Scum of the earth," the cop said.

It wasn't a good hallucination for Malcolm to experience. "Did you see a girl?" he asked.

The officer pointed towards an old Chrysler LeBaron, then looked at Malcolm, "Yeah, I saw her, but consider the company she keeps. That guy would take your life or mine for a nickel bag of China White. He'd cut her up for fun. There's times when I wish a guy would take a pot shot at me so I could exercise a little instant justice."

Malcolm looked at the cop suspiciously, and the cop made a face, "Okay, I wouldn't, but I swear that guy has been arrested more times this year than anyone in Nowheresville. Every time he gets off for one reason or another. One of these days he's gonna have a gun, a cop's gonna have a gun, and somebody's gonna get shot. I just hope it's him."

"One of these days he'll get caught and he'll get put away for a long time," said Malcolm.

The cop looked at him with cold dark eyes, "Five pounds of coke and he's out on bail. The system needs an overhaul."

"So who bailed him out?" asked Malcolm.

"Some mule. Probably one of his whores," Grizeldi replied rhetorically.

"But she was a goddess! Wow! She was hot! Yowser, yowser, yowser!" exclaimed Malcolm.

The cop shook his head, "Forget about it kid. She's a looker alright, but if she's not hauling drugs or drug money she's working on her back, keeping one of his clients happy."

That cop was talking about Malcolm's future wife and it was starting to piss him off. The girl was too nice looking. Not just good looking but she genuinely looked like a nice person.

"I don't think so, man. She's not the type. She was fine. She wouldn't sell herself like that," Malcolm defended.

The cop shook his head, "No, kid... Junkies do some pretty crazy stuff. Things you've never seen before. Don't give her a second thought. If she don't kill you, he will."

Malcolm didn't want to hear it. He shook his head and walked out of the police station.

The cop went to the door and yelled at him, "Hey, I'm supposed to give you a ride somewhere!"

There was no response from Malcolm so the cop ran back into the station to tell the guys about all the clichés he just used. Malcolm went ahead into the dark of night.

VII

There's nothing like the bite of high wind when it cuts through a thin cotton shirt. The gusts rolled through the inner city streets and carried a faint mist over the high rise rooftops. It was cold enough to keep ice sheets on puddles from thawing, but his body still perspired as he jogged through town trying to get to his car before morning. Malcolm's mind was beginning to counter the harsh environment by tuning out the weather, pretending it wasn't there. He focused on his few possessions. A pocket knife, an old photo of his first girlfriend, and a song that was imprisoned in his head, *"Tow truck, tow truck, red light stop, tow truck, tow truck, green light go, tow truck, tow truck, haul a wreck, tow truck, tow truck, crash."* All around him, the world was exhibiting signs of terminal illness. Vagrants were huddling against each other, chasing each other for money, then warmth. Steam spewed from the sewer grates as beacons of warmth. The streets were quiet and the passing cars carried faceless grey drivers who didn't turn their heads at the traffic signals. Drug dealers snatched up their hookers and turned away junkies to get off the streets.

It was getting too late to make it to his car that night, so Malcolm looked for any place that was open where he could get out of the wind and stay warm. He ducked into a side street bar. It was a small establishment in the center of town and it was overcrowded with people, smoke, the smell of leather, and noise. On that particular night some of the bar people were just enjoying a reprieve from the cold air that blasted outside. Otherwise there were all kinds of typical stereotypes hanging around. They were just lounging. Lounge, great thing to do is lounge. The Night of the Loungers. Bride of the Lounging Man. I Was a Teenage Lounger. Yup, nothing like a good lounge to rest the bones. Loungers in the form of yuppies, squares, mods, rockers, preppies, puppies, pooheads, and party animals. Quite a menagerie of meat people. As much as Malcolm wanted to fit in, and as diverse as the crowd was, he wasn't like anyone else in the bar. It really didn't occur to him that everyone there thought of themselves as unique.

They all had their special signature style, with the hair, or the tattoos, or the fancy duds, and jewelry. He only saw them as clique members and none of them were as special as they imagined. Malcolm pegged them all as spoiled, lost, and lonely.

The biggest draw by far for the males was the ever present possibility of finding the perfect one-night-stand. Some of the guys had dates, and some of the guys came to see the band, but women were the main attraction for the rest. Most of the ladies were dressed to kill. As the chickeroos passed the bar, the guys would turn and point and rib the guy standing next to them, who would in turn point and rib the next guy, like dominoes. So basically there were a lot of guys trying to pick up women, a lot of drooling guys, guys who felt pressured to prove not only that they liked girls, but also that they could drink any guy under the table and then beat the hell out of 'em just for effect.

The women were a different story. Two of them wanted nothing more than a physical relationship that would last all night long, or as long as they could maintain consciousness. The other women actually wanted to dance or just watch guys try to pick up on the two promiscuous gals. Fun loving people watchers, with purses full of phoney phone numbers for the fellers.

Now, Malcolm was just looking for a chance to get out of the bone chilling night air, but he did seem to have one admirer that evening. She was sitting at a table with several friends, smiling at him, flirting with her eyes. Many times he imagined exactly how he'd deal with such an encounter. It seemed like a perfect opportunity to put his imagination to the test. He smiled back at the girl and nodded his head giving her his approval. She giggled and put her hand on her heart. The other girls at the table were encouraging her to introduce herself, nudging her, and forcing shots of tequila down her throat. But she must have been shy. She just shook her head and laughed.

Living out his little fantasy, Malcolm gave her a sly look left, sly look right, sly look up, sly look down. Then he raised his eyes and lifted his steely jaw with a big pouty face which he slowly, seductively turned into an entrancing smile. Then he casually pointed to the girl and began rocking his body to the beat of the music. The girl was captivated, just as he anticipated. Still keeping with the music he began pointing left and right and up and down repeatedly. She seemed mesmerized, but also kind of holding back a laugh.

Malcolm, in a surprise move, attempted to spin around, but stopped halfway when something grabbed his crotch. He looked down to see that the fly on his pants was open again (probably had been open for a while), and the arm of a chair managed to slip in there when he made his groovy gyrating dance move. Naughty chair, thought Malcolm. He looked back over his shoulder and saw that the girls were in hysterics. It was a contagious laughter and he would have chuckled under different circumstances, but since it was his fly on his pants, and the chair was jabbing him sharply, he didn't find it particularly humorous, and neither did the woman sitting in the chair. He wanted to reach down and remove the chair's arm from his pants, but he was afraid it would look like he was urinating. So he tried shaking the chair off without using his hands. He held his arms over his head and shook and shook and looked over his shoulder and shook some more. Most of the girls were rolling around in hysterical laughter. He gave his hips one more good shake before the woman sitting in the chair gave him a strategically aimed dose of pepper spray, excused herself, and walked away quickly, grinning over her conquest.

In a last ditch effort to end his moment of infamy and possibly relieve the sudden burning sensation, Malcolm spun around, and sent the chair sailing out of his pants. He buttoned his fly and noticed that the girl who'd been admiring him was unconscious on the floor with a broken chair at her side and a big grin on her face. Things were starting to get back to normal.

Recovering from pure embarrassment was one of Malcolm's strong points. He passed off the aggressive chair incident as rotten bar dharma and went back to being a typical Malcolm. Through the smoke filled room, beyond the crowd of bar mongers, he saw the girl from the police station sitting alone at a table near the end of the bar. She was wearing a tight leather skirt, a blue denim jacket, some kind of nutty go-go boots, and her long blond hair was tied back in a pony tail so Malcolm knew she was a class act. Nonchalantly, she nibbled on nachos with one hand and sipped a Pink Fuzzy Wuzzy with the other. As she pulled a corn chip from her nacho platter, a trail of cheese followed the chip and wouldn't detach. She raised the chip over her head but the tenacious dairy product wouldn't let go. Who knew what would happen if that cheese snapped. Malcolm contemplated the disastrous impact of releasing a string of cheese from such a distance, but was soon captivated by the young woman's helpless expression. She looked at the cheese, then at her Fuzzy Wuzzy. She glanced quickly around the bar and averted her eyes when they met Malcolm's.

"She'll never be more vulnerable than she is at this moment," thought Malcolm as he began to stutter and froth.

He needed a pick up line and he needed it fast! In the spirit of unwitting spontaneity, Malcolm approached the woman while incredible introductions flew through his narrow mind, "Step aside, ma'am, I'm a professional cheese wrangler," or "Say there, fondue temptress, can I give you a hand with your cheese?" or "Didn't I make it with your sister last week?" or "Hello mama love baby, you must be a Scorpio..." or just "Eeeeeeeee, yakka yakka yakka!" Having that repertoire of aphrodisiacal opening lines firmly instilled in his papery cranium, he stopped at the table of the cheese girl, and quietly stood there for a few minutes before she noticed him.

"Oh, hi," she began, "I'm almost done. If you need a table, you can sit here with me and wait for a minute."

Malcolm was bowled over by her generosity, her charm, her warm healthy voice, and her groovy bod. After smiling for a minute, and wiping his mouth a few times, he said, "Uh, uh, no, I mean, I noticed you had a watch on and I was wondering what time it was."

She smiled as though Malcolm wasn't a complete loser, giving him an undeserved and confusing sense of self confidence, and said, "Oh, sure, it's quarter to twelve."

"Quarter 'til," Malcolm rubbed his chin, "Well, I've got more time than I thought. If you don't mind, I will have a seat."

"Go ahead," she insisted, again giving Malcolm a genuinely friendly smile.

"Thanks. This place isn't usually so crowded. They must be running a special," he said, pretending to know where he was.

The girl looked up at Malcolm and smiled, "I don't know, but I've been coming here for years and I've always had to get reservations."

Malcolm waved at several strangers and a flickering light bulb, then said to Matilda, "Oh, yeah, well, the owner, the... actually the president of this place usually has a table set aside for me, but he's been out on a business trip. I think he's in Europe or maybe Sweden, cashing in his Swedish bank account, or something."

The girl looked at Malcolm with a cunning smirk, then at her Fuzzy Wuzzy and said, "Jerry's out of town, but I think he's just up in Toodle Town. He should be back in about an hour."

The gorgeous young lady was quickly working her way out of an ignorant barfly stereotype, but Malcolm wasn't about to be outdone, "Jerry likes to tell people that he's in Toodle Town, but he's really in Sweden. He'll be back here by three. He's, he's the most punctual guy I know. He even flies over the International Date Line to set his watch. He's punctual and he flies around a lot. He and I go way back."

The girl laughed, "What's your name, cowboy? I think I could learn to like you."

He squinted at her, "Do I have to be honest?"

"No," she paused, "But you might give it a try."

"I'm Malcolm," he said shyly, "...Not the movie star."

"The other Malcolm?"

"That's right," he smiled and smelled the rose on her table. "I'm not too good at this."

The girl smiled and bowed her head.

"In fact," Malcolm confided, "I'm terrible at this. The last time I tried to start up a conversation with a pretty woman I actually swallowed my tongue, so I don't do it very often." He began to laugh, "In fact, I don't do this at all. The truth is, I'm should still be standing at the other side of the bar staring at the most attractive woman I've seen in years."

"Oh, that's too bad. The guy sitting across from me seems like a nice guy." She looked towards the other side of the bar, "Are you sure you should be over there?"

Malcolm smiled and looked across the restaurant then back at the girl.

He started to explain himself but she interrupted, "I'm Matilda, and I don't know the owner either. This is the first time I've eaten here."

Where did that come from? She just beat him at his own game. A common bond between Malcolm and a pretty woman? Stranger things have happened. It was good. Another honest attempt at real conversation couldn't hurt.

"Maybe you'd like to meet here again for lunch or dinner or just to talk?"

Matilda smiled, "Yeah."

Malcolm's heart grew 3 sizes bigger!

She leaned towards him, "I'd like to have lunch here again. And I think it would be nice to have some interesting company..."

Suddenly her expression became hard. She collected her purse and sat up straight.

Malcolm surveyed the room and noticed a small but handsome young man approaching their table. The guy had a stupid expression and was taking himself very seriously, but he was obviously a moron. It was Jimmy Shwirl.

He stopped and stared impatiently at Matilda. "Let's go," he spat. "You gotta pick up a package for me and it's gotta be cut and delivered tonight."

Matilda's face turned sour, she looked like she'd just been punched in the jaw. "You can't give it a rest, can you? You gotta push everything to the limit."

The small man turned away and demanded, "Now!"

Pulling her purse from the back of her chair, she looked at him with disgust and stood up. She shook her head and muttered, "You only push things that don't push back."

As she looked at Malcolm, her hardened eyes became soft for a moment. She might have smiled if she didn't feel as though she was being abused. She weaved away through the bar crowd.

Malcolm guessed that the little man probably carried a big gun and shallow ego that lashed out when threatened. He could have crushed the man's head with his bare hands, but the guy was just being impolite and that probably wasn't legal grounds for murder. What the cop said earlier made sense... Malcolm wished he had a reason to attack the man. For some strange reason, violence seemed logical. Maybe it was just the culture, the affluence of guns and fear. He was living in a world where people were looking for excuses to strike. Maybe the world had always been like that. It just seemed that modern society made it too easy to do a lot of destruction in a matter of seconds. Maybe it was good that people could carry firearms to protect themselves, or maybe there were too many hair triggers carrying weapons.

Shwirl walked out of the establishment about five feet in front of Matilda. Neither looked back, and no one really watched them leave, except Malcolm Tent. He sat at Matilda's table and sipped her Fuzzy Wuzzy. The rest of the people in the bar were acting as human as they knew how. A mute woman was signing to a male friend. They chatted for a little while. His gestures suddenly became grandiose, like he was yelling. She sat there and made short signs as if she couldn't get a word in edgewise. He stepped away from the bar and said something inaudible to her. She began waving her hands. She was babbling.

Elsewhere in the bar, guys were laughing about how hard it was to hear, and women were nodding at incredible feats of male accomplishments, like snowboarding, parasailing, and driving their new cars into trees. Malcolm didn't have a car nearby, or a woman and he didn't know sign language, so he said nothing. A waiter stepped up to his table, verified that everything was adequate or at least non-toxic and dropped off Matilda's large drink order.

Her scent and her smile were fresh in Malcolm's mind. He was charmed, enamored, he'd caught the love bug. What a goof. It wasn't particularly uncommon for Malcolm to fall in love at first sight. In fact, he fell in love at first sight quite regularly. Matilda was different though, she was a different breed of cat. Awesome eyes, a smile that could melt ice, a healthy healthy body, and best of all, she wasn't in a beer commercial.

His mind quickly set to scheming. If he ever met her at the restaurant again, he'd do things a little differently. He played the conversation over and over in his head. He'd say, "Hi," (being clever with words like that), and she'd reply, "Do I know you?" because she had that certain cautious shell that prevented her from being perceived as a know-it-all. "Yeah, I met you here the day before yesterday. I bought you a car." She'd laugh and the conversation would gradually develop into a night of passion and a lifetime of love and happiness. Incredibly enough, Malcolm's conversational fantasies never actually materialized into reality. Instead they hung around until the next love-at-first-sight episode came along and the previous infatuation would fade away. Malcolm knew the sad facts about his romantic limits, but carried enough amorous optimism to offset the pessimism that generally pushed him up to the edge of suicide. She was a nice girl. Malcolm loved her.

Damn. It wasn't fair to anyone that he fell in love so easily. The biggest problem, of course, for the inexperienced Malcolm was that he thought that being with anyone at all was better than being alone. He really believed that he loved all those women. Not so much because they were all very lovable, but because he thought that he could accept any short comings they might have had, and he never saw any of their short comings before they ditched him. He also assumed that he could change to meet their needs as he learned more about them. Ha!

He sat at the table for a while with a picture of her in his head. The fragrance of her perfume was still in the air. Her soft soothing voice, the relaxing flow of her conversation, everything about her was as calming as the sound of cool deep river. He couldn't stop thinking about her. The waiter brought Malcolm her check. Malcolm looked at the check, then at the waiter. Apparently she was quite a drinker. Malcolm could appreciate that in any woman. He loved Matilda all the more for it. For her love, he would have walked on water, eaten broken glass, flown to the moon, but there was no way he was going to pay that ridiculous bar bill. He convinced the waiter to run a tab for him as, uh, the crew of a small aircraft carrier would soon be joining him for a drunken riot. Actually there were only four Mai Tais on the order, but Malcolm put 'em away pretty quickly then ducked under the table and snuck out of the bar before anyone could catch him.

What followed was an experience that Malcolm would never forget. It was the first of many blackouts that he'd endure as a result of his homelessness and intense drinking spells. The average person can't understand exactly what a blackout feels like. It's not the loss of memory that's so difficult to stomach, it's looking down at your knuckles or looking into a mirror and seeing someone else's blood, or waking up with no idea how you got home the night before, or vaguely remembering running another car off the road. It's as though a period of time is ripped out of your life... And you're certainly not going to remember any kind of incredible sex. The painful morning memories would be replaced with guilt and self doubt as you wonder what happened and what you actually did and who you did it with. Malcolm had gone into the Haze. A temporary state of psychosis that lasts as long the blood alcohol level is high and the victim is conscious. During the Haze, a person would become invincible, or bring loneliness to a new level, or suddenly develop incredible new singing and dancing abilities. But it would always be temporary, and never real, and again, always a problem. It can be tough and painful to deal directly with the Haze, but it's tougher and more painful to hide from the guilt and self doubt by diving back into it.

As the morning arrived, Malcolm didn't feel immediately hungover, he just didn't know where he was or how he got there. The raspberry jelly in his belly button was also a mystery. He spent several hours contemplating the Haze and the jelly, then climbed down from the water tower and went back to sluggishly roaming the streets of Nowheresville. He took the whole blackout episode incredibly well, but his head, stomach, legs, and stomach and head really hurt. He wandered in self-imposed pain for hours.

That afternoon he ran into a gang of young thugs. They were sitting in front of a night club entry. The evening's venue was hours away from starting, but they were in the doorway anyway. Scum bucket children of the streets. Not orphans, not abandoned kids, not abused children seeking refuge from harsh unbearable punishment. Those brats just hated their parents and didn't feel like going home for a few days. The reasons for their absenteeism were varied. Some of them were mad because they couldn't go out when they wanted. Some had stolen enough money to last them the rest of the week and had no reason to go home. Malcolm had seen some of them around and knew they were harmless individuals, but as a group they could be pretty annoying. He began skipping (because anybody can be annoying).

One of the pseudo-indigents noticed Malcolm's silly gait and pointed him out to all the other self proclaimed rejects. They snickered.

"Hey, you! You got any spare change?" asked a real bad egg.

Malcolm froze in his tracks, "No!"

A rotten apple jumped in, "Yes you do. We could hear it when you skipped. Skipper!"

There was a girl in the pack, just one, and she was cute, but obviously misguided. She dressed like the guys in raggedy duds and swore and spit and pretended to be ignorant, but she never let you forget she was a woman.

"You want me?" she asked, out of the blue.

A sardonic smile crossed Malcolm's face as the young fellers in the crowd looked at the gal suspiciously.

"Okay, here's twenty cents," said Malcolm as he pulled two dimes out of his pocket.

That was all it took, the gang was petrified. Instantly, the confrontation became awkward and volatile, like an unexpected phone conversation with a newspaper solicitor or a cow. The girl had never made such an offer to any of the guys. All of the guys had dreamed that she would make such an offer, but not in front of a crowd, not in front the Bow Wow Club, and certainly not to an outsider. The fact that the outsider seemed to accept the offer (and we don't know that he did) was an invasion of their property, but the fact that he was only willing to spend twenty cents as compensation was insulting and purely ludicrous. Plus! Plus, he lied about having spare change.

The young girl was the first to respond, "Twenty cents? You... You... I am worth more than twenty cents, and, and I am not a prostitute, so you can just put your money away."

She looked around at the fellers, "Aren't you guys gonna do anything?"

They all put their money back in their pockets.

One of them, the closest to being the girl's boyfriend stepped forward and said, "Give us your money and your shoes and any VCRs you might be carrying."

The rest of the guys stepped forward. The girl just giggled.

Anticipating a brouhaha, a scuffle, a fisticuffs, a duke out, a situation where five or six punks could be easily frightened away, Malcolm addressed the girl, "What's your name?"

She looked up from her fingernails, "Jenna Rae."

"That's what I thought. I'm working for your father, Jenna Rae. I'm a young street wise detective who doesn't have any goiters and just lost his job as a bit actor on cheap television show. I'm bringing you in, kid," Malcolm said, giving Jenna Rae legitimate reason to shutter. "You've been out here too long. You're hanging around with a bunch of losers who'll never amount to anything until they go back home and learn to help out their families. You're lucky enough that your father's willing to give you another chance. None of these guys are going to make it. Besides, all of them make fun of your butt behind your back."

Jenna Rae turned around and caught three or four guys snickering. Her butt was kinda sideways.

"Okay," she said, "I'll go with you, but you have to promise that you'll tell my father I put up a fight and that he's a tyrant and I can stay out as late as I want any night of the week. And I like to smoke cigarettes and I can and I will, and I can see anybody I want, and if I need to borrow the Cadillac, I'll take it, and I deserve more allowance!"

"Okay," said Malcolm and he began walking away.

Jenna Rae looked at Malcolm, then at the guys and made a face, "Losers! Butt mockers! I teased you all and it was fun!" She quickly ran to Malcolm, "And I want to have the master bedroom, and I'd like some new clothes, and I want to play my stereo as loud as I want whenever I want, and I get to drink beer and whiskey and chew all the tobacco I want. I want a pony!"

Malcolm nodded and agreed and didn't pay any attention to anything she said until she stopped and asked, "Where are we going?"

"I was going to try and find something to eat," he said as he stopped. "Where do you live?"

"In the Whitehead district. Why?" she asked as she began to turn pale.

He reached into his pocket, "Here's bus fare, take the 63 to Outskirt Avenue. It goes right through Whitehead."

She stood there in disbelief.

He continued, "So go home, listen to your father, and graduate from high school. If you fail after high school, you'll still have a chance to recover. If you fail now, you're lost forever." He looked up the street. "And here comes the 63 now. Get on it, and don't come back."

The bus arrived and she got on it and stared at Malcolm as the bus carried her away. The old gun slinging philanthropist was right to stick his nose into Malcolm's business. Malcolm was right to stick his nose in hers. There were enough prostitutes in the world.

He'd done his good deed for the day and decided it was time to start getting his life back in order. He searched for a motel that charged less than $10 a night but didn't have much luck. Most of the rooms cost at least $30 for the night and those were all run down vermin infested dives, so he gave up on his search for conventional shelter. The following day he could go to the bank and take out some cash. But that afternoon, he didn't have enough cash for a room. He did have enough money for a bottle of whiskey and a hamburger, so he spent what he had on fast food and liquor. Half the bottle was gone in less than an hour. The day still had a couple hours before sundown, but the sun seemed to be falling quickly as the Haze kicked in. Young Malcolm staggered around the city looking for a reason to live.

The late afternoon was incredibly cold. The mood, the air, life was meaningless that night. Birds whipped through the air like paper. They hit the ground long enough to know that they couldn't stay. They'd touch down in a chaotic landing then kind of let the wind throw them along.

That evening Malcolm witnessed a murder. Two beggars were fighting over an old green jacket. The struggle started with a tugging match until the larger of the two pulled out a gun. The smaller one saw the gun and screamed, "No! Mine! Give! ME!" and tried to jerk the jacket away. The larger one yelled incoherently and put the gun to the smaller beggar's chest. Malcolm looked around to see if anyone else was watching and saw grey bodies huddled in stoops facing the confrontation. Round heads with blurring dark holes where their eyes should be looked down from steamed windows of the condemned buildings that lined the street. Two muffled shots went off in short succession, pooph, pooph. The back of smaller one was gushing out blood, and the wind picked up and carried away a few helpless moans. The other beggar clutched the green coat and swore at the smaller one as she pirouetted to the street. The larger one pointed the gun at the smaller one's head, cursed it, and wiped his face. He didn't shoot her again but began running towards Malcolm pointing the gun straight ahead. He stumbled as he struggled to put on the green jacket. The smaller one collapsed and a short gust of wind hit Malcolm as the larger one ran past him.

Cautiously, he walked towards the smaller beggar. By the time she hit the street the cold wind had robbed her of most of her warmth. Malcolm reached down with his fingers sticking through the holes in his glove and touched her neck. There was no life. There was wind... Wind carried the heat out of the body and spent it on lamp posts and boarded up store fronts. Malcolm's hand became cold at the dead woman's throat. He looked up to see the heads in the windows fade into the shelter of darkness. The doorway men were scurrying down the sidewalk shrouded in blankets and jackets they had picked up in their journeys. A police car slowed at an intersection several blocks away, but kept rolling and disappeared.

Malcolm felt the wind tug and slid into an alley.

Diesel exhaust filled the air.

He sought refuge beneath an empty refrigerator carton and began to sleep. That night's sleep was visited again and again by the image of a frail young woman losing her life for a green jacket, a madman rushing past him with gun pointed at his face, his own destitution, and back to the woman. The images cycled through his mind over and over, hypnotizing him, rocking him, bringing him in and out of deep sleep, dark thoughts, evil resolution. What did she think about when she knew she would die? Did she see her killer's face? Did she care? Maybe her death was an early reprieve. Maybe it was the cessation of great possibilities. A glimpse of her disbelieving angry and confused face as her dying body crumbled to the street stuck in Malcolm's mind. The images became dreams, then reality wove in and out of the cracks of the walls. At some point he fell asleep completely. He slept with her memory as though he'd married her.

Through the night, the image of a grey body rolling across the pavement repeated itself over and over in his sleep. The images continued to roll across his mind and eventually formed grey waves crashing down on a tropical beach. He dreamt that he was asleep on the beach, a beautiful young woman was pressing against him, a perfect woman, in his hand was an ice cold Mai Tai, and nothing but serenity called him. Suddenly, in his dream state, someone was rustling him, the whining sound of a diesel engine was approaching him. He looked up from the sand to see a thief stealing his wallet and dashing away. The sound of machinery was getting louder and Malcolm looked up to see a giant bulldozer scoop crashing down on him.

He awoke screaming from his nightmare. When he looked around to see if anyone heard him, he caught a beggar patting him down for cash and the forks of a trash truck were approaching the dumpster behind him.

The trash truck driver honked and yelled at him, "Scat, now. Oooo! Go on! Git! Ssss!"

Malcolm rolled out of the way, and fearing for his life he dove into the dumpster.

The driver laughed hard, stopped and turned off his truck, then pulled out a coffee thermos.

"Break time!" he shouted.

The thieving beggar reprimanded Malcolm for not giving up his wallet, "Good fer nuthin', no good, nurzzelberger."

Malcolm felt silly. Not like, giggly silly, but more like, "why'd I jump into a dumpster," silly. He lost his balance climbing out of the bin and fell on his face and shoulder. Straightening his shirt and brushing cigarette butts out of his hair, he attempted to hold his chin up with dignity as he wandered out to the street. When he looked back, the bum and the trash truck driver were laughing over a cup of coffee and pointing at Malcolm. The bum slapped his knee when the driver yelled, "Boo." Malcolm was irate and considered talking to himself or yelling at an innocent stranger, but no one was around so the tantrum would have been just a waste of time.

Ooooo! Angry! Grrrr! Over the next few blocks, a smoldering orneriness began to percolate with looming fury. Can you just imagine that? There also happened to be a nerd strolling down the sidewalk towards Malcolm. The whole episode with the bum and the trash truck driver coupled with years of repressed hatred towards "easy listenin' music" and self-help books made

Malcolm snap. The nerd was just moseying along, paying no mind to nobody else, just reading entries from a table of logarithms and basically causing no harm. Malcolm didn't know what the nerdy dude was doing and no one could guess why he was doing it, but apparently the guy liked the sound of numbers or something.

"Hey, 'Sound of Music' was a musical," said Malcolm to the nerd, "Would 'Sound of Numbers' be a numerical?"

The nerd laughed.

Completely out of the blue, Malcolm started rattling off random numbers and mocking the nerd's rigid walk. Bullets of sweat rolled down the nerd's greasy face. As hard as he could, he tried to block the irritating interruptions from his mind, but he couldn't, Malcolm was too much for him. To make things easier, he tried extrapolating exponential values, then geometric, then arithmetic, until he was finally reduced to counting his fingers over and over.

"Looks like we've found your lowest common denominator, didn't we!" Malcolm yelled and ran in circles around the defeated mathematician.

The conquest over the harmless nerd was a short lived victory. After the guy ran away (shouting out perfect squares), Malcolm came to the conclusion that he had fallen into the jaws of psychosis. He was acting like the street people he'd seen when he was gainfully employed. It was the meanest thing Malcolm had ever done. He didn't know why he'd hassled the nerd, but he knew he'd gone too far. His life needed purpose, order, direction, and a girlfriend would be nice.

VIII

Ever notice how some people try to solve the rest of the world's problems before they take a good look at their own? Getting his life in order would require Malcolm to reassess the whole world. There was something fundamentally wrong with the every aspect of society and Malcolm had to make things right. Mass hypnosis would be a good first step towards changing the modern woman's attitude towards guys like Malcolm. Next step involved changing the legal system in such a way that he could have anyone incarcerated on a whim. Finally, he needed financial independence. So all he had to do was restructure the system of capitalism, do a little editing on the Constitution, and learn how to sing like Tom Jones. It would take time, money, and many many voice lessons. In order to fund this effort himself, he had to get a job.

Possibly he'd lower his standards and take a fast food job at minimum wage, but that meant he'd have to take orders from some snotty little high school kid who thought that getting into restaurant management was a ticket to great wealth and possibly scoring with the most popular person in the world. Imagine the humiliation of Malcolm actually flipping hamburgers for money. Once you've tasted life as a warehouse warrior, burger money leaves a funny taste in your mouth. He figured he could rough it for a while before resorting to fast food processing. He could bathe in a public bathing facility for a few days and probably take clean clothes from the clothesline of some poor unsuspecting family that couldn't afford a clothes dryer. If he had to, he could always steal food from the trash cans behind fast food restaurants, but his pride forbade him from working for minimum wage. Something good would come along if he just waited.

It seemed to Malcolm that everything would be okay if he just didn't rush into anything. His outdoor sojourn would be a refreshing change from the bourgeois trappings of modern domesticity. The great accessibility of public transportation made him forget that his '68 Toyota was broken down at Armadillo's.

Slurp and Gurgle insisted that it had been stolen by space aliens for observation, but Malcolm was pretty sure they were lying. It didn't matter. Public transportation was anything but a guilt trip. They used that as the motto there at the county transit system. It was true. Malcolm wasn't down and out, he was embarking on a new and exciting episode of the Transient Man, Kerouac revisited, King of the Road, truly a Man about Nowheresville. He was empowered, independent, and strong. Suddenly he really needed to go to the bathroom.

It was too late for personal relief, the bus had arrived. He got on the bus and got hassled by the driver because he didn't have exact change. Then he sat down in an empty seat and bounced along while the driver flew down the urban streets, over the sidewalks, and through the red signal lights. If it wasn't for the gum on the bus seat holding him down, Malcolm probably would have been thrown into the aisle several times.

An old woman in front of Malcolm tried to strike up a conversation, "First time rider?"

It took Malcolm a minute to figure out what she was talking about, but he finally picked up on it, "No, I've been on a bus before."

"I notice you didn't get a window seat," said the lady.

"That's 'cause I'm sitting over a wing," Malcolm replied.

The old woman bristled and looked at the driver. She noticed that the driver would press the right turn signal repeatedly while he was making a turn.

"You know that light will continue to flash if you just press it down real hard," she said.

The driver looked at her in his rear view mirror, "Yeah, I know," he said, "I don't mind."

"Complex guy," Malcolm muttered.

The bus driver slammed on the brakes and yelled at Malcolm, "That's it! You've been disruptive ever since you got on the bus. Now I want you off or I'll have you arrested!"

"But, I..."

The driver opened the exit doors and said, "I want you off my rig right now!"

"Your rig?" asked Malcolm.

The driver pulled a machete from under his seat and went towards Malcolm who wasted no time diving out the door. He rolled on the concrete and got to his feet quickly so he could shake his fist and yell and run away quickly if necessary. His final words to the big grey bus and its dumb blue bus driver were, "I *did* have exact change! Fatso!"

The bus screeched to a stop at the next intersection and made a U-turn and came back towards Malcolm. So he ran and ran and ran and ran as fast as he could. He covered the distance between Bean Street and Noodle Road in 19 minutes flat. If you know anything about Nowheresville, you know that's a pretty good run. It got him from the edge of the inner city to the edge of the suburban residential area. As luck would have it, Malcolm Tent was finally just a few blocks away from Armadillo Cleef's house.

"Armadillo!" he shouted as he got within shouting distance. "Armadillo?"

"I am Armadillo," said... Armadillo, who was whittling on his front porch. "Where you been, Malcolm? Your apartment burned down."

Malcolm rolled his eyes, "Yeah, I did hear about that. I'm okay though, except for the blood and bruises and scars, third degree burns... and the drinking binges and rejections and death threats and lack of sleep and I really need to use the restroom."

"How'd you burn down your apartment?"

"Why do you got to be such a pessimist? I burned it up, not down. Can I go inside and use the bathroom please?"

Armadillo picked up a wood shaving and began picking his teeth. "Sure. Watch out for my little brothers. They don't like you lately. Think you disrespect the Cleef name."

Malcolm stepped into the house and muttered as he went through the living room, "I'm about to use the Cleef Family Toilet. How much more respect do they want?"

The younger Cleefs were sitting in the attic watching Malcolm pass through their domain. If he was going to do what they thought he was going to do, they would have no mercy on his soul. He did it, and little did Malcolm know that when he flushed the toilet, he sealed his fate.

"Much better," said Malcolm as he went back out on the porch. "Thanks."

"Don't mention it. So where you going to stay now?"

Malcolm didn't detect any subtle generosity in Armadillo's question, so he asked directly if he could stay for a few nights.

Armadillo let out a long sigh, "Y'know. If it was totally up to me, and you didn't owe me all that money, and if you had a hot girlfriend with a cute sister, or if you were a party animal, or if you had some kind of personality better than wallpaper paste, I might be able to say 'Yeah, stay for a day or two.' But the thing is, Malcolm, nobody likes you and my brothers will probably bury you alive in some kind of satanic sacrifice, and I really can't have your death hangin' over my head. You understand, don't ya?"

"So even though I lost my apartment, I can't stay here?"

"Hey, at least it burned up, not down."

"Do you have my car keys?"

Armadillo pointed towards the old Toyota at the side of the house, "They're in the ignition."

Malcolm walked over to the car and saw through the open window that the keys were in there, plain as day. Any old goofball could just jump in and crank it over.

He yelled back at his friend, "It runs?"

"Sure does."

"What did you do to fix it?" Malcolm asked as he sat down in the driver's seat.

"One of the cables fell off the battery," Armadillo replied nonchalantly.

Malcolm was no mechanic, but he knew that... the battery cable fell off? That was ridiculous. It just fits over the battery terminal. He was humiliated. "How long did it take that to figure it out?"

"Remember when you dropped it off?"

Malcolm nodded.

"I checked under the hood and saw it right then. Easy to fix. I just slipped it back on. Forgot to mention it before you left."

"That was over a month ago," Malcolm expressed his displeasure in a loud voice and explained that having a car might have helped keep him out of jail and off the street and possibly held back some near psychotic episodes.

Armadillo laughed and brushed a pile of splinters off his knees.

Malcolm faked a laughed and left a cloud of dust as he pulled out to the street. On the side of the street a small car was parked. No one was in that parked car. It certainly seemed safe to pass a parked car with nobody in it on the other side of the street. Malcolm slowed down to 25 because speed kills.

When Malcolm's car was ten feet away from the empty car at the side of the road, a driver suddenly sat up in the empty car, made a lightning fast U-turn and Malcolm smacked right into him. Damned if it wasn't Armadillo's little brother, Gurgle. Gurgle got out of his car, which barely had a scratch on it while Malcolm's front end looked like an accordion.

The young Cleef yelled, "How could you run into me? There isn't another car in sight and you hit mine! Didn't you see me?"

Malcolm grumbled, Gurgle went on, "Of all the imbecilic moronic dumb and irresponsible things you've ever done, this one has gotta be the topper. If you weren't so stupid, I'd have to kill you... But that would just put you out of your misery and I'm not feeling that nice today. You know what I'm gonna do? I'm gonna sue you for everything you got. I'll attach your wages, I'll confiscate your Herb Alpert collection, and I will make your life one living Hell. Do you hear me, you rodent! You'll never work in this town again. I thought I'd seen it all. Jumping Geehosafat! You are a one-man parade of morons."

Malcolm stared at Gurgle, took his Herb Alpert tape out of his cassette player and walked away, leaving his car stranded and Gurgle fuming. Gurgle yelled and jumped up and down until Malcolm was out of earshot then opened the trunk of his car. Brother Slurp climbed out of the trunk, got into Malcolm's car and drove it away. Gurgle followed close behind.

Malcolm's car was the only chick magnet he still had. He'd purchased it from his high school metal shop teacher just after graduation. Several weeks later he learned that most of the chassis had been welded together with scrap metal, which made it very heavy, and he mistakenly thought it was indestructible. Apparently if something suddenly rose up from the center of the earth under the vehicle, it would have withstood the impact, but the front end panels just didn't have such structural integrity. Unfortunately, all that remained of the car were painful memories. He went back into the shelter of the inner city on foot.

IX

The Jack Webb Memorial Park in Nowheresville was well on its way to becoming a national monument, if for no other reason than its incredible goose population. Really! It had more webbed feet per square foot than any other place in the world. The park contained an exclusive goose gaggle comprised of some very well connected water fowl. Once they got in, they didn't get out. And they didn't want to. It was an all-inclusive goose habitat.

The scientific community was baffled by the park's fowl popularity. However, in order for the phenomenon to be studied, scientists would need to relocate to Nowheresville. Anyone desperate enough to dedicate their life to goosology was going to perform their studies at some interesting locale like Canada or Bolivia or Tahiti, but not Nowheresville. The academic aversion to the lackluster city of Nowheresville caused the astounding goose phenomenon to go largely unreported.

As a devoted citizen and a solid pseudo-environmentalist, Malcolm Tent was well aware of the park's wild goose collection and had always been conscientious of the fragile natural balance between man and the overgrown egg. He fulfilled his desperate need for refuge with an ecologically sensitive resolution. He planned to live in a tree or on a bench and promised himself never to eat any of the squawking birds. A few feathers in his bed for a week or two wouldn't be so bad. He even kidded himself that he could make a big down pillow with all those loose feathers. A big down pillow! Feathers! Just thinking about it made him scrunch his nose and giggle. He was quacking up! Quacking up! The guy was hilarious. Oh my! He was!

After spending a few nights on the park's benches, he found that he had to tolerate a lot more than just feathers. There was slippery slimy goose poop everywhere. There was honking all night, goose brawls, marauding pheasants, and parties until 3 a.m. Some of the avian subcultures were very frightening too; Boozer geese, drunken ducks, loosy goosey strippers, and goose gangs. That was all pretty bad, but the real frustration came one morning when he discovered that a renegade goose had lifted his wallet. He spent the whole morning shaking down geese until he came across a stool pigeon that wasn't down with the rest of the birds.

Malcolm found the thief, a big white gander in a black leather jacket smoking grass and drinking Cold Duck on ice.

Malcolm confronted him, "Hey! You there! Ugly duckling! Did you take my wallet?"

The goose just stood there.

"Fork over the billfold, you fiendish fowl!" he cried.

There was no response from the large bird, so Malcolm growled and pounced on it. A horrifying fight raged on for several minutes. The goose sent Malcolm reeling with a left wing to the nose. Malcolm answered back with an upper cut to the beak. It wasn't pretty, but in a ducky duck world, sometimes you have to take the good, along with the bad and the ugly ducklings. After Malcolm gave the felonious fowl a fat lip and ruffled its feathers, the goose cried uncle. But, the bird was just faking his surrender and the battle roared on. There was blood, and spit, and barbeque sauce all over the place. Eventually, Malcolm flipped the bird and put him in a sleeper hold, then recovered his wallet before the goose regained consciousness.

Malcolm was immediately filled with guilt and slight remorse for the all the violence and bad puns he used to subdue the wild fowl. A small group of animal rights activists who witnessed the whole ordeal quietly approached Malcolm, beat him senseless, and made him subscribe to one of their publications. The activists became teary eyed, if not suicidal, when Malcolm told them that he was the only one of his species still living in park and they had nearly driven him to extinction. They apologized to Malcolm for several hours and sang him a song. Then they ran off the Nowheresville Zoo to free the whales. The beaten goose waddled away to get a restraining order against Malcolm.

From that point on, he did what he could to stay away from the geese. There were a few interesting people in the park, but most of them had depressing life stories that made Malcolm's encounters with accidental arson seem like a walk in the park (as one might expect). He didn't spend much time socializing because most of the conversations were limited to guttural noises, obscenities and knock knock jokes. The communication barriers were too much for Malcolm and he quickly isolated himself from man and bird alike.

Aside from the geese, the park had acres of trees. After many nights of contending with waterfowl for flop space, it occurred to him that he could apply an unusual survivalist technique he'd seen as a child. It might have been beyond his abilities to construct such a compound, but he was going to build a tree fort or die trying. It was an act of desperation but he couldn't live like a goose any longer. The guy was a primate for crying out loud. He found a couple trees that had grown close together and stole some 2 x 4's and an old tarp from a nearby construction site. Using a patented architectural design, he built his fort and moved in. He stayed there a couple nights until one morning he was accosted by another displaced citizen who carried a manila envelope in his hand.

"I see you've moved in," said the bum as he surveyed Malcolm's work. "I hope everything's to your satisfaction. Here is your rental agreement."

"Rental agreement?" replied Malcolm.

"Yeah. You know, terms of residence, lease."

"I know what a rental agreement is, pal, but I'm living in a damn tree fort. You think I'm gonna pay rent for a tree fort? You're nuts."

The indigent gentleman scratched his chin, "Well, I may be nuts, but I got a contract, and I can have you shot for not agreeing to follow it."

"It's plywood and a tarp! It's a tree fort! There must be dozens just like it around here! You can't charge rent for a tree fort! You can't have me shot for living in a tree!"

"Technically, it's a custom tree *house*," the bum said as he straightened his tattered rain jacket and tried to hand Malcolm the envelope.

Malcolm smiled, "I hope you're not going to shoot me with that thing."

"Of course not. It's just a letter."

Malcolm pointed to his dilapidated fort, "If that's a house, then your envelope might be a gun."

"Nope, I can have you shot, but this ain't no gun. It's a letter from the City Council. It says I'm the sole ward of the Jack Webb Park and Naturally Selective Goose Habitat of Nowheresville. I have rights to do anything I want to anybody I want, anytime I want. I'm a lord," said the power tripping bum.

Malcolm looked at the letter. "This has got to be a joke. How can they appoint a ward of a park?"

"Indigent Employment and Rehabilitation Act of 1992. They got tired of arresting me for vagrancy so they gave me a job. I have to make sure that anybody who takes up residence in this park keeps their squat clean and pays a fee to help cover all the duck bills. Five hundred bucks a month, first and last up front with a two thousand dollar cleaning deposit."

"It's a tree fort!" objected Malcolm.

Pretending to be embarrassed, the bum said, "I'm just kidding about the money. How much you got?"

"How much money do I have?"

"Yeah, on you?"

"Not much and I'll be damned if I'm giving it to you!"

"Oh, come on. You must have something. It's a tax write off. How 'bout your shoes?"

"No. Get away from me."

"I'll have you shot."

"You're threatening my life?"

"Not me. The cops don't like your type."

"Yeah? No kidding. You aren't working with Slurp and Gurgle, are you?" Malcolm asked as his eyes lit up. "That's it! Those guys are good, but I swear I'm gonna pay them back for all the headaches they've given me. I'm gonna have a long talk with Armadillo. Your job's done, pal. You had me goin', but you're not good enough. You can tell those two little monsters I saw right through their prank and I will get them back."

"Hey, I don't know anything about slurping and gurgling. All I want is some compensation for letting you sleep in the park."

"Forget it. Leave me alone."

"I'm going to call the cops and have you shot."

"Good. Nobody's shot me yet today. See you 'round, Soupbone."

The indigent man was amused, yet concerned. He walked away. Malcolm went back to creating a clever stairway that would get him into his elevated abode. As he was placing an old gas can on his stack of makeshift stairs, he heard a muffled explosion and something whizzed by his ear. He swatted his head to frighten away any gnats or loco mosquitoes and went back to work. The sequence of sounds played again and a chunk of tree bark flew off in front of him. He looked around. Standing directly behind him and pointing a gun towards him was a uniformed police officer. What is up with the cops in Nowheresville?

Malcolm ran away and a short chase ensued. Running through goose gaggles wasn't as easy as it sounded, and he ended up throwing geese at the oncoming cop. He thought about throwing his wallet out to distract the geese, but that wouldn't have worked since all the geese knew his wallet was empty. Finally, Malcolm disguised himself as a goose. He lost the cop, but none of the geese were fooled. In fact, they tried to point the officer in the direction of the idiotic man in the mud and feather suit. The cop didn't get it.

Having eluded the park's resident law enforcement personnel, Malcolm contemplated the possibility of becoming a full time goose. You got to understand, living on the street can cause some pretty serious emotional and psychological problems. Many of the best geese started out as street people.

Given that he couldn't safely sleep among the geese or live in the trees, Malcolm sought refuge somewhere else. Anywhere else. He was alone in the city. Armadillo wasn't around (his brothers, incidentally, were back at the park having a good laugh with the indigent man, a cop, and several thousand fun loving waterfowl). Malcolm thought about looking up some of the people from his former job, but the only person he knew that would possibly offer him a bed was Devlette, and she would have forced him to share it with two or three other people. That was not his bag, man. He was out of luck.

It was time for Malcolm to become an official street person. Most everyone he met laughed when they heard that he'd been kicked out of the park. They knew all about the organization of geese and the hassles involved with living in trees. Malcolm wasn't particularly interested in making any long term relationships with the other street people. Many of them would form little cliques and band together for warmth and protection but Malcolm was a loner by nature. He didn't want to hang with the tired, the poor, or huddle with the masses. He wanted a shower.

Naturally there were no designated public showers (bum baths) in the city. Oh sure, there were private showers. There were literally thousands of private showers in the city. Seems like everybody and their brother had a condo or an apartment with a private shower, but try to walk into somebody's private shower just once and see what happens. They don't like it. Try bringing your own soap? Doesn't make a damn bit of difference. They start shouting, "Hey put your clothes on and get outta here before I shoot ya!" You can't get out fast enough. The alternative impromptu urban showers consisted of water spigots, fire hydrants, and drinking fountains. It's really tough to shower under a spigot or bathe in a drinking fountain, and just try to clean behind your ears with a fire hydrant. Malcolm tried 'em all and it was very difficult. Of course, people still insisted that he put his clothes back on and get lost or get shot.

In New Delhi it's common practice to cleanse one's body and soul in the Ganges. It's reasonable to assume that Malcolm didn't have any Hindu roots, or Asian ancestry, or much of a soul, but his body needed some serious exfoliating or even an exorcism. That dude was stinky. Nowheresville didn't have any major rivers running through it, but there was a major canal that went through town on its way to a neighboring community's irrigation system. The canal would be a suitable place to bathe until a more permanent facility was located, so Malcolm jumped in for a good cleansing. It didn't take him long to figure out that beneath the calm surface of the canal moved a very powerful current that would easily grab the average human and pull that person underwater so far and so fast that it was like someone tied an anchor to his waist. Further investigation revealed that the slick mossy walls of the canal offered very little to grab on to.

Fortunately, Malcolm was able to stay at the surface using an old Indian technique of filling his cheeks with air and breathing through his nose. That didn't keep him any closer to the surface, but it did give him a deeper appreciation for the advice given by Native Americans to invading European cultures. They also must have had a good, if not too vengeful, sense of humor.

Dog paddling and screaming as he drifted along the canal, he stayed afloat for about thirty minutes until he passed a fallen power line that was dangling just above the water. He grabbed for the line and caught it with the back of his hand. The high voltage shot him about twenty yards away from the waterway into a pile of pussywillows. When he regained consciousness he felt clean and tingly all over, plus he had an exciting new tattoo of an explosion across the back of his hand that ran all the way up to his shoulder. The canal experience was cleansing and invigorating, and the electrocution was rejuvenating and exciting, but he figured he'd better stick to bathing in unguarded bird baths from that point forward.

After three weeks of sleeping in door stoops, window sills, dumpsters, appliance cartons, shoe boxes, and empty pop bottles,

Malcolm knew he couldn't go on much longer. He'd been reduced to the level of rotting putrid garbage. This was not what Malcolm wanted to do with his adult life and it was never ever explicitly mentioned in his horoscope. His high school guidance counselor mentioned that it was his most likely career path, so he probably should have seen it coming, but since when does anyone listen to adults in high school. And sinking to the level of putrid garbage? Damn! Things could not get worse.

One day, as he sat leaning against an empty box, he saw a guy that looked like Jack Palance meet a guy who looked like Dylan Thomas. The imitation Jack said, "How's it goin'?" The Dylan look-a-like replied, "How's what goin'?" Jack shook his head and walked on. Malcolm remembered that in some mathematical models two straight lines on a common plane could get closer together without ever touching. Two lines could converge forever and never meet, just like the Jack and Dylan look-alikes. He dwelt on the irony of such dilemmas. It was like the atoms in the epistemological table that combined in a seemingly solid object but they were actually a relatively great distances apart. The atoms never touched, yet their interaction created a bond, a complex system that couldn't be broken without the assistance of, say, somebody who cared.

Malcolm contemplated a similar pseudo-mathematical philosophically useless analogy involving condoms, diaphragms, and his love life but the deep thought process was interrupted by a screaming woman in the Nowheresville Cordon Blue city park. The woman stood and yelled as a young purse snatcher ran away from her. The ever-heroic Malcolm was bored and feeling unusually cavalier, so he took to chase.

The bandit ran across the park and heard Malcolm yelling far behind him. He was a rather portly villain, with a limp, and a cast on his leg that was probably responsible for his irregular step. His crutch may have also slowed him down a little. At any rate, the thief wasn't moving very quickly. He actually dropped the purse when the woman first screamed, because she was really loud, and he needed to cover his ears. Still, Malcolm made a valiant pursuit and caught up with the guy in about ten seconds. Malcolm jogged in place behind the crook for a while, yelling for him to stop. Then he backpedalled in front of the wrong-doer, shouting at him to desist. Then he backed away about twenty feet and hurled himself at the hoodlum, tackling him with a soft thud. The whole chase took about three minutes and Malcolm feared for his life and reputation at every moment. There weren't any cops around so Malcolm had to do whatever he could to detain the rascal. He repeatedly kicked the crutch out from the empty handed purse snatcher. Then took the thief's wallet and told him about the Golden Rule. Eventually the bad guy looked sad enough that Malcolm left him alone.

Feeling completely noble, and pooped out, Malcolm grabbed the purse and sat down on a park bench to contemplate the gravity of his chance encounter with adventure. He doubted that he'd ever do anything so stupendous again in his life. The victim of the purse snatching was the typical goddess type that tended to get him in the most trouble, especially when he was full of enough self-confidence and bravado to offer the woman a date. It was always safest for him to start off small with a casual suggestion. No long term commitments. When he was young he liked to take his dates to those 4-snapshots-for-a-dollar photo booths. It was intimate, it was spontaneous, and it was brief enough that if things didn't work out, they could go their separate ways without anybody caring one way or another. But lately Malcolm could never phrase the photo booth invitation in way that would keep him from getting slapped or laughed at or arrested.

After a short rest and long deliberation, he stood up and went to the innocent victim with a photo opportunity in mind. As he offered her the purse, he tried to think of something witty to say. She was so nice looking. She took the purse without making eye contact and reached into it. Probably wanted to give him a reward. When she pulled her hand out, the only pick-up line he could think of was, "Hi. Those are brass knuckles, aren't they?"

A sharp brass knuckled right jab to his magical charley horse shoulder answered the question.

"How dare you attack that poor crippled man!" she screamed.

Malcolm was hurt that she would think such a thing. He was injured because she thought such a thing.

"Look! I'm homeless," he said.

She smacked him again.

"And I'm almost crippled, too! Just..." he tried to finish his explanation but she kept hitting his head.

After attacking him for about twenty minutes, the attractive purse snatching victim collapsed from exhaustion. He understood that fits of violence can be very tiring and he would have sympathized with the poor woman much more if he wasn't delirious from pain. By that time he hardly even wanted to ask her out anymore. Instead, he just kind of imagined that she was sleeping with him as he lost consciousness.

X

A few days later, he found himself hungover in the middle of the afternoon, ambling around aimlessly through central Nowheresville until he stopped in front of a television store and gazed through the window. Train wrecks, hurricanes, traffic pile-ups, tidal waves, fires, insurance salesmen, electrical shock, earthquakes, bolts of lightning, botulism, floods. So much destruction, so much agony and pain, so much suffering, so much tragedy was just so much comedy for the bitter Malcolm Tent.

He stood in front of the window chuckling, when he noticed that the local news station was covering a story on a street that looked suspiciously familiar. They were filming on Block Street, the same street that Malcolm was standing on. Somewhere on Block Street a news crew was capturing an important event on film and he wanted to get into the action. He looked up and down the street. About a quarter mile away he saw a large throng of observers thronging. It was his big chance to stand behind a news guy and try to act like he didn't know he was on television. Millions of people would be able to see him at his most candid moment. Maybe a beautiful woman would notice him, pity him, locate him, give him a toothbrush, and marry him.

He ran down the street to find out what the commotion was all about. Possibly a circus was in town or a movie studio was filming on location. As he got closer he recognized the lights and the film cameras in front of the Nowheresville Action Witness news teams. They were really making a movie on location in his home town! A movie! It was groovy! And a huge crowd was watching the action, including a little girl with a lollipop. Malcolm considered stealing the little girl's lollipop. He made a grab for it, but as luck would have it, one of the movie's props got screwed up and startled the child. A half crazed giant mechanical clam converged on the little girl. Yup, a giant clam! Giant clam with a hankering for a lollipop tot! There wasn't time for second thoughts, or meditations on good Samaritanism, or introspection, or popcorn, or a long drawn out analysis of the things that are usually taken into consideration in perilous mechanical giant clam attacks. Malcolm had to act fast. There were cameras around, for Pete's sake!

With the skill and timing of an under-aged Eastern Block female gymnast, Super Malcolm did a cart wheel to distract the menacing mollusk, then he straddled the beast. With surgical precision he reached deep into the heart of the clam and groped around for something, anything, and just as he expected, he couldn't find anything. He pulled away from the monster covered with clam juice and melted butter.

"Hey! Somebody boil some water and bring me lemons and some extra sheets! Oh! And a nice chardonnay and sour dough bread, please!" he shouted as he dove at the clam again and wrestled with it until the extension cord that powered the electric clam eventually came unplugged.

The clam was dead. Malcolm had defeated the evil overgrown galloping scalloping little girl grabbing prop. As the small child climbed out of its big mouth, Malcolm was mobbed by grateful citizens who demanded that he accept their financial rewards. Media people surrounded the hero and begged him to pose for the evening news and accept his well deserved fame. Gorgeous and energetic professional cheerleaders embraced him in their arms and smothered him with their ever-loving bodies.

Before he could take advantage of the cash, hype, and chicks, the little girl approached him. Her eyes were filled with tears of joy and she spoke, "Thanks, mister. You saved my life. My father owns the phone company. Would you ever want to be a vice president of a multi-billion dollar company? What's your name?"

Malcolm smirked, but before he could answer, the little girl glanced across the street and screamed, "Five Clean Boys!"

Five Clean Boys were, of course, a rock band put together by a wealthy producer who had nothing better to do than make money off a bunch of puppy love puppets. Malcolm was quickly abandoned and his random act of bravery was forgotten. Once again he was knocked into the dirt.

Several days later he found himself resting against a wooden board that served as a wall on a dock at the Nowheresville Marina. A lonely man was sitting on a bench near the end of the pier. His face was weathered but he was still a young man. A smoke trail slowly swirled from his cigarette for a moment until it was scattered by the wind. There was emptiness in his eyes, a base hatred mixed with a deep passionate love. But there was no object for his hatred, no victim for his love. He just sat there watching the ocean. The ocean had knocked against the cliffs relentlessly for eons, but embraced the sands as well. The ocean didn't care. You could swim in it, spit in it, dump anything you wanted into it and it would keep coming. For all the anger the weathered man carried, he could only gather more. The ignorance of the world constantly surrounded him, and only the most heinous acts of cruelty stuck in his mind. Similarly, the love he searched for all his life would come just within his grasp then fade away before he could take hold. The generosity of a child or the selfless acts of kindness shown by the elderly all faded away.

Malcolm looked over at him and said, "How's it goin'?"

The guy looked back at Malcolm with a vacuous frightened stare then stood up and jumped over the railing on the pier.

Malcolm didn't try to save him.

At some point during the last few days he'd lost his will to care. He reflected on his ability to watch another person jump off the edge of a pier without intervening. It didn't bother him much. His absence of caring didn't bother him. If he were to jump off a pier and no one blinked, it would have been fine, maybe even good. His will to live was gone, but again, his will to die was no stronger. The plan was to go on living until something better came along. It wouldn't take much.

For all that he didn't think he felt anything, the guilt of not caring was running around in his subconscious. The alcohol had made him incapable of acting even if he wanted to care. There was a body in the ocean near Malcolm that no one was going to save. There was a young man looking over the pier, waiting for a feeling to hit him. He could wait as long as he wanted. Malcolm had to make the change happen himself. Nothing would happen until he made that commitment. He wasn't doing anything. He was lost, lost in a bottle.

XI

Many days later, he ran across a sign of destiny, a sign of fame, fortune, and great wealth. It was a help wanted sign. *"Lead singer wanted - must be willing to work evenings - Apply in person at Joe's Garage and Grill after 7:00."* Stenciled under the clever wording was a firecracker and a horn, so Malcolm knew the gig was legit. True, Malcolm had no formal training and it might take some work to become as accomplished as some of the great entertainers, but he didn't care, he was ready for anything. It was one of his life's goals and he thought he'd love it. So what if he failed? At least he tried, and it's better to have lived and failed than never to have lived at all. No, it's better to have loved and failed... wait... lived and loved. He didn't really care.

The search for Joe's Garage and Grill began in the phone book. The search for Joe's Garage and Grill ended in the phone book. Let's face it, he wasn't looking for buried treasure. The location happened to be 2 blocks down the street from the burnt out structural remains of the Hot Diggity Dog Delivery Service and Grill. And while Malcolm had vowed never to set foot on that street again, he figured one exception wouldn't cause him too much bad luck.

When he arrived at the garage there were five people waiting in line. Three of them were there for the audition and two wanted the grilled chicken cheese sandwich. Malcolm waited. When you're on the road like that, you get used to waiting. The line dwindled as the food was served and potential singers collapsed. Within an hour Malcolm was at the front of the line.

He filled out a standard job application listing his favorite colors, next of kin, previous employer's mother's maiden name (Esther) and he was ready to play. It was a tough audition to say the least. Malcolm belted out the fast and slow versions of *Mack the Knife, Red River Valley, Anarchy in UK*, and finished up with a tearful rendition of the *Banana Split's Theme Song*. The band was knocked over. Technically they'd passed out. Between the whiskey, weed, and Malcolm's singing, the band couldn't maintain consciousness long enough to refuse him. When they woke up the next morning Malcolm was still there, so they figured they must have hired him.

As an official band member, Malcolm felt comfortable asking all kinds of potentially embarrassing personal questions to the veterans. First and most importantly he had to know, "How come you guys all have such long hair?"

"We like to think of it as exaggerated hair," said the least menacing member of the band.

"Uh huh," Malcolm uttered, "So what are your names?"

"I'm Slap," said... Slap! "cuz I'm the drummer, y'know. Steel drums, do da reggae riddum, mon. I hate whitey!"

Slap was a big Caucasian guy with a terrible attitude, so Malcolm didn't feel like starting any racial discussions. He just continued with the introductions, "What's your name?" he asked the next guy.

"Dudes call me Muttbrain, but I don't care. I play a little bass, make a little love, get high on life."

"Heh. Heh, that's, heh, cool," said Malcolm like an idiot as he looked at the next member.

"I'm Wire!" said a character who spoke mainly to move his mouth.

"He's what you'd call hyperkinetic... Get it? He's always bouncin' off the walls, but he jams like a demon so I keep him around," said Gary.

Malcolm asked, "So you must be the leader of the pack?"

Gary shrugged his shoulders, "Yeah, I'm Gary. Welcome to Monkey House, Bud. We're gonna practice for a while tonight. But right now we got work to do."

Malcolm hadn't heard of Monkey House and wasn't completely sure that any of them were actually talented beyond their hair growing abilities, but he was in and he liked it. He was ready for whatever came next; groupies, autograph hounds, big money, he didn't care, he was up for any of those perks. Like all great bands, Monkey House had a van. Like all great singers, Malcolm was entrusted with driving the van and delivering pizzas until they got a gig.

The grill shut down early that day so the band could work on one of Gary's new songs. After eight hours of thinking about doing work, they all felt like relaxing (Malcolm included). The band leader slept in his car until he... woke up and then dedicated

7 solid minutes to song writing. When he was done, Gary ran back to the garage with a page of lyrics and jumped to the stage.

"Okay guys, let's rock," he yelled.

Muttbrain and Slap looked at each other, groaned and stumbled to their instruments.

Wire found a spider and was playing with it like a yo-yo, concentrating as the spider kept crawling up a strand of silk to his hand. He was more than a little irritated that Gary interrupted his natural science project. The spider was also quite miffed with Gary for ruining its yo-yo antics. If Gary ever decided to sit on a tuffet he was in for a big scare.

With an uncharacteristic sense of urgency, Malcolm ran out from the kitchen to the stage full of blind enthusiasm.

"Let's go, Wire," shouted Gary. "This one's going to make us famous."

Wire grimaced and shook the spider from his hand, "Yeah, you think everything's gonna make us famous. We don't even have a demo album."

"This one's goin' on the demo," Gary confided.

Wire wandered over to his guitar and started strumming the theme song to *Daktari*.

"Okay! Let's just start with the rhythm for, '*It Ain't My Kid or Yours*' and we'll kind of take it from there."

He handed Malcolm the song sheet and the band started to play. Malcolm got a feel for the rhythm and started to read the lyrics out loud almost like he was singing,

> *"Wakin' up on a good day,"* he crooned and looked around.
> *"Gotta go to work,*
> *Thinkin' about sleepin' in,*
> *But my boss is just a jerk,*
> *I hate my job,*
> *I hate my job,*
> *I hate my job,*
> *I hate my job."*

Right on, brother! The band was jamming, hair balls were flying everywhere. The guys were all seriously stoked.

> *"Kinda feel like quittin',*
> *Just wanna quit today,*
> *But I know I'm only kiddin'*

'cause I really need the pay,
I hate my job,
I hate my job,
I hate my job,
I hate my job,
Got fired from my job,
'cause the boss don't like my hair,
Told him I couldn't cut it,
So now I'm outta there,
I need a job,
I need a job,
I need a job,
I need a job!"

That was it! A lyrical social and philosophical masterpiece that rivaled the best works of Mozart, Rousseau, and Ronald the Electrician. The band loved it.

Gary told everyone that the title was, '*It Ain't My Work or Yours,*' but Malcolm didn't get it.

Wiping the sweat of passion from his face, Wire yelled, "Awesome, Gary! That was so righteous!"

Slap lit up a cigarette and said, "Jus' wait until dat one heets de white man's air waves. Then we'll be seein' some changes!"

"What's it called again?" asked the Mutt.

"How about '*Work Sucks*'?" suggested Malcolm.

"No, it's called '*It Ain't My Work or Yours,*' and it's like about how when a kid gets a job and then finds out it sucks and then, y'know, do you even get it at all?"

"I still think '*Work Sucks*' is a better title," Malcolm muttered.

Everyone but Gary liked the new name. "Look, pal," Gary said, like a wiseguy, "I think that when I spend all that time coming up with a classic song, you can do a little better than spending two seconds coming up with '*Work Sucks*' for a title."

Since Malcolm wasn't sure if Gary was serious he went along with him, "Hey, sorry man. I'm new at this whole far out rock band thing. I wasn't trying to compromise your creative vibrations. I don't know anything about art. I'm just thinking maybe your title is too brainy for your audience. I wasn't trying to mess with you or your title."

Gary smiled and nodded at all the band members. "That's cool. I can dig it. Hey guys," he said, with great satisfaction, "the song's new name is, *'Don't Mess with My Creative Vibrations'*. All I have to do is change the word 'hair' to 'creative vibrations' and we are platinum."

The band was blown away as they exclaimed, "You're the man, Gary."

"Genius, dude."

"Irie!"

"Wow, what a good name for a song," finished Malcolm.

Beaming with pride, Gary nodded at his followers, "So now all we gotta do is change the beat a little so it sounds totally new, and we got a demo tape!"

"Awesome, let's do it!" shouted a small drunken wannabe roadie from behind a stack of milk crates.

For the next three hours the band practiced and perfected, *'Don't Mess with My Creative Vibrations'* and Malcolm recited the words over and over and over, and after a while he decided to add a personal touch to the performance. He started dancing, spinning around, doing somersaults, and what not, and so forth. Then he started snapping his fingers and became a finger snapping sensation. The band members liked it so much they let Malcolm throw a finger snapping solo into the act. It really was good.

By the end of their short but intense rock and roll experience, Malcolm had been transformed from a tone deaf civilian to a tone deaf finger snapping, microphone swinging, hula dancing maniac. With Malcolm's moves and the band's bitchin' rhythms there was nothing those guys couldn't do. They were going straight to the top with a bucket.

Midnight rolled around and most of the band members were asleep except for Malc and Muttbrain who sat and talked about politics and music, and the influence of politics on music, and the influence of music on politics. If the whole conversation had been captured on tape it could have influenced history, or at least filled up an empty tape. They reasoned that the "Bill of Rights" would be easier to remember if it was recited to the tune of *"What's New Pussycat?"* Congressional members would be more productive and accountable if they had groupies, roadies, and theatrical agents. The president would have to play more than just a saxophone to get elected, he'd need be able to pick up any guitar and jam like Hendrix and beat bongos like a Gatling gun. And of course he or she (rockin' presidential babes) would have to be under thirty-five to stay in office. The two political ideologists concluded that history was boring so they got drunk and fell asleep talking about dream analysis.

They woke up around 10:00 the next morning to the rhythmic sound of Slap and Gary pounding pans over their heads. "Wake up, dudes," shouted Gary, "We got a gig and it's not even noon!"

"Where's it at?" mumbled Muttbrain, like a grammatical maroon.

"FGBG! Ha! They love us!" Gary yelled as he ran to the stage and started banging on the drums.

Malcolm looked at Mutt, and Mutt, sensing Malc's naive alienation said, "FGBG's a bar on the East side. It's not that big, but it's better than nothing."

"What's it stand for? FGBG," asked Malcolm.

"Something like, 'Furtive Glances Bar and Grill'. It's not that big," Muttbrain reiterated.

Gary ran down from the stage and continued to boast, "The deal is, we play for tips and we each get a free drink. The guy totally fell for it! Except, Malcolm, um, you don't get a drink, I had to make some compromises. But hang in there, dude, we're on our way!"

It was official. The band had a set of songs and a place to play. That's right, The Furtive Glances Bar and Grill in the old part of town. The contract required all the band members to arrive at the bar alive with their instruments and maintain consciousness throughout most of the performance. They did and Malcolm's debut was a smashing success. The band really was only playing for tips and Malcolm, being the newest member, had to wait tables between sets for tips. Anyway, the audience clapped after every song. They also clapped after Malc dropped a tray of drinks (Malcolm actually ended up losing money that night). Of course the audience also clapped when Alphonso, the fry cook, heckled the band. The important thing was that the band played and nobody got shot.

Malcolm's next destination on his rocket to stardom was at the Moose Lodge and Grill. It was indeed an auspicious occasion because the Mooses (Meese) had a reputation for catapulting acts straight to the top. It was rumored that the Beatles made a killing back in the Sixties after playing the Moose Lodge and Grill. Around the same time, the Rolling Stones played there and performed what became their first hit. The other rumor was that one time there were some beetles at the lodge that were killed when they were hit by rolling stones. That wouldn't have been very exciting, so Monkey House stuck with the first rumor.

"Midnight at the Moose" was printed on the hand bills and it was expected to be the biggest thing to hit Nowheresville since pudding. Everyone was talking about it or at least everyone in the band had heard about it. For an evening so big, the band members needed some costumes. Not just Halloween costumes, but costumes that rivaled the best of the Partridge Family. They needed costumes so cool and so impressive that even if they didn't play, the crowd would walk away happy. The monumental wardrobe decisions required deep artistic insight and some degree of talent. Gary appointed himself costume manager and set out to create the best costume ever seen on any stage in any club in any country on any planet. Just as everyone expected, Gary exceeded expectations and came through with a costume concept that was artistic and cool. Get this, white T-shirts, blue jeans, and real nice dress shoes. Brilliant.

Monkey House showed up at the club and played to an audience that was mostly awake and breathing. Malcolm noticed a young lady sitting with a girlfriend at one of the front tables. Each time he looked at her she seemed to become more attractive. Even better, the more beer he drank, the more attractive he became to all women. She had the smile, the eyes, and the bod. She was basically very good looking. Malcolm smiled at her, she smiled back, truly fantastic smile. He began to favor her end of the stage. As their eye contact continued, Malcolm sang directly to her and she just ate it up. She laughed about it with her friend. Noticing how impressed she was, Malcolm rocked out like a man covered with fire ants and thoroughly made a fool of himself, but she didn't seem to mind.

During a break, he approached her and she invited him to join her. He did and they chatted. Love chat, life chat, doesn't matter, chatting is the coolest. She was very friendly, down to earth, intelligent, and apparently unarmed. Their conversation was pleasant and centered on relationships, music, old cars, and she made virtually no effort to scratch his eyes out.

When the band started up again, Malcolm had to jump back on stage. They played for a while when some tall dark handsome guy showed up and joined Malcolm's girls. Frustration got the best of him and he burst into an old Stiff Little Fingers song. The girl and her new male acquaintance were having a good time, laughing, joking, and ordering drinks, just like friends. It was disgusting.

After the set, Malcolm got up the nerve to return to the table. They invited him to sit down, and he did, but he didn't participate in the chatting. Instead, he listened and learned that the tall dark and handsome guy was actually a decent person who eventually took both girls home. Talk about romance.

Malcolm had a couple drinks to soften the blow that evening as he believed he'd missed another opportunity for happiness with a beautiful woman. Again, he was mistaken and the girls actually took Mr. Goodbar back to their bachelorette apartment, beat him black and blue with a strobe light, and threw him into a meat locker with a frozen team of cryonic suspension scientists.

The next morning Malcolm was awaken at the garage and grill by the sounds of arguing band members.

Gary was explaining his frustration, "Look man! I'm an artist! I can't let financial problems get in the way of my work. Money just clouds things up. Same thing with women. If I want a woman, she should want me. No questions asked. All that thrill of the chase garbage goes right out the window for artists. Money's for managers, not musicians. If I can't work in an artistic atmosphere and you guys won't help support me, I'm gonna have to break up the band, okay?"

"But what about our album?" asked Slap.

Gary snapped back, "Dude, there isn't going to be an album because you people don't appreciate art, artists, or even music. I don't know why I ever got involved with you deadbeats. I'm sure I'll never know. You guys are the worst! I'm outta here!"

"But where are you gonna go?" Muttbrain asked.

"Frisco!" he answered.

"If you're going to San Francisco, be sure to wear a flower in your hair," said Malcolm.

"Shut up!" Gary shouted and with that, he stormed out of the restaurant and never looked back.

"Hey, man. Now that Gary's gone, let's start our own band. The Deadbeats," suggested Muttbrain.

Malcolm knew the band didn't have a chance. He was ready to call it quits. He announced that he had to move on and admitted he didn't have any talent. The guys agreed that he didn't have any talent and it was the best thing to do. They offered to get him stoned, but he declined. Their poignant parting words were, "That's cool, dude, more buds for us. Ha!"

Malcolm left the band with the few tips he'd earned, some extra pizza, a broken guitar pick, and a bunch of false phone numbers from imitation groupies. He wandered into the streets with the complete knowledge that he was once again entering the worst phase of his life. Damn! He needed to get his act together, get a job, and move into a hotel until he could afford monthly rent payments. Then maybe he could start moving up a better path in life.

XII

Things were starting to get desperate, and desperate times called for desperate measures. Malcolm had to commit crime, any crime. It didn't have to be a major crime with guns and car chases and swearing and frontal nudity. A small crime would also serve as an adequate act of desperation. Meditating on all the atrocities that had been committed against mankind over the centuries, he selected one that would meet his needs. Maybe it was a little too tame, but he was learning. He decided to steal an extra newspaper from a paper rack.

He spent maybe fifteen minutes tracking down a likely victim for his plunder and found a newspaper rack that had crime written all over it. Actually the rack had "Free" written all over it, but Malcolm didn't notice that part. Subconsciously he interpreted the word "Free" to mean that the newspapers inside the bin were seeking liberation. The rack had a coin slot, so Malcolm figured it was there for a reason. He put 4 quarters into the machine, lifted the cover, casually removed 1 newspaper, then quickly and violently grabbed another and stuffed it down the front of his pants. A businessman came up behind Malcolm. Malcolm offered him the legitimate paper. The businessman took it. Malcolm gave him a knowing smile, like he knew they were getting away with some kind of sinister act. The business man looked over his shoulder to see if Malcolm was smiling at someone else. Suppressing a deep diabolical laugh, the blossoming thief bolted from the scene.

With his stolen newspaper folded up and concealed in his dirty blue jeans, Malcolm ran stiff-legged down the street until he was out of reach of any paper police. He took out the newspaper, unfolded it, and consciously read the word "Free" written in bold letters on the front page. He looked back, and watched the businessman open the paper rack and put his free newspaper back in the machine. Malcolm's career as a master criminal wasn't starting off too well.

It started to rain, so Malcolm used the paper as an umbrella. He smiled at his sudden burst of ingenuity and looked at the businessman smugly. The businessman pulled out an umbrella, so Malcolm stopped smiling and ran for shelter in an alleyway. As he raced for a refrigerator carton, he stumbled on stray hubcap, landed in a deep pothole, and got soaked by pouring rain as his newspaper fell apart on top of him.

"Malcolm!" shouted his adopted father, who appeared out of nowhere, "Get in out of that rain! What's the matter with you? Is that how I brought you up? Why don't you get yourself a job?"

"Nobody's hiring," grumbled Malcolm.

The self-proclaimed father pulled a strip of newspaper off Malcolm's shoulder. "Nobody's hiring, eh?" He looked at the news strip and began reading, "Help wanted. Forklift driver, cook, delivery, assembler, sales. I see plenty of jobs out there for a healthy white boy." He pointed to a sign on a restaurant window that was two feet away. "Now hiring... You ain't looking too hard, are you?"

The sign at Beauford's Breakfast Nook and Grill didn't impress Malcolm, "Here's the deal, Dad, I'm going to make you rich, but I'm not going to do it by flipping burgers."

His father looked confused. "You're goin' to make me rich? I want to know what's in it for you?" he asked and waited for an interesting answer.

"I figured if I can make enough money to make you rich, I can make enough to make myself rich. I just need something to shoot for. I've never been able to get things done without a goal. Don't destroy my goal," said Malcolm as he stared at the help wanted sign through the rain and soggy pages of newsprint.

Ignoring the obvious logical assumption that his presence in Malcolm's scheme tended to detract from Malc's greater good, the father went along with the game. "Okay, make me rich. And you damn sure better not settle for buyin' me a new pair of shoes."

"I'll make you so rich, it'll make you puke. You gotta believe me Dad. You just gotta!"

His father put his hand on his stomach, "Well, I'm startin' to believe you already." He coughed, "But you better hurry."

Forcing himself to care, Malcolm asked, "What do you mean?"

"You hear that cough?" he coughed again, almost convincingly. "I've only got a few weeks left. I'm hallatocious."

"Hella what?"

"You heard me! Don't back talk your father. I'll smack you like I used to."

"Why didn't you tell me? You should have just looked me in the eye and told me you were …hallatocious. Damn you!"

"I wanted to, but I thought it would scare you off."

Malcolm remorsefully asked the toughest question he'd ever asked anyone, "How long do you have?"

The black man put his hand on Malcolm's shoulder and leaned into him, "It's hard to say. Doctors gave me thirty, maybe forty years. They've seen cases where a hallatocious victim can live longer, but they didn't want to get my hopes up."

Malcolm waved the air from his face, gasped a little, and fought off some tears. His father wanted to bust out laughing, but he didn't want to kill the kid. The garlic fries at the ball game were pretty strong, and he hadn't had a chance to brush his teeth since lunch. But he was lucky enough to watch the game from seats on the 50-yard line (he had a few friends). So aside from his inaccurate pronunciation of some arbitrary medical vernacular, Malcolm's artificial father was actually having a bang-up day. He always liked the rain in the inner city.

"Look, I don't care who you are, father, bum, whatever. I'm going to make you rich and you're going to help me," said Malcolm.

"I can't lift anything," interjected the father.

"You don't have to do anything. You're just my inspiration," Malcolm explained as he wiped some mud out of his eye.

The father looked at Malcolm with deep concern, "Think you better get started." Then he punched Malcolm in the shoulder. "Remember the magic charley horse? You're killin' me, son. Killin' me."

There was something believable about the old man's expression, his countenance, and his right hook. Perhaps he was speaking from the heart. If that was going to be his father's, ahem, the old man's last request, Malcolm wasn't going to let him down. The whole damn world was full shysters and idiots. All around him, people were robbing the poor with false promises for their investments. The poor fell for the scams out of fear and desperation. If one small investment can turn their life around, they'd make that investment even if it was their last dollar. Sirens raced up and down the streets for the victims and the cheats. What a mess. Just one person worth helping, that's all he needed, and that person was his paternal bum.

At that moment Malcolm Tent decided to take action against the world of con-men. He wiped the newspaper off his face and shoulders, tucked in his shirt, put on a great smile, and marched right into Beauford's Breakfast Nook and Grill. He actually tripped over his shoe laces and fell into the little restaurant, but he intended to get himself a job. He had to wonder though, what exactly was the attraction to greasy fried eggs set between two wheat muffins with a slice of chicken and some yellowish breakfast sauce? On the surface it might sound good, indeed, people were buying them hand over fist, but when you break it down, all you're really purchasing is starch, polyglycerides, salt, cholesterol, and a nutritious paper wrapper.

Regardless of the ingredients, Malcolm wanted to check it out. He went through the lobby of Beauford's Breakfast Nook and Grill and gazed up at the plastic menu above the cash registers. An old white man was standing behind the counter watching Malcolm. "Welcome to Beauford's, peabrain, can I help you?"

Malcolm looked at the old man and gave him an awkward smile. Although the word, "peabrain" sounded clear enough, he assumed that he must have misunderstood the old fellow. He motioned that he wasn't ready and mumbled, "Not yet."

The old man grimaced, "What?"

"I'm not ready yet," said Malcolm to the aged cash handler.

A young lady was standing next to Malcolm. "You go ahead," he said to her, like a chauvinistic dog.

She smiled and continued to look up at the plastic menu.

"She's not ready yet either," said the elderly jerk. "Nobody knows what they want," he muttered.

Malcolm looked at the girl and determined that she was still deciding, so he slowly, politely approached the counter. The old guy had been staring at him for a while.

"I have a question," said Malcolm.

"Good for you," said the old cashier to a bewildered Malcolm, then added, "That's the first step in getting a clue. The next step is actually asking your damn question."

"What's in a Chicken and Egg Sunrise Sandwich?"

The old man shook his head, "Well, I'm gonna take a shot in the dark here and guess that it's got some chicken in it, probably some egg, and assuming they haven't changed the definition of sandwich in the last couple of hundred years, it's probably got two of slices of bread somewhere in there. But let's not take any chances with guessing here..." He turned his back to Malcolm and looked up at the sign. "Yup, I got lucky! Chicken, egg, and bread all come with the Chicken and Egg Sunrise Sandwich. You want to ask another question or do you think you've learned enough for the day?"

Malcolm smiled and shook his head (it rattled), dumb question. "I think I'll have a..."

"I don't care what you think. What do you want to order?" barked the old guy.

"Just give me a burger," conceded Malcolm.

"I'm not gonna give you anything. This is America. You want it, you pay for it."

Malcolm reassessed the situation. Things would only get worse if he antagonized the dear old man. "Thank you for helping me, sir. Without your assistance, sir, I would probably end up starving to death. I would greatly appreciate it if you would allow me to purchase a 'Perky Burger'," said Malcolm.

"Sure. You want cheese on that grease mitt?"

"Oh, no thank you, sir. I don't really care for cheese."

"Oh, have some cheese. It's good for ya."

"Well, in that case, yes. Yes, I would like you to make me a 'Perky Burger' with cheese."

"Now you want me to make it? Listen kid, if I was making a burger for you, I guarantee it would be the last thing you ever ate."

Shrugging his shoulders and raising his hands in surrender, Malcolm said cordially, "Such a kidder. You've got a good heart. Hey, by the way, I was curious about that 'Job Opening' sign in the front window."

Old wrinkle puss aimed his beady eyes at the front of the building, "The sign itself? I'm sure it's just an average ordinary sign... Would you like me to get you in touch with the sign makers or do you just want to order some food today?"

His patience waning, Malcolm tried to stay friendly, "Ha! Yeah, I'd like a burger and I'm not all that interested in who made the sign. You are very funny. I was really wondering about the job opening posted on the sign more than who made the sign."

The old man's face turned bright red as he said, "Oh, yeah? Well, let me just take a look and we'll both know."

He climbed up on the counter, clumsily slid over it, then stomped out the front door. From inside, Malcolm watched the ornery cuss as he looked at the sign, read it out loud, scratched his head and looked around the front of the building for another sign. Malcolm sensed it was a good time to roll his eyes, so he did.

The old man came back into the building with a confused expression and climbed back over the counter. "I don't see any signs that say anything about a job opening. I saw one that says 'Help Wanted', but that's all it says, so that can't be the one you're talking about."

"Well, actually..."

"Help wanted," interrupted the old fellow, "Y'know? We all want some help now and then. You want help now and then, don't you?"

"Yeah, but I'm not..."

"I could sure use some help dealing with idiots. Maybe we should all get our own signs."

"Look, could I talk to your manager?"

"Y'know? I bet you can. Been talking to *me*, haven't ya?"

"Yeah..."

"Then I think you can talk to him. Talking's funny that way."

"Can I talk to him now?"

"What's your name?"

"Malcolm Tent."

"You really are a pinhead. Who the hell do you think you've been talking to?"

"You're the manager?"

"That's what I said."

"And you don't have any job openings?"

"Yes, we're looking for idiots. You're overqualified."

That was it. Once they tell a person that he or she is overqualified, the interview is basically over. Malcolm bid adieu, "Okay, then, thanks for your time."

"What about your order?"

"Oh, right, my order. Can I get that to go?"

"To go?" said the old guy.

"Yeah, to go to Hell!" Malcolm laughed, kicked up his heels, and gave himself a high five. What a burn! He flipped the old guy off and ran out of the restaurant while the theme song to the Mary Tyler Moore song ran through his head. For that brief moment he felt liberated, vindicated, bubbly, giggly, perky, self-fulfilled, self-conscious, guilty, pessimistic, bummed out, unemployed... suicidal.

He still didn't have a job and darn it, that's what he really wanted. An anxious employee from Beauford's Breakfast Nook happened to be outside the eatery sweeping a broom very quickly, with short strokes. The sweeping man was intense, yet stupid.

With every stroke of his broom he had to ask himself if the spot he swept was clean enough. If not, sweep again! If clean, move on! What separated that nervous ninny from Malcolm? Nothing, thought Malcolm. He attacked the sweeper and stole his broom. Then he attempted to start sweeping quickly, but the employee tackled him and beat him about the head and shoulders with a dustpan. Malcolm tried to escape, but the employee was relentless. He quickly covered Malcolm in a large green trash bag and began punching him with stale hamburger buns and stabbing him with sticky soda straws.

A crowd of thoughtful business people had gathered near the brawl and watched with great interest as they sipped espresso and patted their lips with napkins. You shoulda been there! It was the fight of Malcolm's life and he knew he'd never win. That employee was frothing at the mouth, his eyes were bulging, and his dander was way way up! Malcolm was no match for such passionate savagery. The sweeping man left him lying on the sidewalk with a bag of soggy french fries sticking out of his mouth. Some mornings just don't start off too well.

Outside the front of Beauford's Breakfast Nook and Grill, Slurp and Gurgle removed the help wanted sign they'd put up and slithered down the street.

That one minute of unrestrained offensiveness towards the old white Beauford man turned out to be more costly than Malcolm could have ever anticipated. The guy had tons of hamburger connections and Malcolm was subsequently blacklisted by the whole fast food industry in Nowheresville. He spent the next several weeks scavenging from dumpsters, stealing tainted cheese from mouse traps, and eating edible pine tree parts. And of course, he found moral sustenance at the bottom of a lot of cheap wine bottles.

XIII

Well, if all else fails, beg. Beg for food, money, love, whatever it takes to keep you alive. Malcolm decided to beg for money for a while. He stood on the sidewalk for about an hour, begging at his best until another beggar approached him.

After a few minutes of observation, the seasoned bum couldn't take anymore. "Man," he said, "You're doing it all wrong."

Shaken by the rude interruption, Malcolm dropped his trick or treat bag and stepped back indignantly. Generally, the indignant reaction was very effective for Malcolm. This time, he got nothin'. No reason.

The bum continued, "I mean, you're on my corner and I'd be pissed if you were stealing my donations, but you're just giving the corner a bad rep. Try looking a little more desperate, and for God's sake, don't tell people you're a loser, it's pathetic."

"Look," argued Malcolm, "I'm panhandling! There's no wrong way to panhandle!"

"Yeah, there is," explained the master beggar. "First, hunch your shoulders."

Malcolm hunched.

"Now hold you hand out," instructed the bum.

Out went Malcolm's hand.

"You're right handed?" asked the bum.

Malcolm nodded.

The bum shook his head, "Okay, whatever. Now put some change in your hand so people won't think you're a lost cause."

After pulling some change from his pocket, Malcolm held the coins out in his hand, and the beggar took 'em all.

"You gotta be careful of that," the transient warned, "People do that all the time. Now put some more coins in your hand."

Malc did and the bum took 'em again.

With genuine concern, the hobo said, "You're not doin' too good, pal. Let's try it again."

Malcolm put some more coins in his hand and the bum took them.

"Honestly, pal, I don't think you're getting this. Have you thought about flipping burgers?"

Malcolm was confused, but still understood his station in life, "I can't. I'm Malcolm Tent."

"Oh," said the beggar, "Well, let's try it one more time."

"Can't do that either, I'm out of change," Malcolm admitted.

The bum lowered his eyes, said, "Sorry, wish I could help," and walked away leaving Malcolm standing there holding out his empty hand.

It had been another rough morning for Malcolm. There was nothing he wouldn't do to regain his pride, or his dignity, or enough money to pay for a roach infested, sleaze bucket, paper-thin-walled little motel room as long as it had a paper band over the toilet seat to ensure some sense of hygiene. He was at his wit's end with money making schemes. Granted, it was a short path to his wit's end, but he still needed some way of making money. A voice in the back of his head was getting louder. Not the voice that kept telling him he was Abe Lincoln's mother-in-law, it was the "Join the Army today," voice. Malcolm spent a long time suppressing both voices, but the army thing was beginning to sound more and more reasonable. There was also a recruiting poster on a bus stop in front of him that displayed a proud confident young man working on a computer. Seemed like a good option. He remembered the jingles that claimed, "We do more in two hours than most people do in an hour and forty five minutes," and he just couldn't get it out of his head. Maybe it wasn't so crazy after all.

The Nowheresville Army recruiting office was just a few blocks away so he practiced begging while he walked that direction. He approached the local recruiting office, came within two feet of the door, and was immediately grabbed and pulled inside. The recruiter abruptly sat Malcolm down in a green vinyl chair and handed him a pen and a clipboard.

"So what makes you think you've got what it takes to be in the Army?" barked the general.

Malcolm belched, "Well, I've seen 'Sgt. York' a few times and, I don't know, I thought it was kind of, y'know, cool. I always wanted to look like Gary Cooper."

"Hey! You're not one of those sissy types? One of those that runs around dressed up like Ethel Merman singing railroad songs with soap bubbles dripping off your fingers, are ya!"

"No."

"Are ya!"

"Well, I guess I could learn. Do you have the lyrics?"

"I think I've heard enough. Fill out those forms and I'll give you a physical."

"Right."

"On second thought, I'll just give you a physical."

Raising an eyebrow or two, Malcolm paused, then asked, "So, what does this job pay? I get medical, dental, all that? What kind of hours will I be working?"

"Hush, hush, let's just get to the physical."

"Look, I just want to know what kind of money I'll be making. I'm not even sure I want to work here."

"Listen, mister, one more word out of you and I'll bring you up on charges of insubordination. Now you get that shirt off, drop, and give me twenty push ups."

"I'm outta here."

"Hey, you're AWOL soldier!"

"Yeah, who needs this."

"I wouldn't have admitted you anyway, Flatfoot!"

Flatfoot. Flatfoot! Malcolm hated that name. He walked out the door fuming. He wasn't half a block from the recruiting office when he decided to take revenge on that, that ...that name caller. There was a kid selling guns and magazine subscriptions on the street corner. Malcolm traded his hand crafted black leather belt for a 9 mm semi-automatic hand gun and a year of 'Modern Boredom' and stormed back into the recruiting office.

"All right jarhead, I've got some work for you!" our hero shouted.

The recruiter frowned and asked, "You call that a weapon? I guess you've never stared down the barrel of a six inch anti-aircraft cannon. I'm not a scared of you," the military ambassador paused. "You're not going to tie me up are you?"

Malcolm shook his head, no-like.

"I'm not afraid of you!" yelled the colonel.

"I'm going to rob you. I want all your money and lottery tickets!" said Malc.

"I'm a recruiting agent. I don't have money and I don't have any lottery tickets."

"All right then, give me all your computer equipment and all that crazy radio walkie-talkie stuff."

The recruiter shrugged his shoulders and shook his head.

"None of that either, huh?" Malcolm was confused and angry, "Okay, give me all your pens and clipboards, now!"

The recruiter began to twitch, "Hey, c'mon guy, not the clipboards. Okay? I'll give you all the pens, pencils, scotch tape... Just leave the clipboards alone."

Without hesitation, Malc snatched four neatly aligned clipboards from the recruiter's front desk. The recruiter winced, "Seriously, c'mon, here's my wallet and, and my Rolex. Let's just leave the clipboards out of this."

"It's too late, Mister Name-Caller. You make me sick. I know you've got a stash of these clipboard babies holed up in a storage closet around here somewhere. Bring 'em out!"

"What are you talking about?" said the recruiter with a nervous laugh, "I don't have any more clipboards. Just those four. Just Billy, Moe, Sammy, and Baby Doc. Just take 'em and get out of here."

"I don't think so. I think you've got at least two dozen unused clipboards around here somewhere and I want 'em. I want them all."

"You're crazy man, you need professional help."

"Yeah, I'm crazy. Crazy like a halibut. Now if I don't see some virgin clipboards out here in thirty seconds, I'm taking one of these nice new military pens, which I also plan to steal, and I'm gonna start scribbling like a cartoonist on a caffeine binge!"

The recruiter was sweating profusely, "You're bluffing!"

Malcolm quickly pulled out a pen and dragged it across a blank clipboard.

"Stop!" screamed the recruiter.

"I've got all the time in the world, General, and a lot of ink to go with it."

The recruiter began to object, so Malcolm gritted his teeth and brought the pen within scribbling distance of the clipboard.

"Okay, okay! Put the clipboard down. Neither one of us wants to see that presswood scarred. Let's both just relax for a second. I'm going into the back room and get all the clipboards you want. Just don't do any more scribbling. Okay?"

Malcolm set his angry bloodshot eyes on the military man and said coldly, "Hurry up. And no tricks! And, and... No funny business!"

The army guy cautiously retreated to the supply room. Malcolm watched the front door. A sudden crash from the supply room sent Malcolm to the back to see what was going on.

"Damn it!" he shouted.

The recruiter was throwing packages of clipboards out a window telling them to run for their lives. Quickly aiming his nine-millimeter at a clipboard on the floor, Malcolm shot it and blew a hole right through its center. Letting out a short cry, the recruiter fell to his knees and covered his eyes.

Malcolm scolded him, "Stupid! Stupid..."

Then he grabbed two packages of clipboards and ran out of the building and vanished in the metropolitan morass called Downtown Nowheresville.

That being his first attempt at armed robbery, he felt both invigorated and nervous. Had the recruiter been held up before? How did Malcolm rate? Would the recruiter like Malcolm to rob him again? He was tempted to ask, but he knew that was rookie stuff. Just the same, he couldn't stop wondering about it. He wanted to rob the recruiter again, but what if the recruiter wasn't ready? Of course, if the recruiter wasn't robbed again... Well, Malcolm knew the whole line of questioning was too stupid to continue so he gave the clipboards to a blind man selling pencils and went back to his business of being a bum.

Bumming in the civilized outback, Malcolm was on an urban walkabout. While he didn't get to wear the gnarly red and yellow paint and rock out to aboriginal rhythms like his Australian counterparts, he was able to enjoy a certain degree of social solitude and self-reliance. The wildlife of the city was as strange and fascinating as any found in the Australian wilderness. There were guttersnipes and sewergators and rare untamed bread eating pigeons. Malcolm eventually befriended a wild street dog and named it Dingo. As the two of them sat under the shelter of a train track bridge sharing a fresh can of dog food in the cold damp night air, Malcolm couldn't shake the feeling that the dog somehow wanted to slit him open and warm his paws in Malcolm's belly.

Yeah, it's a different breed of wallaby that thrives in the concrete jungle. It's a dog eat Malcolm world. If you're a Malcolm, you should probably just get a cat instead. That's street logic. Malcolm used his semi-automatic weapon to force his way into the Nowheresville Animal Pound where he ditched Dingo at gunpoint. He lost the mutt but gained several hundred fleas.

There was another inner city park that offered refuge to Malcolm, and it had no geese or purse snatchers, but it did have cool monkey bars and some of those springy dragon seahorse things, so he decided to crash there for a week or two. The first few minutes were intolerable with all the kids running around in their squeaky sneakers and gooey food substitutes that they carried in their hands, on their clothes and all over their faces.

"Hey, Mister, are you a bum?" asked one charming tot.
"No, I like to dress like this."
"My mom says bums are dirty," said another.
"She's welcome to give me a bath."
"You smell like a trash can," noticed yet another.
"Don't make me steal your candy, all right kids?"
"We don't eat candy. Candy rots your teeth. Mom won't let me eat anything that isn't sugar free."

At that point, all the kids looked alike and Malcolm was getting dizzy trying to field all their questions. "Sugar free, huh?" he asked.

"Yeah, and caffeine free with low sodium and high in riboflavin."
"When I was your age I ate everything."
"Everything? Even chlorofluorocarbons?"
"Yup, especially clorol flubber cabins."
"You're a liar."
"You're a kid."
"Boy bums can't make babies."
"Watch it, ya little brat."
"You're a bum."

After a long argument, the situation deteriorated into a fierce hair pulling, ankle biting, rock throwing melee and Malcolm was subsequently taunted by mean faces, bad words, and chased out of the park.

That was it. Malcolm couldn't take anymore. While the thought of suicide generally annoyed the hell out of him, he decided that things weren't going to get any better. He couldn't stand the thought that things might get worse. He contemplated his state of being: no money, no friends, no car, no place to sleep, nothing to eat. Pretty darned depressing. Well, how was he going to get out of it? The only solution that came to his head involved lying, cheating, and stealing. He had to lie, cheat, and steal to stay alive. What kind of life was that? Is it better to die an honest person or perpetuate life through deception and thievery? Maybe just enough deception to get him back on his feet. We all make compromises.

He'd been scoffed, humiliated, and scoffed again. Malcolm was just looking for a sense of social security (and who would ever deprive him of that?). All the contributions he'd made to his fellow peoples, all the times he said "gesundheit", all the times he passed the sidewalk panhandler and said, "Sorry, Bud" and meant it. Did none of this matter? Was being a nice guy not enough? Couldn't it have been just enough, just enough for the city? Not so thought Malcolm. He was bumming.

He felt like an actor in life's theater. True art is real life. Malcolm was the living artist with the leading role of that miserable play, except he kept forgetting his lines. Alone and without means, the poor soul wandered the alleys searching for scraps of food for nourishment, and scraps of paper for roughage. His was a grumbling belly. He was a mumbling man. Stumbling through an alley, "Earthenware," he muttered, "What the hell is earthenware?" As he spoke softly to himself, and answered, "Must be some kind of organic computer program."

Only the rats were listening. They scurried for the transient shelter of fast food packages that wafted down the alley as the offshore winds raced between the urban constructions. Malcolm stopped and watched as the delicate shanties constructed of temporal trends were blown over, forcing the indigent vermin to dash beneath the next nearest wad of refuse for refuge. He thought out loud of the analogy, "Trash goes into the home, then comes out of the home, then becomes the home. My next house was once owned by a mouse." Yes, he was right there on the edge of psychosis.

XIV

The alley was dark and dull and he contemplated life at such abysmal depths as he slowly waddled into the shelter of total abandon. A small street dweller was peering down at him from the lowest landing of a fire escape. The elfin urchin noticed a solid bulge in Malc's back pocket. A wallet perchance, or perhaps a money fold. At worst, it must have been a valuable pack of trading cards, so thought the observer. It was actually the want ads that Malcolm's self-appointed father told him to use to find a job.

As Malcolm stepped beneath the escape ladder, the child swung down and dangled for a moment in front him. Malc screamed and the youngster yelped, "Hep, hoop, oops!" and fell from the low rung.

"Well, young weevil," declared Malc, "you seem to have fallen to your death!"

The child looked up at the callous man in astonishment, the rims of his eyes turned crimson as they welled up with water, and a bloody scream burst from his powerful young lungs barely preceding the stream of tears. "I'm not dead! I'm not dead!" he demanded.

Startled and slightly disappointed, Malcolm hastily bailed out of the scene.

Behind him the fading cries echoed through the alley, "He tried to kill me!"

Malcolm was reminded of a similar incident that cost him four hours convincing a couple of overly cautious police officers that graveyards were occasionally a good place to find peace and quiet, and it would be virtually impossible for him to have killed all those people, bury them, and still have time to carve out so many heartfelt gravestones. He wasn't about to go through another one of those self defense fiascoes. He started running.

Near the street entrance of the alley, two large dark figures stepped out of the shadows. Undoubtedly they had been alarmed by the child's screams and were curious if they could assist Malcolm in his dilemma. Right. Sweaty homeless Malcolms were generally the first Malcolms to be trusted when it came to a situation like that one. The silhouettes of the two men moved quickly down the alley towards him. He thought about discussing the unfortunate, even humorous "falling child" episode with the two concerned citizens, then he spent some time thinking about single-handedly ending all wars, or becoming an astronaut, and which of those he would be most likely to survive. Damn the distractions. He was in danger!

The walls on each side of the alley towered to the sky. The fire escapes were too high to reach. The bodies at the end of the alley were still moving towards him. There were doorways nearby, but they were all padlocked. The men quickened their pace. He stopped dwelling on world peace and gave some thought to retreating. As he turned, he saw the fallen boy's shape in the distance, but there were several people standing around him. Beyond the crowd the alleyway was blocked off. Those people appeared from nowhere.

The two men approaching Malcolm were running and shouting, "Get the bum! Lactov! Grab heem!"

The crowd around the child came to attention. They were still further away than the two more menacing figures who were shouting for assistance, but Malcolm got the impression that they weren't going to offer much protection. He ran to the doors along the edge of the alley. Each was locked. Malcolm continued to shake and pound on all of them all, but didn't expect any luck. It was going to be another one of those occasions where he'd be beaten senseless, robbed of all his belongings and picked up by angry cops or street sweepers.

The crowd around the child started to move towards him. The rushing men had dirty angry faces and bricks in their hands. Suddenly and without warning, a door creaked open in front of Malcolm. He meditated briefly on world peace, then threw himself into the door. The men were at his heels, but he managed to slam the door shut and latch its deadbolt before they began pounding on it. In the darkness, Malcolm couldn't see anything but groped around quickly and found a 2x4 that served to brace the door shut.

Malcolm knew that the mob outside would soon make its way to the front of the building and nab him on his way out, so he had to get out of the building as fast as possible. The room was pitch dark until his eyes adjusted, so he attempted to find his way out by trial and error. Get it? As he moved forward he tripped and fell and wrenched his ankle, but he seemed to have landed on some packing material or a mattress. Something moved nearby. He got up and with his arms straight out, he moved ahead. His hands felt something soft, fabric. He figured he was in the storage room of a furniture store. Of course a room like that would have been locked and would have an alarm, but it was no time to contemplate bad security measures. He pushed ahead, slowly groping in the blackness with his outstretched hands until he bumped something that wouldn't move out of his way. Soon he remembered that furniture in a storage room was seldom warm, it rarely moved towards him when pushed, and it never felt so much like a woman. Malcolm had a theory and he needed both hands to prove his theory. Yup, he'd finally found the storage room where they keep all the great bodies he'd missed out on all his life.

Forgetting the urgency of his dilemma for just a moment, Malcolm continued his experiment. He seemed to have discovered the necessary shoulders, neck, head, and other body parts that went into the basic female construction. He double checked to make sure none of the features had changed, then he felt the face. Soft skin, a nose, long hair falling over the ears, and a mouth, a mouth that was smiling. Only one head. Malcolm was in Hell. He'd found an actual woman, with only one head, he'd touched her. One way or another there would be a price to pay. He had to escape or talk his way out of getting slapped in the face!

He stuttered, "Duh, I, uh, uh, I gotta..."

The woman silenced him by laying her soft finger across his lips, "Shhh... They'll be gone soon. They won't hurt you. Just stay calm. Relax. Enjoy yourself."

There was no more pounding on the door, but people were still outside. They were talking. No, they were laughing. They were laughing hard. It's one thing to be threatened with your life, but laughed at for talking to a girl, that's going too far! Malcolm turned and kicked the 2x4 from the doorway and pulled the door open.

Outside, a crowd had huddled and was calmly talking. They suddenly looked up at Malcolm with fear and hesitation as he jumped out of the storage room in a fit of anger.

"What the hell is so funny!" he demanded.

The crowd stared at him for a second then looked amongst one another for some kind of clue as to what Malcolm was ranting about. Finally, they looked behind Malc and all broke into spontaneous laughter. Malcolm turned around to see a ravishing goddess standing in the doorway. Her face was sculpted with large brown eyes, high cheekbones, thick lips, and long brown hair that flowed back over her shoulders. She raised her eyebrows, shrugged her shoulders, and the crowd renewed its burst of laughter.

Malcolm recognized the two men who had pursued him down the alley. Again, they approached. The larger of the two (about 6'4", 270 pounds) put his tattooed hand on Malcolm's shoulder and smiled like a gargoyle.

"Hi," Malcolm engaged, "Is there a bingo game in this alley? I know I'm late, so if this isn't the place…"

The man forgot what he was smiling about until his partner put his hand on the shoulder of the woman in the doorway. Then the big man remembered his task and lifted Malcolm off the ground and carried him back into the storage room. The woman smiled and followed them in. Once inside, she turned on an overhead light and the human ox left, closing the door behind him.

"I told you to stay calm," she said.

Malcolm regained a sense of composure, "Yeah, I don't know what came over me. Five hundred pound gorillas chasing me, screaming bloody murder... and all I can think about is my safety."

"Maybe, if you like, you can stay with me for a while. You're safe with me."

The room was filled with candles and tapestries and pictures of Bela Lugosi. "You live here?" Malcolm asked.

"Today I live here, tomorrow I may live somewhere else. Would you like to stay here?" she asked.

"Woo woo!" shouted Malcolm, "You are one hot tomato! Hmmm!"

"Or not," interjected the temptress as Malcolm tried to lick his ears.

"Hey," Malcolm responded calmly, "I'm cool, I'm cool. It's just that I'm really kinda homeless at the moment, and more or less celibate, and without religious conviction, and penniless, and I'm not going to bore you with my medical history, but if I did…"

"…you'd continue with your celibacy."

"What's your name?" asked Malcolm in a nasty, prying, suspicious way.

"Do you like Rowena?" she asked coquettishly.

"Rowena? Sure, but you don't look like a Rowena?"

"I'm not, I'm Jasmine. I was just curious about Rowena."

"Well, I really like Jasmine. It's flowery, yet, pungent."

"That's what somebody told me," she blushed, "just before he called me a beembo."

"Oh, I'd never call you a bimbo. Even if you were, I think you're the best."

Jasmine took Malcolm in her arms and gazed deep into his eyes. Malcolm burped, but it was a discreet burp, almost a non-burp, more like a quick, closed mouthed, spastic exhalation.

Jasmine smiled, "I liked that." She paused, "Wanna do it again?"

"Yeah!" he squealed, and wrinkled his nose.

He contracted his abdomen, but nothing happened. Sensing Malcolm's problem, Jasmine punched him in the gut. It was no use, Malcolm bowed his head.

"I'm spent," he said solemnly and ran out the door, crying.

Jasmine followed him to the doorway and watched him attempt to escape. He didn't get ten feet from the door before he was accosted and returned to her. The crowd was forcing him to spend time with a beautiful mysterious woman. There had to be an angle. He couldn't let her know that he knew something was amiss. He stayed quiet, defensive, stupid.

"You're not used to talking with women?" she asked.

"People," he explained.

"You can talk to me. I want you to tell me all about yourself."

"Why?"

"No one enters my room by chance. You're here for a reason and I want find out what the reason is," Jasmine said as she sat down at a small table.

"Self preservation, mainly."

"No, you naive boy, the reason is beyond your scope of understanding. It's written in the stars and perhaps you are the Chosen One."

"I may have already won a million dollars," Malcolm admitted.

Tossing her hair back over her shoulders, she smiled and motioned to a chair, "Sit down. I need to read your palm."

Malcolm sat in front of a table with tarot cards, crystal ball, Ouija board, the works. Jasmine took his quivering palm. Her smoky brown eyes penetrated deep into his eyes. It didn't take her long to reach the bottom of his psychological depths. Malcolm wasn't as complex as, say, your average egg noodle.

Anyway, she didn't find what she was looking for in his eyes, so she decided to look at his palm instead. As she followed the creases in his skin, she explained what she discovered, "Your life line is strong. It is deep and unbroken. That is good. Do you see how it forks here? It sends life in many directions. That too is good."

Malc was pretty proud of his life line accomplishments. Getting a palm massage from a pretty woman was also a big bonus for the little goober. Jasmine smiled as she continued to study the form of his palm, "You had me worried, my friend, I was looking at your love line, and... well, I've never seen anything like it. You have no love line."

Malcolm looked at his hand, "Well, I admit, I've never actually gone all the..."

"But, here! I see a very very strong line! It doesn't start where it should, but when it starts, it starts off strong! Mmmm!"

Malcolm blushed a little.

Jasmine's smile turned to a frown, "But, here, your love line vanishes."

"Let's just go back to how strong it is when it starts, okay?" said Malcolm meekly.

Without looking up to Malcolm, she examined his palm further, "Malcolm, you have met your true love."

"When? Who?" he begged.

Jasmine stared at his palm, then shook her head, "This is weird, man." She turned his hand over to make sure she had the right side.

"Look, if you just brought me in here to make fun of me, I'd rather go back into the alley and get beaten by the mob," said Malcolm as he started to rise.

"No, no, no... You stay here. I want you to stay with me for a couple of weeks. I need to know if you're the Chosen One. I need to know for sure," said Jasmine. "I don't think you are, but we can't take any chances with the Chosen One."

Malcolm thought about the proposition for a minute, "When you say, 'stay with me'..."

Jasmine stood up, "I mean that is my bed, this is my body, this body stays in that bed. You stay with this body in that bed."

Malc thought some more, "When you say, 'that bed'..."

"Yes, yes, yes. I want you to sleep with me."

"When you say, 'sleep'..."

"I mean sleep. I must protect you until I know if you're the Chosen One," Jasmine said as she draped a black and grey shawl over her shoulders.

"When you say, 'nobody'..."

"Including me. You must be chaste."

"I told you I'd rather go out in the alley and get mugged."

"Don't worry. If you're the Chosen One, you'll get more love than you ever imagined. You'll have to father the new race. But until then, you must remain a virgin," said Jasmine with a sheepish grin.

"A virgin! A virgin! I'm no virgin! I've had tons of women. I'm a livin' lovin' titan, I am! I know every position in the book. I've heard the stories! I've seen photographs! I am not a virgin!"

"The love line never lies. You have never made love."

"Oh. Well, love and sex are two different things," said Malcolm with a shred of dignity.

"Which one did you want to lie about?" asked Jasmine.

"So I get to stay with you?" he conceded.

"And you can fantasize all you want."

"Okay."

"And you'll get food and shelter, free coffee. We've got a lot of perks around here."

"This, uh, Chosen One. How will you figure out if I make the cut?"

"The Chosen One has the power to rise out of the ashes and prove his greatness by bringing prosperity to the tribe. He shall lead others through strength and devotion. He will gain reverence through his wisdom and power."

"But... but, what if I'm not the guy you're looking for?"

Jasmine ran her fingers through his hair, "Don't worry about that, you just stay with me until it is time." She went on to explain that she and her extended family were nomads, often called gypsies or Bohemians. They lived in a tight social circle that was extremely spiritual and self-reliant, and was never understood by outsiders. For anyone to be accepted from outside the tribe was a rare honor.

Malcolm agreed and spent the next two weeks at Jasmine's side. After the first week, she was pretty confident that he was the Wrong One, but didn't want to tell him and give him the idea that anything other than sleep was a possibility. She let him stay in her bed as long as he wanted, but strongly encouraged him to interact with other gypsies whenever he could. He took advantage of the gypsy ways while he had the chance, playing mostly with children and insane people. They sang gypsy songs, danced gypsy dances, baked cookies. It was a wild time in the gypsy world.

One night Malcolm was sleeping alone in a room of an abandoned building where the gypsies had temporarily taken residence. The room was sparsely furnished, containing only green leafy… no, not parsley furnished, sparsely furnished, containing only a mattress, a Malcolm, and a rope for decoration. The windows had been knocked out and there was no door in the doorway. As he slept and dreamt of better times, his nemeses, Armadillo's younger brothers were plotting nearby. They'd heard that Malcolm was hanging with gypsies and they were delighted to find him.

Given the limitations of objects available, all they had to work their craft was a blanket, a stack of old newspapers, about 100 yards of rope, and Malcolm. That was enough. The next morning Malcolm woke up and found himself wrapped in a blanket covered with strips of paper slowly descending from a third floor window into the middle of a piñata party. The party eventually ended when the piñata stopped screaming and the children determined that someone had swapped all the candy with blood. Kids. When he regained consciousness, the pain in his shoulders reminded him of the magic charley horse he received from his fake father. Maybe there was something to it.

After several weeks of living with the transient dilemma, Malcolm had seen the gypsy lifestyle and had come to a turning point. His willingness to accept their strange ways and means was no longer enough. Zarathustra, the elder, came to speak with Malcolm. His long white beard and grey features were contrasted with his youthful optimistic expression. He wore a faded brown leather jacket and jeans stained with automotive grease. He approached Malcolm in his usual friendly manner and put his hand on Malcolm's shoulder. They sat down in a pair of worn out beach chairs.

"So, you know you can't live with us forever, right?" he asked.

Malcolm wasn't completely hip, but he knew that Z-man had more wisdom of the world than all the *International Farmer's and Goat Herder's Almanacs* from 1976 to 1977 excluding the winter editions. Humbly, Malcolm replied, "Yeah, wise guy, but I don't have anywhere else to go."

"You can't stay here," said the elder, softly, reading Malcolm's dopey expression.

"I don't understand. It's not like I'm living under your roof. You're trying to kick me off the street," Malcolm was truly distraught. "I'm supposed to live in the sewer now?"

"I'm saying you can't remain in the clan."

"But we've been getting along fine. I thought everything was cool. Why are you doing this?"

"Everything is not cool. Nothing is cool. You think this is a 'neat' way of life, a nice change from paying rent and making commitments to people who want to control you and your money. This is our way of life! We can't pay rent because no one will let us move into their apartments. No one will hire us because we have our own set of standards and they don't include working eight hours a day, five days a week for someone who would rather see us in jail. This isn't a choice, Malcolm. This is our culture, this is our life as much as forty hour work weeks are your life." The old man stood, "Get out! Follow your own path!"

Malcolm stood up too. "Hey! I know living like this isn't your first choice, but it is a choice. Like it or not, you chose this alley and these people. Nobody's holding a gun to your head making you live in this or any other city. I also know that it would be hard for you to live with the status quo."

"It would kill us."

"So you think it's easy for me to change my life to fit into your culture?"

Zarathustra smiled and spoke, "It may kill you."

Malcolm thought about gulping for effect, but decided that it would be too silly, and would probably go unnoticed. Zarathustra gestured for Malcolm to stay where he was, then went over to two young men about Malcolm's age. Tshyshe three of them stood and spoke for a few minutes, laughing occasionally. Two others joined into the conversation and also laughed occasionally. Malcolm sat back and watched the little gang chat and laugh and point and make exploding sounds.

Suddenly the group broke up. One of the young men, Glib, ran off out of the alley. Two of the other gypsies, Yoke and Clammer, slowly approached Malcolm. Zarathustra gave him a nod then walked away.

Yoke stopped in front of Malc. "So you want to hang out with us..." he stated contemptuously.

"Yeah," Malcolm cheerfully replied.

Clammer shook his head, "You gotta do the rites."

"What do you mean?" asked Malcolm.

Clammer looked at Yoke briefly for reassurance then at Malcolm, "Zarathustra says you gotta either 'Bite the Snake Back' or 'Smoke Steal'."

With a small grin, Yoke hissed, "or get the hell outta here."

"So what's, um, bite a snake?" Malcolm asked hesitantly knowing that the gypsies put a lot of faith in rituals filled with symbolism.

Before Clammer could answer, Glib returned carrying a weighted pillowcase which he handed to Yoke. Yoke reached into the case and pulled out a diamondback rattlesnake. The snake writhed and wrapped most of its body around Yoke's forearm. Yoke kept a tight grip just below the reptile's head. "This is the interesting part of 'Bite the Snake Back'."

Malcolm gulped, noticeably.

Yoke began explaining, "We all sit in a room..."

"We have guns, you don't," interrupted Clammer.

Yoke continued, "We have guns, and you don't because if you back out, we don't expect you to shoot yourself. But we sit in this room, with this snake and this sack. You put your arm in the sack until the snake bites you."

"Show us the holes," Clammer interjected.

"After the snake bites you, you'll pull it out of the sack and tear it in half, or cut it in half if it's too hard to break. Then you suck the blood out of the half with the head."

"And if you back out, we shoot you," Clammer added with an air of sophistication.

Malcolm scratched his head for a minute. "That's a rattlesnake," he said to Yoke.

Everyone agreed that it was a rattler.

"People have died from snake bites," noted Malcolm.

Clammer objected, "Some people don't die!"

Malcolm was excited, "Okay, um, this is some kind of wiggy Pentecostal truth or dare, but I'm up for it. I can handle it. Obviously you've thrown in an element of justice since I get to bite the varmint back, but this might just be a little too tame for me. What's the smoke steel deal?"

Clammer rolled his eyes.

Yoke started to explain, but Malcolm interrupted, "Let me guess. I take a steel pipe and warm it up for a few minutes with a cutting torch, then I stick my tongue into the red hot end of it.

After my tongue ignites and its remaining ashes settle in the pipe, I blow them out the pipe and take off my shirt. Then I heat the pipe up again, and stick it right..."

"Stop! That is gross-o-rooni," shouted Clammer. Clammer and Yoke looked at each with disgust.

Yoke shook his head, "Don't be stupid, all you have to do is go into an all night liquor store and steal a carton of cigarettes. God! A little sadistic today, aren't we? Sheesh!"

Malc meditated on his options, he could visualize the whole snake thing along with the blood, the fainting, the bad breath, and all that, but he couldn't see himself stealing cigarettes. He hated cigarettes. He didn't actually mind the cigarettes or the smoke, but the anti-smoking commercials really annoyed him. The self-righteous band of pasty skinned whiners that had nothing better to do than to tell hard working Americans how to live their lives somehow bothered Malcolm. Stealing cigarettes might just be the payback those wimps deserved. Free cigarettes for everyone!

The time had come for him to embrace the gypsy culture or move on. The nomadic band had only a small initiation requirement. Decisions, decisions: Malcolm had to slay and drink the blood of a diamondback after being bitten by said snake and possibly provide the clan with a marketable death scene; Or! ...or, he had to steal a carton of cigarettes from a cigarette store. The gypsies were real flexible and honestly didn't hold one method in higher esteem than the other, but Malcolm wasn't absolutely sure that he wanted to enter into their wild world of free spirits.

He thought. He wrung his sweaty palms. He thought some more. He wrung his hands some more. He was deeply troubled. He'd suddenly discovered that he couldn't think and wring his hands at the same time. Finally, he made his decision.

"Fellas," he spoke with a sense of relief, "I wanna do both!"

Yoke and Clammer smiled, and shook their heads. "Okay," Yoke responded, "but could you snag the smokes first?"

Malcolm leaned back and let loose with a hearty laugh. "Ha! Haa haa haa," he said. "The next time you see me... The next time you see me, I'll have cigarettes for everybody!"

The two young gypsy men shook their heads and walked away. Malcolm knew they had no faith in his cunningness. He had to prove his mettle, prove that he could survive on the seedy side of the city. He was officially entering the underworld. His life as an upstanding citizen was coming to an abrupt end. Before long, he expected to see his face on Post Office walls. Tough guys would cower in his presence, children would cry and run away when Mighty Malcolm approached, and women... women would turn into quivering dollops of gelatin at his touch. The good life was heading his way. The only thing standing between Malcolm and the dashing daring jet setting sleaze troopers was a few little sticks of crushed tobacco leaves. Tobacco leaves and solid thieving experience were the only obstacles facing Malcolm at that important junction in his life.

Since Malcolm didn't know how to smoke, he had absolutely no idea where he might find some cigarettes. He'd always ignored the cigarette signs because they were supposed to be designed for kids. He started walking. An urban indigent stopped him on the street.

"Got a smoke?" the bum asked.

Malcolm ignored him. He didn't realize there'd be competition to get into the gypsy club. His quest for fire sticks would surely be an arduous one. He stopped at the first phone booth he found and went straight for the phone book. He knew he was cheating, but he didn't feel like wasting any time getting to the next stage of criminal desperation. Malcolm was crushed when he discovered that some lecher had torn the cigarette page out of the book. He couldn't fathom the irony of his predicament until he remembered the parable, and was suddenly consoled by its power, cheaters really never do prosper. Mmmm. Slim consolation there.

In the same cosmic moment, Malcolm's world was rocked again. There, right there, in front of that dope was a convenience store and it was having a sale on High Brow Cigarettes. The last bastion of capitalistic venturism was marketing the means to Malcolm's passage into becoming a gypsy. Those convenience store employees were a vital part of the community who provided goods and services that the world desperately needed. Anyone who's ever found themselves in dire need of a plastic airplane, a small can of Cheez-Greez, and a breath freshener at three in the morning can vouch for the subtle necessity of those handy dives. He'd found his gateway to gypsydom at Betty's In and Out All Night Convenience Store and Grill.

He was nearly bowled over by a desperate teenager who needed some late night malnutrition. The kid passed Malcolm mumbling, "Got to... Get me... a... weasel dog."

Malcolm admired the juvenile's focus and determination. Malcolm was on a similar quest and simply needed to formulate the actual task of illegally acquiring the contraband. His life was guided by the premise that all his plans were doomed to failure. He fully intended to abide by that philosophy in his cigarette heist. After consciously planning nothing, he marched into the store, looked up and down all the aisles, and he couldn't find a single cigarette. He walked out of the store and double checked the cigarette sign. Yup, they were on sale. He went back into the store.

Suddenly things were getting complicated. There were cameras all over the place. The clerk, an overweight grey haired belcher, was minding the counter. Behind the belcher were the cigarettes. Tons of cigarettes; menthol, regular, filtered, diet, hand-rolled, hickory flavored, smokeless, second-hand smokes, and plain tasteless cigarettes; the selection was fantastic. If Malcolm ever wanted to learn how to smoke, that was the place he'd go to buy his own educational training cigarettes.

He approached the belcher. "Hey, guy," said Malcolm in an annoying voice (disguised to sound like a preppie).

The clerk stared at him.

"Say," Malcolm continued, "You don't have any more cigarettes in this store, do ya? I mean like somewhere in an area that isn't behind the counter, and preferably where there aren't so many cameras?"

The clerk stared at him.

Malcolm deduced that he did speak English, but chose not to exercise his vocabulary. "Okay, um. How 'bout those 49ers? What a year?"

The clerk reached under the counter and pulled out a shotgun and propped the weapon on his shoulder.

Truly a show of force, yet Malcolm figured it was merely a clever sales tactic. "I will buy one of your delicious Mango Slush Cups," exclaimed Malcolm in response to the clerk's clever and effective sales tactic.

The proprietor walked to the end of the counter, behind the slush cup dispenser.

Malcolm was no longer in the employee's field of vision, and he had a brainstorm, he reached over the counter and grabbed a pack of cigarettes, when the clerk yelled suddenly, "What size!" startling Malcolm so that he dropped the cigarettes.

"Um, give me your Hella Big Ice Bucket size, please, sir, now."

The clerk silently went to work filling an enormous waxed paper cup with artificially frozen fluid. Malcolm made a second attempt to grab a pack of cigarettes and managed to pick up a handful of rolling papers and some chewing tobacco. He stuffed them down his shirt.

"Damn machine! Ain't enough Mango Slush to fill the bucket. You want Chilly Chicken flavor instead?" asked the overweight clerk.

"Uh, what else you got besides chicken?"

"We got Iceberg Lettuce and Cool Blue Goo. The blue stuff makes your tongue change colors."

"That's what I want," said Malcolm with genuine interest.

With a nod, the clerk went back to filling the cup. Malcolm leaned way over the counter and took hold of the cigarette case. One of the panels slipped off and three cartons of cigarettes fell on the floor. Malcolm didn't get any of them.

The clerk stepped back from behind the quaff spewing device and placed the gallon size slush cup on the counter. "Seventy nine cents," he bellowed.

Malcolm smiled, pulled eighty cents out of his pocket and laid it on the counter next to the beverage. The clerk made change and gave it to Malcolm.

It was kind of an awkward moment for Malcolm because he still hadn't snagged what he came in to get. He took a big sip from his slush cup and raised his eyebrows at the clerk. The clerk stared at him. Suddenly, Malcolm doubled over in pain. "Agh!" he shouted, "My head! It's exploding!"

The clerk stared at him.

"Call 911!" screamed Malcolm.

The clerk shook his head. "Happens all the time. Shake it off, kid, the ice in the slush cup's just swirling through your head on its way down to your stomach. You'll get over it. I only seen one person die from it, and she just had herself a skull with a brain that was too big to hold the slush, too."

Disappointed, and at the same time enlightened, Malcolm shook his head and the pain soon vanished. He smiled and took another sip. Same thing happened and he shrieked in agony. He did it a few more times. The clerk watched him to make certain that his diagnosis and treatment were effective. Malcolm wasn't getting any closer to stealing the cigarettes, but the sudden increase in cerebral activity gave him a new idea.

"Say," said Malc, "When I saw that gun on your shoulder I thought you were gonna, maybe do some trick shooting... I mean there's a mirror right in front of you. I bet you can't hit that, oh, say that lock on that cash box in less than three shots."

"The hell I can't," bragged the proud, yet ignorant gunman. Eyeballing the cash box through the convex mirror in front of him, he held the gun over his shoulder and pulled the trigger. The gun recoiled and flew from the clerk's hands to Malcolm's. The shot blasted a pumpkin sized hole through a lottery ticket display.

Carefully gazing down the gun's sights, Malcolm aimed towards the clerk's head and explained coldly, "You missed. Shoulda aimed lower. Back where I come from, we don't take too kindly to anyone who can't hit a cash box from less than 20 feet."

He steadied the gun and the clerk began to shiver in fear.

"Let's make this interesting. I want a pack of cigarettes," said Malcolm as he moved the gun's barrel towards the clerk's face. "Try again, and if you miss, I get a pack of cigarettes."

The clerk was apprehensive as he asked, "What if I hit it?"

"Well, then you get the cigarettes."

The clerk blushed and took the gun. He tried his trick shot again and blew the corn dog cycler completely off the rear cabinet. Boom!

"Ha," said Malcolm, "I get the cigarettes."

The clerk snapped his fingers and gave Malcolm a pack of great cigarettes.

"Better luck next time," said Malcolm as he skipped confidently out of the store.

During the whole stupid little episode, a band of local hoods was stealing cases of beer, bags of chips, boxes of cereal, and stale Valentine's candies from the store shelves. Those boys had seduction on their minds and every woman's dreams in their hot little hands.

Malcolm ran past the horny hoodlums and back to the gypsies' alley. The bustling crowd was gone. Not a single gypsy was in sight. He walked the length of the alley and saw no one. He walked out of the alley and started up the sidewalk when he heard something crash in the alley. He looked back down the same alley and saw all those gypsies doing the "Crazy Gypsy Hustle".

Incidentally, the historical significance of the "Crazy Gypsy Hustle" was never adequately documented, but if nothing more than Hitler's expulsion from the Austrian gypsies due to his inability to gyrate his hips and shimmy in front a woman had been recorded, justice would have been served. Unfortunately, all the best gypsy dance steps from the "Machiavellian Mambo" to the "Transylvania Two-step" had been lost in the tea leaves of time and the world was just a little crummier because of it.

"Hey! All you gypsies!" shouted Malcolm as he raised the cigarettes over his head, "I return with cigarettes for everyone!"

The group looked at Malcolm like he was nuts. He wondered if maybe he was boasting his bounty to the wrong gypsy band. No. They were the right gypsies, but something had gone awry, dare say, amiss.

Yoke came up behind him and tapped his shoulder, "Hey man, that's great, but we were thinking more along the lines of a carton of smokes. You just got a box."

Visibly disappointed and wrought with feelings of inadequacy, Malcolm thought. He thought and thought and thought until he stopped thinking and said, "You know what? I'm gonna go back!"

With feigned interest, Yoke smiled and responded, "Good. That's neat. We'll be sure to save the last dance for you."

It was a tough job for any crook, but Malcolm had to go through with it. You can't really understand how important it is to prove your credibility in the underworld until the opportunity comes along. It was one of those semi-plausible honor among thieves deals.

Regardless of his stupid motives, Malcolm went back into the convenience store and found the cash register drawer open. Silly clerk. As Malcolm started to close the drawer, an evil deceitful thought went through his head; he could just steal the money and use it to buy some cigarettes. A great idea, yet his conscience wouldn't permit it. He closed the drawer and accidentally slammed it on his thumb. "Argh!" he said.

The fat man with the lousy aim appeared from behind the pastry aisle. "What happened?" he asked through a mouthful of powdered-sugar mini doughnuts.

Malcolm was holding his thumb in agony. "Oh... I'm such a klutz, I was just closing the cash drawer here and my thumb got in the way and I squished it."

"Squished it, huh? Y'know, I think you could win a lawsuit against your thumb," said the clerk with absolute conviction.

"Yeah! It hurt me, man," whined Malcolm.

The proprietor looked at Malcolm for a minute, then at the sore thumb, then at cash register. "You're not thinking about suing me, are ya?"

"No," said Malcolm as he rubbed his throbbing thumb.

"I mean, I can't be held responsible for the actions of my cash register. If it up and hurts somebody, that's not my fault, right?" asked the cashier as he patted his forehead with a handkerchief.

"No, I don't think so," said Malcolm as he began to walk out of the store.

Fidgeting and looking around for some sort of compensation, the clerk shouted at the thumb crushing victim, "Listen, I don't know what you're up to, but what's it gonna take to settle this out of court?"

Malcolm stopped and calmly admitted, "Nothing. Don't worry about it. I'm fine."

The clerk opened the cash register, "One hundred, two hundred, five hundred? C'mon I'm just a working guy trying to make ends meet. Give me a break."

"Look, I'm okay. Really!"

Sweating like a pig and muttering biblical phrases, the clerk pulled his gun out, pointed it at Malcolm's head, and yelled, "Hey! I don't know what you're after, but if you don't take everything out of my cash register right now, it'll be the last thing you never took."

"Listen, I can't take your money. I've got principles and all those deep pocket lawsuits give me gas. I only came in here to steal a carton of cigarettes! You're gonna to have to settle for giving me that ...or kill me."

The clerk began to relax, "You can have five cartons."

Malcolm was beginning to sweat, "One carton! That's it!"

"Okay, okay. One carton of cigarettes and I'll donate four more to charity."

"That sounds like a good compromise."

Malcolm got his cigarettes, the clerk was absolved, and somewhere in Nowheresville a group of underprivileged citizens would be able to pick up their smoking habits where they left off. The only problem was that Malcolm was asked to steal the smokes and he actually won them in a settlement. He stuffed them into his underwear to give the gypsies the wrong idea. Street life was infiltrating his judgment like a coyote's call infiltrates the cold prairie night air or like a stinky perfume infiltrates the sinuses of a sommelier. It was street life in action and Malcolm was smack dab in the middle of it.

He returned to the gypsies and gave them their smoke, thereby officially completing his first rite of passage. Yoke and Clammer were visibly upset by Malcolm's success. Jasmine and Zarathustra couldn't stop smiling. They didn't want him in their tribe, but they had to respect his tenacity and the purity of his ignorance.

The next step of the initiation was the snake bite deal. A group of young gypsies escorted him into a dimly lit janitorial supply room. They released a hostile rattlesnake into a corner and pushed Malcolm towards it. At first it coiled up and rattled its... rattle, but the snake wasn't biting. Malcolm tapped the serpent's belly with his shoe, then leaned in and blew on its head. For several minutes, he teased and insulted the snake and even made fun of its ears. The snake coiled up again, shook its tail, and then began to fall asleep. Using his index finger, Malcolm poked the snake between the eyes, but the darn thing wouldn't strike. What else could he do? All he could think of was to lie on his back and hold the snake over his face and make razzberries at the reptile. The snake looked like he was about to take a bite out of Malcolm's nose, but it was just yawning. Finally, it fell asleep again.

The death defying ceremony was interrupted when Zarathustra entered the room and assessed that things weren't going too well. "What's going on, here?" he asked.

Yoke whispered in his ear and Zarathustra chuckled, "Hey, bud, I'm sorry about this. Nobody's ever actually had to perform the Bite Snake Back ritual. It was really supposed to just frighten you away, but you seemed so enthusiastic, we didn't want to disappoint you."

"So, I don't have to get bit by that rattler?"

Zarathustra shook his head, "No..."

The snake woke up and let out a sigh of relief.

With a big ol' smile, Malcolm declared, "So, I'm in!"

All the gypsies looked at each other and walked out of the room feeling very discouraged, but none of them denied Malcolm's remark. As far as he knew, he was a full fledged gypsy convert.

XV

That night he slept well. There were no dreams or nightmares of getting squashed by a tractor while lying on a white sand beach next to a beautiful woman. He didn't wake up in a cold sweat with thousands of fire ants tearing away his leg hairs and toenails. No looking up from the bottom of a grave to find Slurp and Gurgle throwing buckets full of dirt down over his body. He just had a good night's sleep. It was another sign that the gypsy lifestyle was more attuned to his own. Perhaps the niche he'd never found in the mundane "civilized" world could be found in the gypsy kingdom. That sentiment was reinforced as Malcolm spent the following day making lanyard keychains and playing dominos with some of the older gypsies.

He felt a bond, an affinity, and warm fuzzies with the gypsy people. Never in his life had he wanted to be a part of a group more than he wanted to be a gypsy. His chance to gain further acceptance presented itself early that evening.

"Okay, Malcolm. Here's the deal," said Zarathustra, "We need you to pick up some wheels and meet us back here early tomorrow morning. We've got some very important business to take care of on the West side. Political business...You know anything about politics, Malcolm?"

"Well, I've read about some of the corruption that goes on in the city, but your people don't look like they're involved with organized crime," admitted Malcolm innocently, bowing his head like an ignorant Sherpa.

Zarathustra smiled his masterful smile, "Gypsies are connected, pal. We're networked throughout the city, throughout the country, really... Hey, Clammer," he shouted, "Malcolm didn't know we had political clout."

Clammer laughed and threw his arms in the air.

Sensing an urgent need to restore his place in the tribe as a valuable and necessary member, Malcolm quickly went on a quest for an unattended automobile. He was quite aware of his deep desire to acquiesce, but he also decided that he had been assigned to the busy work that that no self respecting gypsy would stoop to.

"I hate being a gypsy," he mumbled as he wandered down the street. "Malcolm, King of gypsies. Malcolm, Earl of gypsies. Malcolm, Jester of gypsies." He kicked a can and started singing *Knick Knack Paddywhack* under his breath.

It was just another night in the cruel dark city. Steam rose up through the sewer grates as it had since sewers went underground. Steam rose from the humans that paraded up and down the side streets long before the sewers went underground. Smoke spewing automobiles, and people and stray animals formed endless paths of soulless lights and images. Malcolm thought of their futility and felt no remorse for the crimes he'd committed or planned to commit. How could he tarnish such a rotten world? How could he scar it? There was no part of the planet that remained untarnished and unscarred. The idiot couldn't see past his nose, but he did lay his eyes on a sleek black 1969 Buick Wildcat. Nice ride, baby.

The Detroitian denizen roared down the street and came to a stop in front of a topless bar. Three drunken college students fell out of the car and stumbled into the bar. Those guys were having a lot of fun. The amount of fun they were having was a lot. The fun they were having could have ended when they went inside the bar. Malcolm could no longer see them, so they might have continued to have a lot of fun, they might not have. At that point in time, the only people in the world who knew whether or not those three college guys were having fun were those three college guys and possibly the bouncer, the bartender and several topless women in the bar. That was beyond the scope of Malcolm's immediate knowledge. He was disappointed with his dysfunctional omniscience, so he frowned, and just hoped that the guys were having a bad time.

He had to rationalize his impending criminal action by convincing himself that the owners of the car didn't deserve such a fine piece of steel machinery. The fact that they were in a bar with lots of women while he was out on the street was sufficient justification for his actions. He jumped into the unlocked car, and was shocked to see that the keys were still in the ignition. Knowing full well that the deed he was about to commit was felonious grand theft auto and that dreadful consequences would follow if he were to get caught, Malcolm drove away before anyone could see him. It was an important step in bringing his pseudo-father great wealth and substance. With a resale value of roughly forty five dollars, Malcolm needed to steal and sell only about 22,221 more Buick Wildcats to make his dad a millionaire. The thought of being an heir to that much moola made Malcolm droola.

As images of rich and famous lifestyles danced through Malc's head, he pulled into a vacant alley and parked the car. A while back, he'd overheard some of the tougher gypsies discussing the finer points of car theft and learned that the first thing he had to do was swap the plates. Seemed easy enough, but Malcolm didn't have a screwdriver. The risk of driving out to get a new screwdriver in a stolen car with unswapped plates presented a risk too great even for Malcolm Tent. He had to go out and scavenge the streets for a screwdriver and leave his prize temporarily unattended. Recognizing the value of the car and the hazards of leaving it in that dark dingy alley without a guard, he knew it would be foolish to leave it sitting out in plain sight. He had to bury it. He needed a shovel. Damn! There he was in the worst part of the city with a stolen car and with no screwdriver and no shovel. When he went to steal the next 22,221 Wildcats he'd try to be better prepared.

Waiving the risks, he walked out to get a screwdriver or a shovel. He was astonished at the lack of preparedness exhibited by the general inner city population. After asking about thirty people if they could spare a screwdriver or a shovel, and getting the same negative response, he thought he might just ask people some general first aid questions (for scientific purposes). The results were frightening.

"Excuse me, ma'am, do you happen to have an extra shovel?" he asked a random pedestrianette.

"No," said the gal.

"Well, have you got a screwdriver I can use?" he wondered.

"No," she replied, trying to ignore him.

"When performing the Heimlich maneuver, do you place your clenched fist above, below, or directly on top of the sternum?" he asked on behalf of the scientific community.

"Pervert!" she deduced.

"Idiot!" he figured.

Similar conversations with unsuspecting strangers continued for several more hours until Malcolm finally gave up. If an urgent need for first aid or a mass car jacking should ever occur, Nowheresville would be in big big trouble.

The car theft just was not working out. About the time he'd given up all hope, he found himself standing at the edge of the Hangagas River seriously contemplating a final leap into the cold dark chasm. However, it just wasn't all that deep, and it was pretty darned empty, but that didn't matter because Malcolm felt about as hopeless as he did at his Senior Prom when midnight rolled around and his date didn't, and he concluded that he'd been stood up once and for all. The painful memories, the futile prospects for success were too much for him. He jumped in and fell three feet into the thick puddle of muck. Suicide never felt so humiliating, but he perked up when he noticed a utility company truck parked at the edge of the Hangagas, right next to him. The truck had a shovel and a screwdriver sitting in its bed. In his improvised muddy camouflage, he swiped the tools and ran back to the alley where his stolen car was parked.

As he arrived in the alley he saw a tow truck pulling away with a 1969 Buick Wildcat trailing close behind it. That damn tow truck. The tow truck song ran through his head as he pursued his stolen car through downtown Nowheresville. *"Tow truck, tow truck, red light stop, tow truck, tow truck, green light go, tow truck, tow truck, haul a wreck, tow truck, tow truck, crash."* Malcolm dropped his stolen tools and chased the truck for three blocks until he caught up with it at a stop light and was able to latch onto its bumper for another block or so until it stopped again and he could jump inside through the car's window. His ride came to an end at the Acme Towing Yard and Grill. The driver unhooked the Wildcat without checking the seats and went home for the night.

Suddenly and without warning, Malcolm remembered the Swiss Army knife in his pocket (he forgot about it earlier... We all forget sometimes. Now might be a good time to check your pockets). It was the perfect opportunity for him to swap the license plates. He was surrounded by other impounded cars, it was dark, and he had a screwdriver in his pocket knife. He jumped out of the car, looked both ways, and went to work swapping license plates. He took off the front plate and put it on the back and put the back plate on the front. Task completed. Then he made the best of an uncommon moment of sheltered peace and solitude to sleep until morning.

He curled up in the back seat of the Buick and fell asleep immediately. After a few hours of deep and rewarding slumber his dream of lying on the beach next to a beautiful young woman began to take shape. She lay on her stomach gazing at Malcolm. The white sand contrasted her light brown hair and soft tan complexion. As she lifted her eyelids revealing her pale blue eyes, she gave a Malcolm an alluring smile. He tried to tell her that he loved her, but his voice was drowned out by the sound of a diesel engine. Again, he attempted to say it, but couldn't overpower the engine noise. The young woman appeared confused. He finally tried to yell, "I love you!" but woke himself up in the process.

He sat up in the car's back seat and watched a search helicopter pass overhead. As the chopper moved out of earshot, the sound of dogs barking in the distance became more noticeable. He was pretty annoyed about being awaken, so he rolled down the window to give those dogs a piece of his mind. A large Doberman pinscher instantly jammed its entire head through the open window and tried to take a piece of Malcolm's head.

Jumping back to the other side of the car, he contemplated his options. He could have cowered, shivered, and wept, but that wasn't his style. A lesser hero might have miraculously presented a raw juicy T-bone steak to distract or appease the foaming monstrosity, but not Malcolm. Others might have told the dog to scoot and rolled up the window. All those acts of self-defense required logical reflexes.

Malcolm wasn't about to let logic cloud his mind. Instead, he started singing. He sang like he'd never sung before.

"How much is that doggy in the window?" he crooned, *"I do hope that doggy is for sale..."*

Unfortunately those were the only words he knew. It was enough to confuse the dog, but not enough to scare it away. Malcolm started the car and crashed through a chain link fence to get out of the storage yard. Aside from a slightly bruised ego, the killer dog wasn't injured. Dobies are a tough breed, nothing to call the SPCA about.

He drove back to the eastside tribal squat and proudly displayed his four-wheeled prize to the gypsy leader. Zarathustra stared at the car as Malcolm proudly drove it up and down the street for about thirty minutes until he ran out of gas. With a scrutinous air, Zarathustra paced around the stranded vehicle, stroking his long white beard, giving Malcolm a sense of acceptance with his warm paternal smile.

"You did good, kid. I'd send you out to put some gas in it, but we need to get moving," said Zarathustra as he snapped his fingers. A young boy immediately appeared toting a gallon can of gasoline.

Malcolm stepped out of the car and leaned against it while the young attendant emptied the gas can into the tank. Malcolm was pretty excited, "So! I got your car. What's next? Kidnap the governor? Run down the mayor? I won't take part in a drive by shooting."

Then he scratched his chin and lowered his head, "Is that what you expect of me now? That's crazy! That's it. I'm calling the cops and turning myself in. I can't live with this anymore."

It was more than Zarathustra could take, "Malcolm! Calm down! We're just going to the other side of town to vote."

"Vote?" asked Malcolm.

"It's our civic duty," said Zarathustra.

"But I thought this was going to be a big deal," said Malcolm.

"It is!" said Zarathustra, "Everybody show Malcolm your voter registration cards."

The gypsies formed a line and held out their registration cards. The first three gypsies jumped into the car and waited as Malc stood and stared.

Zarathustra clapped his hands at Malcolm and shouted, "Okay, let's go, the polls won't stay open all day! Get those people in the voting booths and bring 'em back quickly so everybody gets a chance to vote at least once!"

"You know I could have been killed or arrested last night," Malcolm explained.

Zarathustra laughed, "Well, let's not see your troubles go to waste."

"Oh no, we wouldn't want that," muttered Malcolm. He certainly didn't want to interfere with their civic duty or waste his criminal acts, so he got in the car and drove off with a small brigade of gypsies.

For the next eight hours, he chauffeured gypsies back and forth across town, three at a time. He didn't mind the busy work so much, but the trips were the same in one very irritating respect; on the way to the polls the gypsies argued vehemently about the appropriate candidate to vote for, and on the way back they debated just as strongly about their right to privacy when asked who they voted for. Oh, and of course, every time they crossed over railroad tracks, they all lifted their feet, shouted, "neener, neener," and smacked Malcolm in the back of his head. After the first few trips, a groggy Malcolm stopped taking shortcuts directly through the train yard and reduced each trip to only about four such rituals.

When the day was over, Malcolm's head was pounding so badly that if he didn't get a drink, his head would have exploded. He located the gypsies' private distillery and poured himself a bottle. They made a pretty decent grain alcohol. His head did explode, but he was too numb to feel it.

XVI

The next morning met Malcolm with a cold blanket of fog. It was damp, it was dreary, it was on a one way street to Blusteryville. Lucky for him the bed he just rolled out of was filled with a sleeping Jasmine. He looked straight into the fog and belted out a couple verses from the theme song to *Shaft*. It may not have been appropriate, but the human mind is a very complicated network of randominity. Skipping over the psychological justification for his song belting, he was in a good mood.

There was something magical in the air that day, something warm at the heart of the gloom, something like the sensitivity that surfaces at funerals. The Nowheresville waterfront was several blocks from the gypsy hangout. Malcolm had lived in the city for years and never visited the waterfront. He always feared it and thought of it as a place that offered solace to drug dealers and murderers, but Marlon Brando got his start on the waterfront, or was it Marlon Perkins, or was it just a marlin? Could have been Flipper. In the back of his mind, Malcolm knew something might have been happening on the waterfront at that very moment and whatever it was, he didn't want to miss it. To the waterfront he went.

When he got there he discovered a whole new world. There was the stench of stagnant water, the solitude of abandonment, the carcasses of poisoned fish, and the soft echo of small waves pressing against the dock walls under the dock in a non-rhythmic irritating pattern. The drug dealers, murderers, Marlon Brando, Marlon Perkins, and Flipper were either hiding or had gone on to better things. The waterfront was romantic in a kind of 50ish stupid pathetic way and Malcolm was about ready to wretch when suddenly the silhouette of a woman appeared through the fog on the pier. His wondrous eyes stared as the figure became clearer. She became more beautiful with every step.

Trying to be as inconspicuous as possible, Malcolm studied her as she came closer. Her hair was dark brown and cut just at her shoulders, her body was slender, it was no use... Malcolm fell in love just by looking at her. Their eyes met, she smiled, he drooled, it was magic. She began to pass him without stopping, so he stuck his leg out and tried to trip her. She stepped aside and stood watching the annoying stranger. The annoying stranger knew that her agility and premonitory skills were as mystical as her presence on the wharf. He attempted to communicate with the vision. "Na, na, nake, nake... So, you come here often?"

The vision laughed, "You must be Malcolm!"

It was another demonstration of her extra sensory perception and it truly astonished Malcolm. "Are you an angel?"

"No," she blushed, "I'm Debra. I want to go to the movies and one of the gypsies told me you might be willing to take me."

"Yeah, um, let me check my calendar and see when I can fit you in..."

"Well, I kinda wanted to go today."

"Today's okay, I suppose. We'll have dinner at seven, a movie around nine, and after midnight we can let it all hang out."

"The movie starts in half an hour and I don't want to miss the opening scenes. Okay, Malcolm?"

Malcolm smirked, "Y'know, most mysterious women I meet on the waterfront want me to take 'em to Disneyland right away. You're different. I like that. So what's the movie you want to see?"

Debra rocked her head from side to side and smiled, "Actually, it's a Stanley Kubrick film festival. It lasts about twelve hours. It'll be fun."

"Kubrick, Kubrick... He did all those Jerry Lewis movies," he guessed as he looked into Debra's eyes for some kind of affirmation, and found none. "Oh, I mean, yeah, he's the guy in all those slasher movies. Those flicks are so underrated. When you think about the how much talent is really required to convince an audience that your head has been chopped clean off... it's, it's, uh... It just makes you appreciate..." there was still no connection in Debra's eyes. "So, I'll get to spend the whole day with you!" There he got a connection.

"Yeah!" she bubbled, "But we have to get going, okay?"

"O-Kay!" Malcolm said as he took her hand and led her back up to his stolen Buick. As they walked, she swung her arm and his arm swung with it. The whole thing looked pretty silly. He imagined Debra sitting innocently in the theater twirling a finger through her hair while he casually put his arm around her shoulder. She'd pretend not to notice until he whispered in her ear, "What year was this movie made?" then she'd start to answer and stop when their smoldering eyes met and they'd spontaneously embrace in a long hot passionate kiss. His imagination continued to thrive, but reached that critical point of pure incredibility when the theater seat folded out into a waterbed and "Cat Scratch Fever" began blaring through the THX audio system. That's when he got back to reality. They got in the Buick and drove off into the morning mist.

The festival was being held at an old college theater, and the venue ranged from *Lolita* to *Full Metal Jacket*. Attempting to be a male chauvinist pig, Malcolm demanded that he pay for the tickets. Being the New Age of Romance and all, and male chauvinistic pigism being once again fashionable, Debra allowed him to pay for the tickets as long as he agreed to pay for the popcorn and chocolate covered raisins as well. He went along with the male role thing and challenged all the other guys in line to a duel. They declined and stopped laughing after he and Debra entered the theater.

Once inside, Malcolm opened a credit line to get some popcorn and beverages. Debra chatted feverishly with a small band of unruly Droogs. Popcorn and Droogs, that's what movies are all about. The popcorn was stale, the soda was flat, the bon bons were crushed, and the clerk short changed Malcolm three bucks, but Debra looked hot and he was happy. They left the Droogs and went to find some good seats. The theater was nearly empty except for the drunken ushers and the remnants of the previous night's Lost Weekend marathon.

As Malcolm tried to guide Debra down each of the choice center aisles, she tugged his arm and led him closer to the front row. She noticed his resistance towards her blatant manipulation and quickly offered an innocent explanation, "I want to capture the grandeur. It's being shown in 35 millimeter."

"That's pretty small!" yelled Malcolm.

Sensitive to the strange quirks that permeate and propel the art world, he followed her down to the first aisle. He got to sit next to her and that's what he really wanted. Still, he was curious how anybody in the back row would be able to appreciate the craftsmanship that went into a movie that was only 35 millimeters wide. The screen must have been at least twenty feet tall. Malcolm suddenly deduced that the small film must have been the reason they invented theater glasses! He was instantly enlightened and happy to have an understanding of everything he needed know about classy people.

As the theme music for *Lolita* began, Malcolm looked at Debra from the corner of his eye. How would she react if he held her hand? She'd laugh, they always did. He needed to be aggressive yet respectful, sensual without being grabby, romantic, and not some kind of freakish dork. He began to run his fingers slowly through her hair. She smiled at him and leaned against his shoulder. Green light! He quickly glanced around the theater looking for an empty bed, but saw none. He smiled at Debra, but she was concentrating on the film. Green light! Gently he placed his arm around her. She didn't resist. She may not have even noticed. Using an old army trick, Malcolm tried to distract her, he whispered in her ear, "If that film's 35 millimeters, I'm Tom Thumb."

She looked at him, smiled, and shook her head. He had successfully confused her. Now he was ready to go all the way to second base. Gradually, cautiously, ever so lightly, Malcolm's hand found its way down towards her bra. It groped, and groped, and groped, but found no bra. No bra, green light! His hand descended nervously. It was approaching hand heaven, carefully, gently, closer and closer and closer and... "Bam! Bam! Bam!" Was the sudden sound of a loud knock on the steel theater door that sent Malcolm leaping ten feet from his seat.

Debra smiled at him sympathetically, "You okay?"

Malcolm squared his shoulders, nodded his head, and counted his fingers, "Yeah!"

Again, someone pounded at the exit door. "Go see who it is, Malcolm. Maybe it's an emergency."

"Oh yeah," Malcolm responded sarcastically, "Probably some ax murderer lost his whetstone. I'd better go see if I can help him out."

He returned to his seat.

"Please..." begged Debra.

He stared at her for a moment and decided he liked the way she said, "Please".

"Hold that thought," he said and went to the theater exit. The menace on the outside rapped a third time. If he didn't open it, he'd never get to second base with Debra. If he opened it, ax murderer. He pushed the latch, cracked the door, and jumped back in an unparalleled act of quick thinking. A strange hand pulled the door from the other side. A strange head peeked through the opening. The strange head was a gypsy's head, little Salvador's head. Malcolm was relieved to watch the young sprite dart into the darkness before the drunken ushers took notice.

With a cheerful smile on his face and a devil in his head, Malcolm strutted back to Debra. She brushed off his chair and motioned for him to sit down between her and little Salvador. Just an observation, but movie theaters should sell beer and have eject buttons that could launch neighboring seat occupants through the roof. As he leaned back in his seat, the knocking door beckoned again. He looked at Debra and shook his head. With an incredibly compelling pout, she seductively mouthed the word, "Please..."

With a sinister leer on his face, Malcolm returned to the exit and threw open the door. To his delight, another gypsy appeared. It was Melvin. Nobody liked Melvin, but Salvador was the only kid in the tribe that hadn't actually insulted him, therefore Sal was his best friend. Malcolm didn't get three steps from the door before another knock sounded. He didn't even look towards the Debster. It was another gypsy, then another, and another, and on and on for about fifty more gypsies, each one being sensible enough to let the theater door close completely before knocking.

Finally the drunken ushers caught on. "Ay!" the two ushers yelled out in three part harmony as Malcolm opened the door.

The last knocker stood outside the theater exit with a strange expression on his face. He didn't look familiar to Malcolm. He was big guy with a serious speech impediment that sounded more like an angry grunting boar than a human. There were ground squirrel tails resting on his shoulders and sticking out of his pants pockets. Malcolm smiled and waved and stepped backwards quickly into the theater. The big guy looked up at the sky and expelled a long breath through his teeth.

One of the ushers pulled out a gun and aimed it at Malcolm. "Git out!" he shouted and took a shot at the *Lolita* film character.

Malcolm's jaw dropped as looked up at the screen. "Debra!" he shouted, "Are you watching this? That's gotta be way more than 35 millimeters!"

Malcolm glanced at Debra and her collection of gypsy friends, just as the usher took another shot in his direction. After one more shot, he dove out the door forcing the strange man backwards as he lunged. The strange man looked at Malcolm and Malcolm smiled and turned and pounced on the theater door. It was locked closed. He smiled one more time so that he would appear friendly, non-threatening, and happy. Nicest guy any ax murderer would ever want to meet.

Reaching into his utility belt, the tall smelly man pulled out a hatchet and distinctly asked, "What so funny?"

Thinking quickly, Malcolm challenged the madman with his rapier wit, "Okay, two prostitutes walk into this bar and the bartender pulls out a talking banana..." Before he could finish his potentially humorous anecdote, the hatchet whiz passed his ear. Undaunted, Malcolm pointed out, "You're going to miss the end of *Lolita*, ya know."

The giant grabbed Malcolm by his shirt collar and lifted him off the ground. He carried him back, raised him up against an alley wall and removed his hatchet from a wooden pallet leaning against the wall. More and more, Malcolm's date with Debra seemed to be going downhill.

"Just a little off the top there, big guy. Heh, heh, heh."

It was obvious that the ax murderer was playing that stereotypical Nothing's-Funny-Now-I-Kill-You role. A role that unjustly condemned too many breakaway ax murderers to lives of persecution and bad hair styles. Hanging there at the end of the killer's arm and watching the killer draw back the hatchet with his other arm, Malcolm thought seriously about starting a neighborhood watch program. Too darned many communities were being overrun by bad apples and serial killers simply because people didn't want to get involved.

Sensing his demise was imminent, Malcolm knew he had some final requests, "I call last rights!"

The big guy checked his swing.

"One last cigarette!" Malcolm demanded.

The murderer thought for a moment and nodded to indicate that the request seemed fair. He lowered Malcolm and set the ax down next to his bare feet. He patted his pockets and smiled, "People say smoking bad, but I find smoking relaxing." He pulled a pack of cigarettes from his shirt pocket, shook out two cigarettes, and gave one to Malcolm.

Malcolm thanked him and took the cigarette while the lunatic searched his pockets frantically for a pack of matches.

"This country was started with the trade of alcohol, tobacco, firearms, and slavery. People today think they're making progress by outlawing all that stuff, but what most people don't realize is that two hundred years ago, most other civilized countries had already banned most of it," explained Malcolm.

The ogre nodded in agreement as he lit Malcolm's cigarette.

Malcolm added, "All I'm saying is that before you pull the plug on all these goods and services because of their adverse affect on health, take a moment and think about how much good they've done."

The ax man smiled and agreed by making hissing noises.

"Cough," Malcolm coughed, "cough, cough, cough."

The sociopath looked at Malcolm suspiciously.

"Cough!" Malcolm finished.

"You don't know how smoke!" shrieked the lunatic. With lightning fast reactions, he grabbed Malcolm and his weapon of individual destruction. "You trick me, you liar! Liar bad. Liar die!" he yelled and brought back the ax for a terminating swipe.

"Webster!" echoed a voice from the end of the alley.

The giant looked back over his shoulder.

"Put, the, liar, down!" the voice shouted.

Malcolm thought, "Hey, not so fast."

And to his surprise, the killer complied.

The voice was emanating from a familiar figure. It was Malcolm's squatter pop. What was he doing there? Was he an angel? How did he know Webster? Was there a possible connection to the Kennedy assassination? Too many questions. Malcolm was suddenly confused.

"Hey, son," said the surrogate father. "I see you've met my friend Webster. He's not so bad once you get to know him."

"Yeah, I was just thinking about spending my dying days with my new best buddy," said Malcolm.

"Well, let's not go overboard here, Sonny. Webster went a little crazy when the draft board told him to go home because of his flat feet and he hasn't been the same since the war ended. You'd best just part friends."

The lunatic's eyes lit up, "You are friend?"

"To part friends," Malcolm quickly responded, "means saying good-bye on friendly terms. It has nothing to do with splitting them in two."

"I love you," said Webster.

"Love means never having to say I'll chop your head off," explained Malcolm.

If only someone had a camera, the moment was too precious to miss. Webster dried his eyes and ran off, yelling at the walls.

"Thanks," said Malcolm to his surrogate father, "I owe you."

The father squinted, "You owe me? Hell! I brought you into this world, boy! Damn right you owe me! Make me rich! Win the lottery! Inherit a million dollars! Break open the stock exchange!"

Malcolm felt silly. His father shook him by the shoulders and could tell something was wrong. "You feel silly, son. You need to straighten up and get back on you feet," he said as he pushed Malcolm to the ground.

Malcolm looked up but didn't have anything to say. His dad felt bad and said, "I've done everything I can for you, junior. You gotta take some responsibility. You gotta be committed."

Malcolm looked at the clouds and let out a deep sigh. There was nothing to be responsible for, nothing to commit to. The world had let him down and even his father, his self-appointed father, was letting him down. "How can you stand there and tell me that I have to take responsibility..." he said as he looked to his father, but his father was gone. He'd vanished as mysteriously as he appeared.

The stock market! Malcolm knew nothing about financial investments. All he understood was the basic idea was to buy low and sell high. He pondered the prospect and wondered if he had the resources to make it happen. He found an old newspaper and looked for anything that made sense. And there it was in the business section, staring straight at him, rudely. The key to wealth and prosperity was hidden in an obscure article at the bottom of the back page... where no one else would see it.

That afternoon, he concluded that it was time to get his cash and make an investment. He also knew that no woman would ever marry him, regardless of how big dowry was. Malcolm took his $400 out of savings and bought 200 shares of a small secret company at two dollars a shot. It was all the money he had. The next day he sold that same stock at five dollars a share. Excellent! The same morning he picked up 500 shares of another business at two dollars each. Next day he sold those for five dollars a share. He went back and forth between only two companies for about two weeks. He made roughly $4,000,000 over that period and then cashed out. Only in America. His secret was highly confidential so, without disclosing the company names, he invested all his day trading cash in rival yo-yo manufactures. Sound stupid? Yeah. Four million dollars worth of stupid.

He went back to the gypsies and he was treated like a king until he signed most of his money over to the Nowheresville School for the Blonde. The NSB fundraising drive promoted

Charity and Hope, both of whom were blonde. It seemed like a worthy cause. The fundraising infomercials made Malcolm very sad and ashamed of how selfish and wealthy he was. Those blondes had canned goods, but no can openers. Worst of all, they had no formal can opener training. What's a can worth if you can't operate a can opener? Hmmm? Watching the girls fumble with the cans, trying to open them by yelling at them and teasing them gave Malcolm a hollow feeling inside. He bought Hope and Charity 700,000 cans of instant soup, 5000 can openers, and paid their tuition for an intensive highly concentrated 2 week session at the Cannagy Institute for Cans and Bottles Opening and So Forth. He also sent flowers, flashcards, and hair styling tips. Ultimately, the Nowheresville School for the Blonde got all of his money and then they dumped him like a heavy bag of recyclable aluminum. He was okay with that.

Then it was back to gypsy busy work and there was plenty of it. His most notorious task required him to take a biology test for Zarathustra's ignorant nephew Ned (who was not a blonde). As much as Malcolm wanted to help, he couldn't stand biology. All that talk about reproduction, and dissecting frogs made Malcolm queasy. So when the question about dissecting a frog's reproductive organs showed up on the exam, Malcolm vomited all over the test paper and Ned ended up receiving a C- in the class. The bad test score haunted Malcolm. He was taunted by local gangs, the police knew him as a crumb, and the high school kids wouldn't even let him buy beer for them.

Some of the gypsies tried to support him, but it was difficult, he really was a failure. One day, all the gypsies had abandoned him so they could go on a nature excursion in the storm drains beneath the city. They said it was good to get off the beaten path to learn more about the substance of their souls. Soul searching wasn't on Malcolm's agenda for the day, so he went down to the Marina to look for lost metal detectors or something.

Well, ya see, it was like this... Malcolm shows up on the Marina, right? And he runs into this yuppie sailboat guy, right? The guy's got some hot babes in clean clothes watching him talk about sailing. And so Malcolm says about the sailor's shoes, "Are those deck shoes?" Okay? And so the guy says back, "No way!" So like Malcolm gets like, um, really mad and he starts yelling at the guy, so the guy pulls out a gun, okay? And then Malcolm says, "Hey, that's so uncool," y'know, because like Malcolm's sitting there without a gun so the guy goes, "Okay, meet me back here at sundown, and try to remember to bring a gun." And Malcolm dude says, "No way! It'll be too dark, you'll bring all your buddies to hide in their sailboats and before I shoot you they'll jump me. So I say we meet back here at high noon."

"That's just ducky! Yer on!" says the yup, and they left.

Woo! Ducky duelin'!

The time was set, the motive was unclear as was the case with so many primitive altercations, but the duel would take place at noon ...and at 12:01 only one of the two daring young idiots would be left standing. Preparations for the event had to be made. Malcolm's role required a pistol, or an Uzi, or a sawed off shotgun, something, anything more menacing than the impromptu slingshot he'd fashioned out of old underwear elastic.

Knowing the tough streets like the back of his head, Malcolm had little or no difficulty finding a gun. In the process, he also learned that police officers aren't as generous as everyone makes them out to be. But anyway, he found a gun for twenty five dollars outside a candy store and he hoped that in some small way he'd improved his society by preventing some hapless youngster from acquiring the instrument of death. He was ready for dueling.

The yuppie was there at noon with his gal, Nell, and her sis, Bess. Both of them were armed with attractive matching derringers and pepper spray. Malcolm wasn't worried. "Girls!" he thought, and gave them a knowing wink. They winked back with all their eyes. The yuppie had a very tasteful looking hunting rifle. It was clean as a whistle. He carried a whistle in his pocket as backup. He also donned a white cap which tipped the scales in his favor.

Armed only with a big gun and a smile, Malcolm Tent was ready for anything.

After staring at his expensive digital wristwatch for a few minutes, the yuppie said, "It's twelve o'clock."

Straightening his stance on the pier, Malcolm asked, "Don't we need to take twenty paces or something?" He knew that twenty paces would send the yupster right off the edge.

Yuppie didn't go for it, "No. I prefer to simply shoot you." With that, the urban protégé took aim at Malcolm and fired a round. He bagged an innocent seagull and fell to his knees, accidentally pulling the trigger on the second barrel when he fell. The second shot hit the bow of a small yacht. The craft began sinking quickly so the yuppie ran away.

For some inexplicable reason, the honor of Nell and her sis, Bess, was still besmirched. Malcolm hadn't insulted them or made a pass at them or even met them before. Maybe that was the problem. They wanted revenge for all the men who'd never met them. They wanted to shoot Malcolm, but they were afraid of the sound of the guns, and the smell of gunpowder was so icky. They took aim at Malcolm, then tried to cover their ears and hold their noses before pulling the trigger. It was scary for Malcolm because they kept mixing their hands up and pointed their fingers at Malcolm with a gun up their nose or in their ear. They were both very cute! He didn't want to see them get shot in the head. Finally they tried to put the guns down before shooting Malcolm. That wasn't working. They tried a few more times then talked it over. The two decided that Bess was going to cover Nell's ears while Bess shot, but Malcolm pointed out that Bess would need someone to cover her ears. Nell begged Malcolm to help, but he refused because he knew that one of the girls would inevitably get hurt. That would be much worse than the original honor besmirchment and he'd have to kill himself if such a tragedy ever occurred. The girls recognized that Malcolm was willing to die for them and felt that justice had been served. He was openly invited to call them for gossip and gun talk if he ever got a cell phone.

He'd never own a cell phone. He was worthless. The girls were too good for him. All girls were too good for him. Sob. He rolled a drunk for a half a cigarette and 39 cents. He used that to trade up to a can of beer, which in turn he traded for a clean toothbrush and a bar of soap. He found an old hubcap and some fresh water and made a little wash basin and managed to get halfway tidy. Then a delivery truck sped past him and bounced through a muddy pothole and converted him back to a dirty bum. He spent the rest of the afternoon covered in mud and gloom and wandered back to the gypsy hang out. His host Jasmine was nowhere in sight, so he went to the rooftop of an abandoned building and contemplated the world he'd created for himself.

XVII

Sleeping in the warm shelter of a sleeping bag on the top level of a fire escape, Malcolm dreamt of his tropical beach hideaway. It was the usual dream, beautiful beach, breathtaking woman, and again, a bulldozer nearly crushes him before he wakes up. He was relieved to wake up before his demise, but horrified to see that he was staring into the ugly eyes of a strange and large grumbling gypsy man.

"This one?" asked big ugly.

"Yeah," replied a voice from across the roof.

Before he could get a formal introduction, Malcolm was gagged, blindfolded, and taken to the other side of the roof. Once he was out of shouting distance he was ungagged and unblindfolded so his captors could get a better look at his face.

"So what's all this about? Are you guys with the evening news?" he asked impudently.

The leader replied spitefully, "No! We are the Avocado family. You been kidnapped."

"Avocados, eh?" asked Malcolm. "I've heard some crazy things about the Avocados. I don't think I want to mess with you."

"You don't have a choice featherface. How much you think we'll get for you?"

Malcolm counted his fingers and answered, "Millions."

"Think so? All we want is your Laurel and Hardy laser disc collection," explained the big ugly gypsy dope.

"I don't have any laser discs. They all went up in the fire."

"Not you, stupid! Zarathustra!" demanded the leader, "He covets them like gold. We want 'em. We want 'em all."

Showing legitimate concern, Malcolm tried to clarify their blunder, "No... You got the wrong guy. The best I can I can do is get you some used Abbott and Costello video tapes and a Charlie Chaplin poster, and maybe a Felix the Cat soundtrack, if you're lucky."

"Shut him up," said the leader to the ugly dude and Malcolm was quickly gagged again.

Under the cloak of darkness, in a Rambler, he was taken to the bad side of town. When they arrived, Malcolm was tied to a chair and the gag was removed. He assessed his surroundings and his captors. Apparently he was in a tree fort, but it was a neat one. It had a phone. Hans Avocado used that phone to call Malcolm's tribe. The telephone conversation was terse, yet audible. Malcolm listened as well as he could to the one-sided dialog.

This is what he heard: "All right, you rat molesters, we've got one of your soldiers here at gunpoint. We want your Laurel and Hardy video discs."

"Oh, I don't know," Hans covered the phone and asked Malc, "What's your name?"

"Malcolm," said... Malcolm.

"Malcolm," he paused again. "It's a shotgun... Of course it's loaded! ...No! We're uh, short on ammo and we're not going to waste it!" the kidnapper's patience was wearing down. "You know that would kill him, right? ...No, *you're* bluffing! ...Let me talk to Zarathustra... Oh, hi Zman. I'm serious about this y'know... Okay, well, I'll give you some time to think it over... Okay, bye... Huh? ...Okay, real soon... Yeah, they did... Oh, isn't that terrible? ...Okay, bye now... Okay. M'bye," and abruptly Hans hung up the phone.

Malcolm looked at the kidnapper, "Told you, you had the wrong guy."

"We'll see. They must be worried if they have to try and make us think you're not worth saving. A lesser hostage would have drawn a low bid and that would be the end of it. You're a prize."

Once again Malcolm assessed the tree fort, "I'm sorry, but I gotta know, you guys pay rent here?"

"Shut up! We'll give your people the night to think it over," Hans told Malcolm, then turned to the big ugly gypsy. "Lock him in that giant paper bag we picked up at the Democratic Convention."

"But it's all wet!"

"That's okay."

So, Malcolm was trapped in a great big wet paper bag for the night. He thought about busting out, but judging by the graffiti left by former vice presidents it would have been impossible. Instead, he just went to sleep. Slept fine, thanks.

Negotiations started up again early the next morning. Malc overheard the conversation as he entered the tree fort lobby.

"...We *will* kill him! ...Yes we will! ...Look, this is ridiculous... No, no, no... Well, why didn't you? ...We're not murderers either! ...Okay, we'll send him back, but we're not going to feed him... Okay! We'll feed him... How much? ... No way! ...Ten, twenty bucks, and that's it... Alright, alright... Mm hmm... Okay, bye... Yes, she is... Mm hmm, bye... Mm hmm... Mm hmm, bye... Okay... Okay, bye now... Oh really? ...Yes! ...That's great! Bye! ...Mm hmm... Okay... Okay, bye," and Hans unexpectedly hung up the phone.

As Hans approached him, Malcolm knew there would be bad news. "Okay, here's the deal," said Hans. "We had to pay Zarathustra twenty bucks to take you back. Here's your twenty, there's the door, now beat it."

Dejected, Malcolm went out the door without a word. About an hour later he returned. "Guys, could I bother you for a ride?"

Hans spoke to the big ugly man, "Look, take him back to the alley, drop him off, and don't stop the car. And blindfold him so he can't figure out how to get back here!"

Finally, somebody was doing the driving for Malcolm. When he was dropped off, he found Zarathustra waiting with his favorite wife, Helga.

"Glad to see you're back in one piece," he sighed.

"Yeah, they were rough on me but I'm okay."

"You're okay? Who cares! If they kept any pieces of you they could exercise voodoo on the whole clan," Zarathustra was trying to control his anger. "You know how bad it makes us look to have one of our guests kidnapped? We could become the laughing stock of the West Coast. And that lousy biology test score has left a permanent bad mark on our academic record. How could you be so thoughtless!"

At that point in his life, Malcolm had little sympathy for Zarathustra. "That does it!" shouted Malcolm. "You've been initiating me for weeks! How much longer until I'm accepted into the clan?"

Zarathustra scratched his beard, glanced at Helga, and said to Malcolm, "You want to get into the clan?"

Helga said with a smile, "Well, Malcolm, I hope you believe in reincarnation."

"Reincarnation," Malcolm echoed.

"You are born a gypsy. You can't 'join' the gypsies," explained Zarathustra, calmly.

Malcolm was astonished, "But when I first got here, you said if I stole a carton of cigarettes you'd let me join."

"I was trying to get rid of you. You're not a thief, you're not even a smoker, but you are persistent and that's going to look good on your next job application."

"Well, I'm a thief now," said Malcolm shamefully.

Helga laughed. Zarathustra smiled and said, "I wouldn't put that on your application."

Malcolm was steaming, "You can't get away with this! I'll show you!"

"I'll show you all!" chimed a team of eavesdropping gypsies.

"You're mocking me? I don't even like you guys... Well, Jasmine's nice, and Debra is a total fox, but the rest of you are mean and your political affiliations are all shallow and fleeting!" Malcolm grunted and stormed away.

As he walked down the alley, a crowd formed behind him and began laughing. The laughter became louder as individuals tossed out jabs like;

"Don't go! How will we get into the movies?"

"Wait! We need more cigarettes!"

"Call us when you get to Vegas."

By the time he got to the street, he was furious. Noticing a big old chunk of cement on the sidewalk, he picked it up, and cocked his arm back to throw it, but a passing policeman saw him and grabbed his hand.

"Looks like we got ourselves a rock thrower!" the cop said as he looked down the alley. It was miraculously abandoned except for a stray cat that was sitting there licking his paws. "Y'know, I have two cats at home," said the cop, "Some people think it's funny to hurt cats."

He took the rock from Malcolm and threw at his foot. "Funny, eh? Let's go," he said as he began to cuff Malcolm.

Malcolm glanced down the alley and saw Zarathustra leaning against a wall of the alley, covering his mouth and pointing at him.

"It's him!" screamed Malcolm.

The cop drew his gun and hit Malcolm on the head with his baton. "Who?" he asked.

After checking his head for blood, Malcolm replied, "That guy down the alley. He's selling cat burgers!"

The cop quickly looked down the empty alley then asked, "Cat burglar?"

"No! Yes! A cat burglar. He's dangerous! I'll go around the other way!" yelled Malcolm and he started running.

"Okay!" shouted the cop as he took off down the alley.

XVIII

Malcolm ran down the street and didn't look back. He was a fugitive from justice and possibly a heartless cat murderer. No longer could he blame his actions on the gypsy hazing rituals, he was working alone and he felt the power that his alter ego brought forth from the evil depths of his soul. He saw an unattended flower stand and swiped a dozen roses. The rush was incredible. It was purely invigorating to be a fugitive and accused cat killer and thief of roses. The only problem was that he didn't want any other killer fugitive thieves to see him running around with flowers. It's just not done by veteran criminals.

In the heart of that rough and tumble town called Nowheresville was a famous statue of the first horse that entered the town. It wasn't actually a town at the time, but that's where the horse came in. Back 1861, that horse (Old Foof) threw her rider (Jake) and killed him. A grave site was constructed with a tombstone shaped like a horse, but heavy rains kept the grave full of water for three weeks, so they couldn't bury Jake. During those three weeks, a small camp was set up and that camp eventually became a small outpost and eventually a small town. A century and a half later, the mud hole designed for dead Jake had developed into the bustling Nowheresville that surrounded the statue of Old Foof. Malcolm sat down at the base of the Old Foof statue and wondered how he could get rid of a dozen red roses when suddenly, without thinking, a pretty girl walked out of a nearby restaurant. She probably wouldn't have noticed Malcolm if he hadn't capitalized on his ingenuity and keen ways. He approached her intending to give her the flowers (his back up plan required him to tackle her and whisper to her slowly in French).

"Excuse me," said Malcolm playing out plan A with calculated designs. "Did you drop this?" he asked as he held up a red rose to the unsuspecting lass.

"No, it's not mine," she replied.

"Yes," smiled Malcolm, "Yes it is."

"No, silly, I swear, I'm allergic to roses."

Malcolm pleasantly insisted, "Look, you're not getting out of this so easy. I've got about a dozen of these stupid dead flowers and I'm only giving them to beautiful women, so take the damned plant!"

"Help, Police!"

In a fit of fury, Malcolm threw the rose at the helpless waif and ran away. Her eyes opened wide as she picked up the flower and chased after him. "Help, Police!" she shouted in her pursuit. Malcolm ran faster, but in his cheap tennis shoes, he was no match for her "Dashing Comfy Puppies." She was on him like water on a duck. She kicked his cheap tennis shoes with her "Dashing Comfy Puppies" and tripped him up so he fell down.

She stood over him and proceeded to yell, "You men are all alike! You stuff us with flowers and candy and Spanish fly until we feel so guilty that we have to sleep with you. Then you abandon us like so many tired lines. Well I've got news for you, buster! This rose means nothing to me, do you understand? I wouldn't touch you for all the roses in the world even if I was the horniest woman on the planet and you were the last man on earth."

"I've got money," said Malcolm from under her sharp knee.

"Liar!" she shouted and stabbed him with the rose's thorns.

Malcolm cringed in pain, "No, really, I'm fabulously wealthy. I've just got poor taste in tennis shoes."

The assailing woman let up a little. "I'll say," she ...said as she stood up and brushed herself off.

Malcolm got to his feet and regained his composure.

"So how rich is fabulously rich?" she asked.

"Well, let's just say a dozen red roses didn't hurt my pocket book much," Malcolm explained cunningly. "Hey, speaking of shoes, I couldn't help noticing the little numbers you've been trodding around in. I must say, they are spectacular. Simply boss."

"You really think so?" she asked humbly.

"Sure! Mind if I have a closer look?" he asked as he motioned to her shoe.

The woman blushed, took off a shoe and handed it to Malcolm. He took the shoe, gave her the roses and ran away as fast as he could.

Well, it was completely official. Perhaps the rose swiping could have been passed off as a lark, but his criminal status had been escalated to the level of a true thief, an honest to goodness thief, a shoe thief, the worst kind. His gypsy antics were part of a structured social norm. The shoe thing was certifiable thievery.

Once a feller gets started in that line of work, he cain't just walk away, he just cain't! The thrill of the chase was brief, but the guilt of shoe theft would last forever. He'd have to live with himself as a bad guy. He had to live with himself... Sartre was wrong. Hell isn't other people, Hell is yourself.

His self-pity was crippling him, and he was leaning on alcohol as a crutch. He swapped a bum three rose thorns for a bottle of ripple and fell into oblivion.

A day later, as the alcohol wore off, he found himself wandering aimlessly through the heart of the Nowheresville business district. He needed to steal something. Something big, something that would generate the kind of criminal reputation that a street savvy dude needed to survive in the jungle called, "Down Town." He looked around and saw a wealth of opportunities ranging from wristwatches to brokerage firms, hand bags to hotel chains. There was something out there just waiting, no, begging to be stolen. What to steal? What to steal? Purse was too small, and a hostile takeover would take too long. Then he saw the golden opportunity. The chance of a lifetime. After taking it, he'd have a reputation; he'd have power, mobility, stature. People would look up and point at him and say, "It's him." Men, women, and children would run from him and say, "Sorry, we gotta go." It was risky, but he had to do it.

Inconspicuously, slowly, cautiously, he approached his victim, most of all, inconspicuously. If the prey caught his scent, the heist would be botched. Malcolm thought up that last analogy himself. The job would be big, too big. He wandered onto the construction site, took a flying leap, and shoved the bulldozer driver out of his seat. The mechanical leviathan was still running so Malcolm didn't need to do much but steer.

"Hey! What da!" shouted the driver, "Come back!"

Malcolm laughed and drove away in his beautiful big yellow bulldozer.

The foreman walked up to the driver and asked, "What do you suppose he's gonna do with it?"

The driver shrugged. "Think we should call the police?" he asked.

"Yeah, I suppose," the boss said with disgust.

"Okay. One stolen bulldozer heading east on Wallop?"

"Yup," said the boss.

The driver began to walk away.

"Oh, hell, let it go," said the foreman as he shook his head, "It's not my money."

"Well, what do you want me to do now?" asked the displaced driver.

"Um, go help Tom watch that shovel."

The driver nodded as he tried to remember who Tom was.

Back out on the open road, Malcolm was touring in his brand spanking new bulldozer. Nothing like commuting with an attitude. If the high school girls he lusted after could have seen him in his greatness, they'd truly regret passing him up for college guys and movie contracts. Maybe he'd just go back to high school and see if those girls were still around making fun of the nice guys. Then again, maybe not, maybe that's just what they were expecting Malcolm to do.

It didn't matter. Malcolm had the power to do anything he wanted. He just didn't know what he wanted. Damn it! All gassed up and no place to go. He spent about an hour driving around the city. He must have stopped at a half dozen construction sites and challenged their best bulldozer drivers to race him out on Old Man Harrington's farm road, but he couldn't get any takers. Bunch o' wimps. Finally he gave the bulldozer to a bum. It was just another good deed that would go unnoticed.

So there he was, without a bulldozer, in the middle of a metropolitan fishbowl. Purposeful, well-dressed men and women walked along the sidewalks, in and out of offices and nice cars. He felt out of place in his own town. In front of him was a giant fountain. Well, it wasn't actually a fountain because the water had been turned off years ago, result of the drought. It wasn't actually a drought, it was a plausible excuse for the existence of the water management bureau. Drought is really just a meaningless word, but it's kind of tricky to spell and tough to pronounce, so it keeps a lot of city workers employed who are trained in both spelling and pronouncing. At any rate, the non-existent drought created a non-existent fountain, and gave Malcolm a sense of non-existent pleasure which quickly turned into a non-existent fear when he saw his self-proclaimed father attempting to drown himself in the depths of the fountain. Granted, the fountain itself was deep enough that it could drown a yak on stilts, but empty enough to keep any yak thirsty.

The whole situation disturbed sensitive Malcolm so he shouted, "What is this?"

His father, who may have known that Malcolm was present, or may not have, wasn't there, couldn't tell you, looked up at Malcolm and announced mournfully, "It's all too much for me. I'm gonna end it all right here, right now."

"Well, if you're going to kill yourself, this is probably the best place to try. Let's just hope you don't get depressed by failure."

His father shook his head to shatter any train of thought Malcolm might have created. "This world's just too awful. I can't stand it anymore. Mercy me."

"What are you going to do?"

"I'm going to kill myself, you idiot," said the desperate man as he picked up and pocketed a coin.

"No," said Malcolm with the conviction of a child eating beets. "No, don't. It's not, um, worth it."

The old man smiled sardonically, then filled his eyes with tears, "You saved my life."

"Aw. Twerent nuthin'," said the humble hero.

"What's that supposed to mean? You sayin' my life ain't worth saving?"

"Not in so many words. After all, you were going to throw it away... sort of."

"That mean nuthin' to you? That how I raised you? Where's all the money you was gonna get me? Maybe if you didn't treat your poor old dad the way you do, I might not be so anxious to knock down St. Peter's gate."

"You think I can make a million bucks just like that?"

"I heard you did pretty good at the stock market!"

"Well, I did, but..."

"But why didn't you give me the money instead of those gypsies?"

"I didn't! I gave it to a school for blonde people. And the gypsies were helping me get on my feet."

"And you gave away everything?"

"Well, the SEC found out I was pulling some strings with the yo-yo industry. I didn't do it on purpose, but I might have bought some of those companies three times over and there was some kind of talk about fraud."

"So you ripped off a bunch of investors and made me look bad again. Damn it, Malcolm, what were you thinking of!"

Malcolm felt low for a minute, "I'll try to make it up to you, but... but what the hell do you care? The only reason I tried to make that money was to help you. I just wanted to give somebody a chance to turn their life around and hopefully turn my life around in the process. But it doesn't work. I'll never get rich honestly. Honesty. What a joke. There's no such thing as an honest buck." He stopped and looked at his adopter with renewed conviction, "I'll make you rich for your sake. You better not care how... and if you're really worried about looking bad, say so now."

Considering that he was wearing his oldest worn out clothes, the quasi-suicidal pseudo-father couldn't comment on concerns about his appearance.

"Now get out of this stupid fountain before you die of thirst," said Malcolm as he turned around and went back to finding fast money.

The old man smiled and winked at Armadillo's brothers who were hiding behind the spray of a broken fire hydrant. As Malcolm stomped down the street, away from the dried water feature, he wondered how he could get rich. It wasn't easy. He'd been rejected by gypsies, shunned by the babes, and distrusted by his father. His motivation was pretty much tapped out. He knew things couldn't get much worse unless he imagined that they couldn't get worse. He should have known better.

As Malcolm sat back on a streetside bench contemplating his misery, another miserable person came up and sat down beside him. There they sat, two more or less miserables with nothing left to do but contemplate their worthlessness.

Malcolm looked over at his miserable companion and smiled, "At least it's not raining."

The stranger's ears turned bright red and he stood up and faced Malcolm. The guy was about seven feet tall, smelled like old gym socks that had been used to collect fertilizer and fish. He wore a trenchcoat that covered his otherwise bare ankles. Malcolm guessed that he'd just come from the opera or something.

"So you don't like rain," howled the gangly giant. "Let me tell you something about rain. Rain is like mud without dirt. It has no artificial coloring."

Malcolm looked around to see if there were any witnesses to the impending violence. There weren't, so he smiled a mouthful of teeth and blinked his eyes.

"Rain makes the toast soggy, rain knocks mosquitoes out of the air. Rain is good! You better appreciate it!" said the sad man.

"I guess I forget about the wonderful things that rain does," Malcolm replied softly.

"Rain makes you forget," the miserable man said as he sat down, put his head on his knees, and fell asleep.

"Thanks," said Malcolm. "I'll try to remember that." He stood up and quickly tip toed away.

And then it started to rain. Rain wasn't going to affect Malcolm's memory. The only thing that helped Malcolm forget was alcohol. But he didn't want to forget anymore, he wanted to fix his life. When he thought about the terrible way the gypsies treated him, he recognized that he didn't need any of them. He really could create a better criminal life on his own. He'd move ahead with his modest unlawful ambitions. He remembered his experience of trying to steal newspapers and laughed. How naive, how foolish, he put 4 quarters in the free newspaper vending machine, when he should have just robbed it at gunpoint. If he had never attempted to be dishonest, maybe he could have obtained a good job and led a happy life, but that one criminal act was too much. Malcolm Tent was an outlaw and, by gum, he was going to be the best damn outlaw on the planet!

Organized crime is always the best way to go if you want the big bucks, so Malcolm got organized and planned out a masterful crime. Hubcaps! Hubcap stealing was the only way to start a truly menacing or at least annoying crime ring. Malcolm found a quiet suburban neighborhood that had lots of cars on the streets. His first victim was an old green Gremlin. Nice hubcaps. Slowly, stealthily, silly Malcolm somersaulted up to the car. He took the first hubcap from a rear wheel and stuffed it in his pants. Nobody saw him. He shimmied to the front of the car and stole a hubcap from a front wheel. He stuck that hubcap under his shirt. Again, no one was watching. Quickly, he crawled to the other side of the car. He was feeling pretty good about his crime spree until he noticed that the two remaining wheels had no hubcaps. Crazy like! Naturally there's no point in stealing half a set of hubcaps. That was rookie stuff. Malcolm put the wheel covers back on the car.

He thought he'd have better luck with the next car, a Pacer. But when he got to that car he discovered that all its hubcaps were gone. The next car he targeted didn't have any hubcaps either. Malcolm soon discovered that none of the cars on the street had hubcaps. Damn it! How's a guy supposed become a master criminal if he can't even steal hubcaps. He'd have to begin his career with another crime. Knowing something better would come along, he wandered back to the heart of Nowheresville and left the suburbs in their peaceful misery. He also left Slurp and Gurgle in the suburbs. They were having lots of fun returning their freshly stolen hubcaps back to their original wheels.

Crime, crime, crime. This one had been kind of dream of Malcolm's ever since he was in high school. He'd seen the big beer delivery trucks driving by with their larger than life signs begging people to buy beer and tempting alcoholics to steal trucks. Malcolm was at another low point in his life and life's low points often inspire simple acts of desperation. Terribly tragic things like suicide, murder, disco dancing, and, yes, beer truck hijacking. Under normal circumstances, Malcolm would have deplored and protested such thoughtless and shameful acts, but he was having another poopy day. Strangers asked him and he told them, "I'm having a poopy day." The guy was bummed. So when a Schwarzenlager Beer truck barreled up next to him and stopped at a stop light, there was nothing he could do to keep himself from latching on the side of the truck and rolling away with it into beer truck heaven.

Generally, even in the small cities, a hitcher gets noticed when he or she is latched onto the outside of large moving vehicle. Malcolm knew he might attract attention (think he's stupid?), he's not that stupid. He stood on the bumper of the truck and smiled with one hand on his hip and the other pointing to the gigantic bottle of beer painted on the back of the truck. He made a very convincing advertisement and was the envy of all the other homeless people on that beer truck's route.

His initial plan was to steal a case or two at the first stop. That would have been effective, it would have been safe, but it wouldn't have been Malcolm. Instead of jumping off at the first unattended beer truck stop opportunity, he decided to ride out the whole trip, all the way back to the beer distribution center. It turned out to be a long route. Perhaps the most painful portion of the day was during the driver's lunch break. Malcolm stood on the bumper of the truck in the hot sun in front of a ten foot tall beer bottle posing like some kind of potato head for a little more than an hour. The truck got rolling again and eventually took Malcolm back to the distribution center. The damn truck driver had the nerve to park outside the warehouse, forcing the sober Malcolm to sneak into the warehouse while no one was looking.

Security at the facility was tighter than Fort Knox with all the doors and exit signs and everything. Malcolm felt like a regular spy or something as he quietly knocked on the doors. Luckily he stumbled on a loading dock and looked up to see 6 open bays with their rolling doors all wide open. He hunched over and covered his eyes as he snuck through the big door on the first bay. In the world of espionage, people who do this kind of sneakin' around are called "spooks". Malcolm was a spook, man!

Once inside the warehouse, Malcolm needed a place to hide until the workers went home. He'd seen movies where the spy would hide in an elevator by somehow climbing to the top of the elevator and wedging himself (or herself) in by pressing his (or her) hands against one wall and its feet against the other. Inevitably the arch-enemy or an armed guard would step into the elevator and the protagonist would use all his (or her) strength to remain above bad guy and stay quiet (no small task for her) and not drip sweat all over the place (because he is a sweaty pig). Malcolm didn't see any elevators in the warehouse, but he did see a bathroom and made a beeline for it. He went into a men's room stall, locked the door, and then wedged himself in the top of the stall. By locking the door, he eliminated the possibility of an armed guard entering the stall, and thereby ruined any chance for tension and drama, but it was just toilet, and not a good place for drama. Suspending himself between the walls was uncomfortable, but he imagined all the beer he was going to hoist as soon as all the beer workers went home.

After several hours of wedging, and annoying knocks on the toilet door, he heard someone outside the bathroom shout, "Fred's workin' graveyard shift again! That'll teach him to belch louder than the boss!"

Malcolm determined from those remarks that he was going to have a long wait. He didn't want to stay wedged in a toilet stall through an entire graveyard shift (he's really not that stupid). He climbed down and crawled out of the bathroom and gradually straightened his back as the blood began to circulate again.

He needed another plan and miraculously he had one. Recalling that a large tub of bottle caps was sitting about twenty feet from the bathroom, he crouched down outside the bathroom door and performed five sharp and successive cartwheels directly towards the bottle cap tub. All the workers were caught off guard and Malcolm took advantage of their emergency unpreparedness by grabbing handfuls of caps and flicking them at their knees and feet. He had no idea who he was up against. Those people were well trained professional bottle cap flickers and they snapped their caps with deadly accuracy. Some of them worked special missions for the Navy SEALS. The wild cap fight raged on for several hours and miraculously no one was killed. Malcolm was fortunate enough to escape by throwing the driver from a passing forklift and escaping with a pallet of beer.

Luckily for Malcolm, the beer cappers union forbade the workers from driving forklifts or chasing forklift thieves. The forklift drivers perceived the beer cappers actions as a wildcat strike, and they all went on a sympathy strike for the rest of the night shift. The security guards weren't part of the union and they took advantage of the opportunity to shoot bullets at Malcolm instead of bottle caps. Aside from a few stray bullets that grazed the forklift and his head, Malcolm was in the clear. The guards weren't actually shooting at Malcolm anyway. They were just having fun knocking cans off the forklift.

XIX

When he returned to the business district a few days later, Malcolm found himself standing outside the Vape Software Corporation building. There was a sign on one of the glass doors that said, "No shoes, no shirt, no service" and that just seemed totally inappropriate. Were they selling food? Was it some kind of high fashion outlet? That sign really irked him. Immediately, he took off his shoes and shirt and ran inside. It turned out to be some kind of crazy high tech development center. He dashed into the stairwell and ran up four flights of stairs. That was high enough, so he burst out of the stairwell onto the 5th floor.

The receptionist looked at him and rolled her eyes.

He rolled his eyes back at her and screamed, "All right! Nobody move! I want all your latest software!"

One of the bolder programmers sat shivering and loudly objected, "But it hasn't been tested yet!"

Malcolm mulled the consequences of stealing untested software. "Okay, how stable is it, you woodpecker?"

"It's not stable at all. We just added a new feature that upper management said it had to have and we're behind schedule, and, and... Ugh," the programmer collapsed for effect.

The other programmers were humorless robots who refused to assist because he hadn't been certified in UML, OMT, or BFD. Oh, sure, there were a few exceptions who were nice and cheerful and fun. If only they spoke English as goodishly as Malcolm they might have helped. Malcolm had no other choice, "Give me your latest software and one of your quality assurance people."

One of the software testers stepped forward, "I'll go. This is sure to get me a promotion."

She was, of course, a female. That's what made her a she. Her gender was of no importance, but the correlation between gender and pronouns is inexorably interwoven. Malcolm felt no attraction to her even though she carried his preferred pronoun and was basically darned attractive. His rutting boar instincts told him he should be making feeble advances towards the girl, but his solid business sense told him to complete the task at hand which was stealing uncopyrighted software.

"So, what's your name?" he asked.

"Fickie," she responded seriously.

"Fickie? Short for Felitia?"

"No. It's Fictitious. Fictitious Ducharme"

"Fictitious, eh? Now that's an unusual name."

Fickie shrugged her shoulders, "Not really."

Malcolm knew he could have belabored the Fictitious name issue, but thought the conversation might sound contrived. He certainly didn't want that. He put his arm around her waist, blew into her ear, and dragged her into a test lab where he tripped over tons of unread product specification documents. Scrambling his way to a developer's desk, he grabbed a small portable computer, a stack of software disks, and some chicken scratchings that were intended to suffice as user references until they hired back the technical writer who actually motivated people to complete their work.

With his arms full of technical materials and equipment, Malcolm knew he'd have a hard time managing a hostage. He explained that he was seriously abducting the lovely young Fictitious woman and it could be very dangerous. She didn't mind. He gave her every chance to escape by walking through crowds of vice presidents and directors, but they didn't pay any attention. Then he wandered around in a maze of cubicles that most people found inescapable and she followed closely. He even let her take the elevator by herself. Five minutes later he took the elevator to the first floor and there she was, just waiting and shaking her head at the delay. He explained that he got lost in elevator and she should be thankful he wasn't on an escalator or he never would have found his way out. She laughed. He laughed. Malcolm and his stolen quality assurance resource ran out of the building laughing.

As they walked down the sidewalk, Fickie followed without asking any questions or starting any arguments. Chances are she was critiquing every step he made. Malcolm didn't really want a hostage at that point, so he told her she could go back to work if she felt like it. Initially, her eyes expressed a sense of relief, but soon they got all squinty, suspicious-like. She demanded to test the product under the new untested kidnapping conditions. Her only reservation was that if the conditions were too complicated, the programmers would mock her and tell her she was just imagining the problem.

After a few minutes of walking around the downtown sidewalks, Fickie tried making small talk. Obviously she was attempting to get on Malcolm's good side so he'd let her in on any secret problems that might exist in the software. Not the biggest dope in the world, Malcolm tried to change the conversation from small talk to allergies, and sneezing, and anti-histamines. She got all mad at him because she was pro-histamine and spent the next 20 minutes telling him how rude and inconsiderate men can be. He happened to pick up an empty soda can and tossed it in a trash can, and she went into a lengthy diatribe about litterbugs and caffeinated soda and giant dumpsters under the ocean. Eventually Malcolm decided she was too flaky to work with and she was a terrible hostage and she'd never approve the software. He didn't really want the software and so he canned the whole spontaneous act of software piracy project. Software laws were all just legal rhetoric anyway. As soon he installed the stolen software, the manufacturers would release an upgrade and he'd have to steal a new version if he wanted technical support. Besides, who needs a software application that tells you don't have the hardware to use it. That was all it did. It was called LockDownSoft and it would never run because it was incompatible with all hardware and was a security threat to everything. He bought Fickie a hamburger then ditched her when she dissected it and took it back to the cook because the tomatoes weren't red enough.

He probably should have spent more time trying to get to know this Fictitious Ducharme, but why? Once he got to know her, she'd dump him for some debonair dude with white teeth and a fast car. She was really cute, but he had to lower his expectations. He began his search for less goddessly gal. He headed west to find himself an average cowgirl.

XX

So there he was, after travelling 30 miles in 3 days, breaking out of a slight hangover, waking up on the beach, covered with seaweed and seagull poop. It must have been around 6:00 a.m. and four or five kids in their late teens - early twenties appeared on the beach. Yup, they were southern California surfers. It didn't matter where they were from. Over the years, surfers all over the world had devolved. In the olden days, they were young flakey unemployed transients who carried an uncontrollable urge to ride the ocean waves and experience the thrill of acquiescing with nature. In the newen days they'd become young flakes that wanted to look good with sloppy hairdos and bright fluorescent colored duds. Except for Mike, the college student, and his whole family, the surf culture was a private club that drew strength from arrogance and cheap tattoos. Malcolm tried to surf once, but the locals (who couldn't surf worth a damn) ganged up on him and broke his friend's board. He had been ridiculed unjustly. He felt so dejected, so insignificant, so un-local. He maintained an unrequited spite within him ever since. Later in the week he dumped toxic medical waste into the ocean where the locals hung out and that made him feel better, but he still didn't like the modern surfers. Their boards looked cool, but he hated the surfers. He sure liked the boards.

On the beach, the locals stuck their spare boards in the sand to show off their great taste in Styrofoam coloring techniques. After watching them for about an hour, Malcolm set out to steal their sticks. All he needed to swipe those cool flotation devices was a bad attitude, a lot of rope, and some really big blankets. He had the attitude, he could use kelp as rope, and there were more blankets on the beach than all of Babylon. He spent two hours sneaking up on surfboards from behind misshapen sand castles and attacking. He'd pounce on the boards, knock 'em out with a karate chop, and drag them back to an empty life guard tower. Then he was ready to hit the nearest swap meet and make some big money.

As he collected the last boards, a young kid with green and blond hair approached him and shouted, "Hey dude! You see somebody walkin' around with about like twenty surfboards?"

Malcolm scratched his head and looked around, "Sorry, surf dude, I can't say that I have."

"Oh, man, that's so bogus. Those are the best boards on the beach."

The depressed surfer noticed twenty sandy blankets rolled up around some large flat objects sitting on the beach behind Malcolm. "Whoa dude! What's that?"

Malcolm looked at the blankets and replied, "Those are... airplane propellers."

The surfer was stoked, "No way! Dude! You're a pilot?"

Malcolm nodded in affirmation.

Local goes, "Ha! That's awesome! Maybe we could go flying one of these days."

"Wull, it's gonna be a while," Malcolm cleverly replied, "I'm building the plane from scratch, starting with the propellers."

"Dude, that's the most important part! One time I tried to build a board from scratch, but all I had was the wax! Ha," confided the small brained surfing child as he burst into laughter.

Malcolm smiled and walked off, dragging his airplane propellers behind him. When he got to the parking lot he decided that he really didn't want to drag those damn boards thirty miles to the nearest swap meet. He certainly didn't want to guard the boards in a parking lot until a swap meet came to the beach. We've all been there before; bunch of hot surfboards disguised as unfinished airplane propellers and no swap meet in sight. Acting unexpectedly rational, Malcolm did exactly the same thing everyone does. He threw the boards into an unattended recreational vehicle, drove back into town, and abandoned the stolen RV at a nuclear test facility.

Things went downhill from there. His maniacal antics were becoming more grandiose. His next escapade was the decision to climb Mount Everest in an elephant's pajamas. Sure he'd been drinking. A person doesn't just decide to put on a pair of elephant's pajamas and climb Everest. The deal was, Malcolm was standing outside a television store watching four or five different shows at the same time. On one channel, some famous explorer was risking his life by crossing a giant chasm on a human bridge of Sherpas, a comedian on another station was ruining his career with the old, "Last night I shot an elephant in my pajamas," bit. Malcolm finished his bottle of bourbon and laughed uncontrollably as he decided that climbing Mt. Everest in an elephant's pajamas might be a good idea.

He found a gigantic set of pajamas in a dumpster behind a used parachute store. He put on the pajamas and started running as fast as he could towards in the general direction of the Himalayas, but he tired himself out and fell asleep just about 7500 miles short of his goal. His dreams of climbing Mount Everest in an elephant's pajamas were crushed, but at least he had some dreams. His dreams were washed away once more when it began to rain and he woke up. Still tired and a little light-headed from the bourbon and the air in his skull, he took advantage of the weather by doing a Gene Kelly imitation and started singing in the rain. He happened to have several packets of hand soap so he was actually bathing in the rain. He eventually took shelter in a Laundromat and got some solid rest.

The next thing he knew, it was another beautiful day in the park. Another perfect day to relax, catch some rays, maybe even sit on a park bench with a pretty girl. There was a great bench right in front of him. Yup, that would have been a very nifty treat if only he had a pretty girl to talk to and pass some time with. Nothing especially romantic or underhanded, just some pleasant conversation. Was that too much to ask? Anyway, he wasn't going to spend any time on that beautiful spring day in the park talking with a pretty girl. Most of the pretty girls that he would have liked to sit with had better options. They were all probably on the phone. He wasn't bitter, dejected, filled with self-pity. He'd grown accustomed to his solitude, his alienation, his inability to fit in. Of course, if he could fit in, he had a perfect park bench to fit in on. He cringed. If he couldn't sit on that park bench with a pretty girl, nobody could. He wanted that bench and he was going to get it.

No one else deserved that stupid nice little bench. Hell, if they deserved it, they'd already be sitting on it having pleasant conversations, stealing Malcolm's pretty girls! No one in sight, no happy loving couples, no pretty girls, no witnesses whatsoever. He snuck up on the bench, slowly, discreetly, careful not to... possibly frighten the bench away! He lunged! He couldn't get far while the bench was chained to a steel stake that was buried deep in the earth's crust. It was going to be tough a bench to bag.

As Malcolm wrestled with the chain he heard a soft voice from over his shoulder. "Hi," is what the voice said. Just then the bench flipped him. He looked up to see Matilda holding back her laughter.

"I was just thinking about you," confessed Malcolm as he dropped the chain.

"Yeah?" she asked still smiling.

"You were at the restaurant," he noticed.

"Your restaurant," she mused.

"Yes, yes. Y'know, it's not really my restaurant. Let's think of it as our restaurant."

"Okay. What, um, what are you up to?"

"Oh, I was just taking a seat here, and I fell over. Why don't you join me?"

"Okay, but not today."

Malcolm scratched his head for some unknown reason, "Okay... that's fine. Whenever it's convenient. I'll be sitting right here. Waiting."

Matilda smiled. She knew he wanted her to sit next to him. She knew and she knew it would drive him crazy! Ha! "Well, today's a nice day. A perfect day. I think I will join you."

Smoothing out her yellow sundress as she sat down next to him, she took an avocado and ham sandwich out of her lunch bag. Malcolm's stomach grumbled. She set a soft drink on the bench so she could unwrap the sandwich. Consuming every move she made, Malcolm watched as she brought the sandwich to her mouth. He opened his mouth as she took a bite out of the sandwich. Noticing his silly reaction, she laughed and covered her mouth after spitting some green stuff out on Malcolm. Still laughing a little, she said, "Oh! I'm sorry! Do you want a bite?"

Malcolm nodded his head, "You're going to spit on me and bite me too?"

Matilda continued to smile, "I am sorry. How 'bout some diet soda?"

"No thanks, diet soda makes me feel self conscious. If you have an extra napkin, I'd really appreciate it."

Matilda gave him her napkin and accidentally knocked her diet soda over on Malcolm's leg.

"Oh, that's nice. You don't have any spaghetti sauce in that bag, do you?" asked Malcolm. He didn't think it was all that funny, but she just started busting up.

"I'm sorry, I'm sorry!" she laughed.

Malcolm mimicked her, "I'm sorry, I'm sorry," and she doubled over in laughter. Well, spontaneous romance gave way to humiliation and Malcolm had to excuse himself. She really didn't see him leave.

Walking away from Matilda was the best thing he could do. His frame of mind was not stable, and he was physically drained as well. He spent the next several days avoiding alcohol, doing what he could to find clean clothes and hopefully take a real shower.

XXI

Even after doing enough work at the Nowheresville Homeless Shelter for Wayward Thieves and Grill to earn an old shirt, some used shoes, and a small bottle of mouthwash, he still found himself facing another day of depression. Every day was depressing lately. Malcolm knew that it couldn't last forever. Something would come along and cheer him up. It wouldn't take much; a smile from a pretty girl, a child's laughter, his 8th grade gym teacher getting tarred and feathered, something, anything. But there was nothing. Nothing except his own pointless miserable mindless self pounding the sidewalks another day. He needed a reprieve, a sanctuary; a place to stay that wasn't filled with grey lifeless bodies that echoed his pain when he saw them. He went to a museum of modern art. If nothing else it would distract him for a few hours.

Inside, Salvador Dali and George Braque had left symbols of discontent, icons demanding change, arduously constructed paintings that forced a generation to look at their world differently or wander in blindness. The paintings were completely different in style and content, but their messages to the world said similarly, "Hey! You've been looking at this all wrong." While it was arrogant of the painters to assume that their artistic expressions were superior to traditional artists and that the general public was ignorant to the broader perspectives in life, it would have been equally arrogant for Malcolm to deny the artists any credibility.

He stepped back from Braque and viewed the works from several angles and watched the meaning change and evolve, but more importantly Malcolm changed. He saw content and purpose in an old stained canvas. He saw life in a life's work. He felt that others must have experienced similar metamorphoses over the decades and felt that perhaps the part of society that embraced its new appreciation of art was succeeding its lifeless predecessors.

He stepped into Dali and absorbed the meticulously positioned paper thin brush strokes that eventually created intricate images from an alternative realm. Dreamscapes and visions, nightmares and awakenings filled the gallery walls. Dali presented impossible scenes that seemed real enough to step out from the oils and grab the observer.

Malcolm found a bench in the museum and sat down to watch people observe the art. Some of them laughed, some shook their heads, most stared as they made a silent procession through the museum halls. Being as creative as he could, Malcolm tried to interpret the art patrons through fresh perspectives, imagining that one might have been born an hour before and another might have only an hour to live. The halls were no longer filled with art patrons, but suddenly filled with soldiers and doctors and morticians and nuns and other lives that Malcolm imagined they might possess.

He continued to watch them for hours until a pretty young docent sat down beside him.

"Hi," she said as many docents do.

Unprepared for an attractive woman to sit down beside him, Malcolm responded with typical tact, "Erf."

She smiled, "I noticed you've been sitting here for a while. Is everything all right?"

Malcolm thought about the world and its wars, and death, famine, pestilence, drugs, terrorism, and prime time television cartoons, but knew that it was all beyond the scope of her question.

"Yeah," he replied. "You work here?"

"Uh huh," she said to indicate yes. "I just wander around telling people about the paintings and make sure no one tries to steal anything."

The thought hadn't crossed his mind until she mentioned it. Some of those art things might have been worth bucks deluxe. Too bad there weren't any wallet sized paintings. Malcolm looked at the paintings then at the docent. She had the most captivating eyes he had ever seen. Going from hours of interpretive viewing of oil paintings to looking into her eyes, Malcolm was astounded by her natural beauty and charm. Then he remembered that he'd seen her before. She was the woman who didn't jab him in the spleen when he offered to lick her ears at his last job.

"Do you remember me?" he asked.

She started to shake her head, no, but suddenly her eyes lit up, "The delivery service."

"Yeah. You're Sharon," said Malcolm with a warm smile.

"I am! You're the guy who has trouble coming up with words for hello."

Malcolm blushed, "You remember."

"Yeah, my mailing didn't go too well, so I haven't gone back. It's nothing personal."

"Oh, that's alright. I'm not working there anymore. It wasn't a very good job. Long hours, low pay, tough working conditions."

She asked him sympathetically, "Did you get burned out?"

Malcolm shrugged his shoulders, simultaneously. He began to look away, but she started to smile and he couldn't take his eyes off her. He probably would have sat and stared at her forever if he didn't think it was rude, and if he didn't think he'd starve to death. Instead he attempted to strike up a conversation. "So, which is your favorite?" he asked with atypical relevance.

"I like the surrealists, but I really prefer the impressionists to anything we have here in this wing."

Ah, yes, the impressionists, Rich Little, Frank Gorshwin, Uncle Bob's Bogart, they truly were preferable, but Malcolm didn't see how they applied to art.

"Monet's water lilies just seem so natural, so pure. It's like the essence of fluid beauty. They look so soft that you just want to touch them and so fragrant that you want to smell them, but as you get closer they start to fade away. Still they retain their beauty at any distance and you kind of understand that you just can't ever possess them, but need to love them as they are. You warmly accept that they can never be yours. I think a lot of things are like that. Don't you?"

Malcolm noticed he was staring and drooling but he had no idea what she was talking about. "But which paintings do you like?" he asked again.

Sharon smiled and looked at the wall, nearly throwing Malcolm off his chair as he tried to follow her eyes.

"Oh, I don't know," she said and she stood up to move closer to the paintings.

She walked slowly, so Malcolm decided she wasn't trying to ditch him. He got up and cautiously began to follow her.

"I think Dali was ahead of his time," she said. "I still think he's ahead of his time. His work bursts with life, with energy and color, but it's almost like eating too much chocolate, y'know? It's too much of a good thing, overindulgence for the eyes."

Malcolm rubbed his eyes and tried to focus on the painting, but he couldn't. He really was interested in the conversation, whatever it was, but she was so damn distracting. She was marvelous to look at and listen to... he really needed to focus on what she was saying. Again, Malcolm thought how rude his behavior must have been and looked at his shoes so as not to stare.

"Do you like Dali?" she asked.

Malcolm thought for a moment and concluded that she probably wasn't talking about Dolly Madison or the Dalai Lama so she must have been referring to a painter. She was in fact referring to the painter of the paintings that Malcolm had been staring at for several hours.

"Dali's great!" he exclaimed, "I have to tell you, and I don't know much about art!"

Sharon thought for a moment and concluded that he probably wasn't referring to Art Linkletter or Open Art Surgery.

"Well, there's a lot to know," she said, "But the great thing about art is that it speaks for itself. You don't need a Ph.D. to know whether you like it or not. Your appreciation might change you as learn more, but the great paintings are great because the average person feels passion about the work."

Malcolm smiled when she said passion. Some people are extremely passionate, but don't express it capriciously. You can see from their eyes or their movements that they're dying to let it out, but can't because they want to share it with the right person, someone who values it as much as they do. Sharon was like that, but Malcolm didn't know it. Still, something about the woman inspired a new emotion in Malcolm, something almost magical. It was more than physical attraction, or admiration, or lust. As he tried to get past her stunning physical qualities he sensed something much deeper, something like the true beauty that can only come from the heart. She had a natural energy that Malcolm had never encountered. Even though she was a genuinely nice person, gorgeous, with a great personality, it went beyond that, and it confused the hell out of him. He felt something that words couldn't describe, something quintessential and fleeting, but the feeling was there and it was strong. It wasn't gas, or an allergic reaction to shellfish, it was love. But he hadn't known her long enough to truly love her. What if she was a communist or a murderer or a cross-stitcher or something?

He had to get to know her better. He could try to marry her or just spend the day with her. It was a tough decision, a big decision, and he had to go for it, "Will you mm, mm, mm, maybe go to the beach with me?"

Sharon smiled and said, "Yeah, when?"

Damn! He hadn't even hypnotized her and she said "yeah".

"When?" he repeated as though time meant something. "Whenever. Today. Now."

"Okay. It's been so quiet here lately," she said and waited.

Malcolm raised his eyebrows to himself.

Sharon said, "That was a joke."

"Good one!" said Malcolm.

"It's always quiet in museums," she clarified. "Anyway we have some extra volunteers today, so I'm pretty much just hanging around. I'll meet you out in the lobby, okay?"

"Groovy!" said Malcolm.

About fifteen minutes later, Sharon showed up in the museum lobby with a canvas tote bag and an enthusiastic smile. Malcolm had his polyester knapsack and a goofy smile that complemented Sharon's positive outlook quite nicely. They walked out of the museum and stood on the street for a few minutes. He approached several nice cars parked at the curb while he tried to figure out how to break the news to her that he didn't have transportation. To his amazement, he was saved when a solution to his problem suddenly appeared.

"Stop!" shouted Malcolm before jumping into the street.

The vehicle came to sudden halt startling Sharon and everyone else within a 50 foot radius. Malcolm gave Sharon a wink and took her hand. She giggled as they boarded.

"I've never been on a real bulldozer before," she admitted.

"It's a nice one," said Malcolm. "This guy owes me a favor."

Malcolm turned to the driver and shouted, "To the beach! Bum!"

The man behind the steering wheel leered back and smiled a maniacal smile. Then he maneuvered a dozen of his shopping carts into an alley and drove west.

They arrived at the beach about an hour later and Sharon went into a bathroom to put on her beach duds. With the spontaneity and tact of a drunken derelict, Malcolm took off his shirt and pants and tripped and hopped around and fell face first into the sand. Clever as he was graceful, he always wore shorts under his pants just in case a sudden beach excursion was ever to present itself. It's a good thing, if he had been naked when he was hopping around and falling in the sand, people might have thought he was a politician.

Waiting on the beach for his lovely new friend, Malcolm sat and watched a good looking couple, named Victor and Vanity, as they basked in the sunshine. There was hardly anyone else on the beach. Sharon came out of the changing room wearing a one piece bathing suit. Words couldn't describe how good she looked. He compared her to the other beautiful woman on the beach; Vanity's French bikini accentuated her graceful, sinewy figure. She was cute, yet merciful. A second glance at Sharon and he noticed what a graceful figure she had, darned sinewy too. The guy at Vanity's side was well built with a bronze tan that told everyone on the beach that he knew how to take care of himself. Malcolm, as the result of a very limited wardrobe and hours of nude sunbathing on the roof of the Laundromat, had picked up a pretty good tan himself. Sharon was at least as attractive as Vanity. Malcolm was like a much skinnier slightly paler Victor, with lighter hair and a faint hangover aroma, and... yeah, well, Malcolm looked more like an emu than a Victor, but at least he was on the same beach.

It could well have been that Malcolm had finally made his way into the jet setting lifestyles of the rich and famous. Perhaps he was just rubbing elbows with the drunk and stupid. There was no point in splitting hairs. He was on a beach with beautiful people. Victor and Vanity were lying on their backs gazing into each others eyes. Sharon was relaxing in the line of sight between Malcolm and Team Beautiful. He figured that Sharon sure had good eyes. Staring into Vanity's eyes, Victor was reminded of the coastal waters off the North Shore of Oahu on a clear morning. Malcolm noticed that Sharon's eyes were really really pretty. Victor thought of the ageless beauty that filled certain parts of the Mediterranean and understood how the Grecian tales of Venus had been passed down through the ages and felt suddenly that Vanity must have been a direct descendant of that goddess. Sharon's eyes had suddenly been transformed into brilliant azure pools that reflected the sparkling waves that crashed timelessly on the world's most pristine beaches, they shimmered with life and danced with innocence. If all the beauty in the universe could have been concentrated into a small delicate essence, it would find no better resting place than Sharon's eyes. Malcolm smiled. Victor looked over at Malcolm and sneered.

"The afternoon reminds me of the one we spent in the catamaran off the coast of Bermuda last summer," said Victor as he leaned over and kissed Vanity softly on the nape of her neck.

She closed her eyes and softly laughed, "We never left the boat's cabin!"

Victor feigned shock, "I did too! Long enough to get some ice out of the cooler. While I was up on the deck, I just happened to notice that it was a gorgeous day."

Vanity pretended to pout.

Victor quickly added, "I was thinking of you the whole time. The sunshine just reminded me of the heat in your passion."

Vanity laughed and pushed Victor's shoulder. He lay back on his beach towel and relaxed. She began making circles with her finger on his chest until he took her hand and held it gently between them. Still feeling playful, she filled her other hand with sand and let it slowly sift out onto Victor's arm. After a moment, he realized what she was doing and let out a yell. Vanity jumped to her feet and kicked sand across Victor's legs then ran down the beach. He sat up for a minute and began to brush off the sand. He watched her run a little longer, just admiring her firm healthy form as she ran. Slowly he raised himself up then took off after her.

With avid curiosity, Malcolm observed the ritual of two beautiful people in love. He could have been like them, he was sure of it. All he needed was money. If he had money, he could get into a health club and get in great shape and bathe. He could buy anything any girl could want. He could even buy some nice clothes that hadn't been worn by anyone else. He wasn't particularly beautiful looking, but he took great pride in the fact that he didn't have any goiters, which is not to say that goiters are all that bad, they just weren't for Malcolm. If he had money, he could hang out on beaches all day long, go to museums and meet beautiful women any time he felt like it. He thought about it for a minute. He looked at Sharon, he thought some more, and looked at Sharon some more and wiped his mouth. Maybe he didn't need money. Maybe he could have goiters. Maybe all he needed was a personality that was more interesting than a tuna.

The answer to all his problems was right there in front of him. The beautiful people had personalities! It seemed crazy enough to work. Malcolm had never had a personality before. If he could just get a personality quick and do something to keep Sharon interested, he'd be set. Maybe not set for life, but possibly long enough to turn his life around without robbing a bank or something equally implausible. Of course, he wasn't out to use the girl just to turn his life around. He wanted to pledge a lifelong commitment to her, rub her back and shoulders, and maybe even help her in some way. If the relationship lasted forever, great, but deep down, he knew that she was too good for him. He didn't want to confine her to a relationship with a guy that started off with no personality.

Anyway, he needed to get that personality, so he decided to mimic the beautiful people and hope that some of the imitation personality would stick. He'd caught an eyeful of their sand tossing antics and figured he could try the same thing with Sharon. The only problem was that the beautiful girl had instigated most of the activity and Malcolm was a guy. Does that sound right? No! It was the modern world. Malcolm could do anything a woman could do. He began to make little circles with his finger on her chest. He was starting to enjoy it, just before the pain of his fingers bending backwards began to set in.

She looked over at him with a surprised expression. Almost looked like she was afraid she might have hurt him.

"I'm sorry! That's just a reflex. I get a lot of guys that ask me to hold up paintings so they can examine 'em and the next thing I know, they're trying to look down my blouse."

"Yeah, I know what you mean," said Malcolm, for some reason.

Sharon smiled and put Malcolm's finger back on her chest. Fool me once, shame on you, fool. Fool me twice... um... shame on? Once bit, twice shy... Malcolm cleverly pulled that hand away and used his other hand. Smiling at his clumsiness, she gently pulled his hand away and held it still between them. It was one of those incidents that gave Malcolm the impression that he was finally getting a personality. He also seemed to be falling in love. Everything about Sharon was perfect and he thought she was outta sight. He hadn't honestly felt that way about a girl in a long time.

The beautiful people chased each other for a few more minutes until Victor caught Vanity in the ebbing tide. They held each other in a warm embrace and looked out across the Pacific as tiny waves rolled over their feet on the ocean's edge.

That was Malcolm's next move. "Hey, Sharon, let's chase each other on the beach for a while... Okay?" he asked.

Sharon wasn't paying much attention to him, but she responded, "Um, I could go for a jog..."

"Okay," said Malcolm.

She was more spontaneous than he thought. She got up and started jogging. Best damn jogger he'd ever seen. He got up and tried to remember the steps. Lift left leg, fall forward, repeat. They jogged for about a half a mile until Malcolm slipped on a jellyfish and fell into the water.

Sharon stopped and helped him up. "You okay?" she asked.

Malcolm knew he'd maimed the jellyfish, but he tried not to make a big deal out of it. "Yeah, I'm okay, but that... If that had been a peanut butter fish..."

"Or a spiny urchin," she said without acknowledging his stupid joke.

"Yeah. Huh?" he said as they began walking back to their beach plot.

Victor and Vanity strolled hand in hand along the beach. Malc and Sharon walked behind them. Awkwardly, Malcolm tried to grab her hand, but she kept pulling it away. In an effort to get her into the romantic hand holding mood, he looked around the sand for a pair of handcuffs. No cuffs, but he did notice a starfish. He imagined what Victor might have said to Vanity in the same situation, and gave it a shot.

"Y'know Sharon, sugar toosh, there wasn't enough room in the sky to hold all the stars, so some of 'em ended up on the beach," he said and laughed to himself like a fool.

"Oh," said Sharon. "That's um, neat. Yeah, that's neat."

Malcolm raised his eyebrows, "but the prettiest stars are in your eyes."

Sharon smiled and took his hand. She could have taken his hand to feel the warmth generated from his heart and to sense the energy flowing from his soul, or she could have been leading him to a psychiatric ward. We can't be sure, she wasn't thinking too clearly. Malcolm laughed out loud.

Victor looked past Vanity towards the ocean and meditated on its vastness, its indomitable presence. He felt the same way about his love for Vanity. Malcolm was trying to check out Sharon's legs. Vanity rested her head against Vic's shoulder. As they walked, she thought of all the beaches they'd been on, all the times they'd made love on warm secluded sands. There were millions of beaches in the world, but she couldn't dream of setting foot on any of them without Victor. Still she imagined strolling down all of them. Sharon looked at Malcolm's shoulder and noticed he was kind of sweaty for a skinny guy. She imagined throwing sand on his chest to see if it would stick. Then she thought about knitting. Malcolm leaned his shoulder towards Sharon and she rubbed a handful of sand on it. Everyone was having a nice time.

Suddenly and without warning, Vanity and Victor ran out through the surf and swam past the breakers. The water was shallow enough for them to stand neck deep and rise and fall with the slow moving powerful waves. It was a romantic opportunity too perfect for Malcolm to pass up. He'd never gone out in the ocean with a girl. He'd gone out on a surfboard, but he knew Sharon was no surfboard and he was almost positive sure she wouldn't float. Spontaneously, he ran out into the water, but she didn't follow. He came back and threw mud at her, so she got pissed off and chased him. They spent all afternoon chasing each other with rocks and mud and kelp and apologizing for one thing or another.

It had been a long day for Malcolm. Sharon gave him good vibes, but then, while he was in the middle of a good vibration reception, she'd throw in a bad vibe. Just like that! Good vibe, good vibe, good vibe, rank vibe! Bogus vibe! Good vibe, good vibe, etc. He smiled and sulked accordingly.

The thing that confused him most was why she was still hanging around with him. Maybe she really liked him. Maybe she wanted to marry him. That was probably the reason. He considered asking her, but decided that she was just hanging with him because he had bulldozer connections. He never asked her. The two of them sat on the beach watching the waves roll in. Occasionally, Malcolm observed Victor's interactions with Vanity as they sat on some nearby rocks.

It occurred to Malcolm that Victor probably never had a moment of self doubt when it came to women, he had the looks and charm and confidence that appealed to so many of the breathing human women, and all Malcolm had was his self-pity, alcoholism, and calluses. Sharon looked great with her tan skin and the wind blowing through her hair. Victor and Vanity looked pretty good for similar reasons, they looked good together. Good looking couples suddenly seemed important to Malcolm. Victor was tall, Vanity was good looking. Sharon was beautiful, Malcolm was there.

He described his observations to Sharon, "They make a good couple don't they?"

Sharon looked down the beach at Victor and Vanity, "The hunk and the girl?"

Hunk. That guy looked nothing at all like Malcolm, and she thought Victor was a hunk, "No, I'm talking about those birds."

"Oh," said Sharon as she noticed a pair of seabirds in the sand nearby, "I guess they do."

"They're terns," said Malcolm.

"Great!" Sharon said.

"One good tern deserves another, I say," ...said Malcolm.

A stupid grin crossed Sharon's face as she leaned back on the sand and closed her eyes.

After dwelling on the significance of the relationship between Vanity and Victor, Malcolm realized that he was nothing but a tremendous bore. In an attempt to do something incredibly unpredictable and exciting, he jumped to his feet and ran towards a flock of seagulls. At first the seagulls were alarmed. They jumped and squawked and ran from Malcolm, but as he got closer they started to fall asleep. He was able to walk right up to them and push them over without waking them up. It didn't create the effect he was looking for. He yelled at them and, well, if you've ever heard a seagull snore, you know it's pretty funny. There were a few laughing gulls on the beach and the gulls that weren't looking at him with a straight face were snoring, but Malcolm wasn't laughing or snoring. He was just boring.

He looked for something to help him rile the birds in order to get that spontaneous carefree chase-the-seagulls-down-the-beach-on-a-whim-type-of-guy effect going. About forty yards away a couple kids were playing with a golden retriever. Energetically, the dog a fetched a stick from the ocean as the children threw it into the oncoming waves repeatedly. If a golden retriever couldn't frighten those stupid seagulls, then they weren't seagulls. Malcolm went over to the kids and asked if he could throw the stick. They yawned and shrugged their shoulders. Malcolm took the stick from the slobbering dog and it jumped in the air and barked and paced back and forth in front of Malcolm as he feigned a monumental toss. After another fake throw the dog sat and wagged its tail. Then the dog lay down, and by the time Malcolm actually threw the stick towards the seagulls, the dog was asleep on the beach snoring. Malcolm gave up on the spontaneous exciting thing and went back to Sharon.

As he got closer, he noticed that she was also dozing off and he decided that she was probably worn out from all the excitement. He sat back down on his t-shirt and watched Victor and Vanity. Vic stood up and brushed the sand off his butt as Vanity laid on her stomach watching him. Turning and noticing that she was staring at him, Victor tossed his shirt over her eyes and walked towards some beachfront bungalows that were lined up along the back of the beach. Behind the small vacation rentals, a lush green canyon opened up to the hills. Malcolm couldn't figure out why Victor would need to bother the local residents for anything. He was pretty bold about his approach. Undaunted by the legal restrictions that should have kept him away from the private properties, he went to the closest bungalow, jumped over the wall and went inside. What nerve! He was robbing the place in broad daylight.

Malcolm looked up and down the beach for a cop or a lifeguard, or anyone who was still awake, but no one was in sight. Acting on his sense of good citizenship and jealously, he got up to nab the burglar, but before he got to the condo, Victor was on his way out carrying a couple of tropical drinks. Victor had just stolen two tropical drinks from a beachfront bungalow. Yes, obviously he lived there. Malcolm didn't want to admit it. How do people manage to pay for stuff like that?

Anyway, Victor took the drinks back to Vanity and they sat together in the afternoon sun watching the waves crash down along the beach. The sound of waves breaking and children playing and seagulls snoring created a unique natural orchestra that played daily, but never the same song twice. The smell of sea salt and suntan lotion, the light reflecting off the ocean, and warm bodies relaxing all around was a poetic magnet that attracted the soulful and silent people throughout the world. A cool breeze rolled down the beach. Victor and Vanity got closer to stay warm, then finished their drinks and went back to the bungalow.

Sharon had fallen asleep, but was beginning wake up as Malcolm covered her with a blanket they'd brought along. She sat up and wrapped the blanket around her shoulders.

"This is nice," she said to Malcolm.

"Yeah, I'm glad you're enjoying it. I thought maybe I was boring you," Malcolm said.

Sharon replied with a yawn, "Oh, no. I'm just tired from all the excitement. And I've been working a lot of long days lately."

"You like working for the museum?" he asked.

"Yeah, I love it. It doesn't pay very much, and I do get stuck with a lot of tedious work, but my boss is pretty nice and I get to learn a lot about art."

"You probably meet some interesting people."

Sharon answered hesitantly, "Yeah, I guess so. There are a few snobs who don't think I deserve to talk to them, but there are also some real nice people." She paused and smiled, "Some strange people, and some wild people. Every so often, I get to work directly with the artist when I'm setting up an exhibit and they want everything just right. Sometimes it's just, 'No. That won't work. Move this, and move that,' but others try to explain why they don't like something and that's really interesting. Like, the light in the museum might be a different type than the artist uses in her studio or the light might come from a different angle, or the background for a sculpture might be completely opposite from the way the artist expected it to be, so it's hard to make sure everything's just right... I think a good artist can make their art work in any light in any setting."

"Have you ever done any painting?" asked Malcolm.

Sharon looked across the ocean, "I've played around with charcoal and pastels, but I don't have as much control with paint as I do with drawings."

"What do you like to draw?" asked Malcolm as he looked out over the ocean.

Sharon looked at him and smiled. She went on for hours about capturing beauty on paper and the evolution of the art world. Malcolm took in every word she said, but for all she talked about capturing impressions of light and color, he knew nothing in any museum could compare to her natural beauty.

The afternoon cooled quickly so Malcolm and Sharon started a bonfire and talked a little longer. It was a very nice conversation, personal without being pretentious. Then Malcolm tried to keep her warm by sitting closer to her, but managed to burn himself on some of the embers instead.

"Y'know," he said, "I don't know what it is, but I've been trying to be romantic all afternoon. I just can't do it. Am I expected to do things that other people think are romantic, or should I do things that *I* think are romantic... or things that *you* think are romantic? Riding across the desert together on a camel, or a picnic beside a lake, or sitting in a candlelit room overlooking the lights of a city on a rainy night? Personally, I like the beach and I've heard it can be romantic, but I don't know. Making those little circles on you chest with my finger could have been annoying."

Sharon looked down and laughed.

"Or just embarrassing," he finished.

"Well," she said, "You realize that by answering that question, I pretty much wipe out any possibility of you and I having a romantic afternoon."

Malcolm jumped back, "Don't say anything!"

Sadly, Sharon looked at Malcolm for a minute, then at the sand and said, "Hey, it's not gonna happen. You're a nice guy, but let's face it. You don't have what I want."

"But... I'm a nice guy."

"There are millions of nice guys in the world and there's nothing wrong with you, but there's nothing going on between us. You act like my brother," said Sharon. For a moment she worried that she might have hurt his feelings, but he was an adult, and she was being honest. Honesty was the least she could give him.

Malcolm made a permanent mental note, "Never ask how to be romantic."

He sat and shriveled as she continued, "You'll find somebody, and you'll do something with her and you'll feel something special. You'll forget about everything going on around you, you'll forget the past and the future, and you'll realize that the woman you're with is taking all your attention. I know it sounds old-fashioned, but you'll know it when it happens. Romance happens more than it's planned, but the beach is good place to start."

Malcolm had forgotten that they were at the beach. He'd forgotten himself. He was sad, but he knew there'd be other perfect women in the world. At least he'd tasted romance. Maybe he'd only smelled it. He was certain that he'd seen it, and that would have to suffice.

"Do you feel like grabbing some dinner?" he asked, "I'm starting to burn out on hanging around down here. I have to sweep up all this nasty sand when we're done, but it can wait until after dinner."

Ignoring his lame humor, Sharon went on to more practical matters. "Have you ever eaten there?" she asked, pointing to a restaurant on the cliff.

Even though she'd pretty much eliminated any possible future plans between them, she still looked good and he couldn't deny that she had a great personality. He could just take her to dinner for some very non-romantic interaction. They could talk about construction work and life in Sudan, then maybe he could just casually suggest that they spend the night together.

Perched on a prime piece of real estate overlooking one of California's most spectacular beaches sat Gatti's Fine Seafood Restaurant, the best food in the entire Nowheresville coastal area. Malcolm looked up at the restaurant and knew he could never afford to pay for dinner, but maybe he could find a way... maybe he could steal some food... or get a very temporary cooking position... Nah, he had to find a legitimate way of having dinner with Sharon, she was worth it. It occurred to him that most good restaurants accept gas cards and two-for-one coupons. Besides, they wouldn't bring the bill until after they ate. They could take a joke and Sharon would probably understand... if she didn't, the old adage held true, "It's better to have dined and been dumped, then never to have dined at all."

His eyes glazed over, his face turned crimson, his voice cracked, "Would you, um, er, duh, how's what... I. Would you like to have dinner with me now there?"

It's not totally unheard of for a guy to pass out after asking a girl out, and when Malcolm regained consciousness he found Sharon standing over him smiling. Cute smile. The bucket in her hand and water on his face led him to believe that he'd ruined the moment once again.

She laughed then let him have it, "Dinner sounds like fun. I'm starved!"

Always ready for rejection, Malcolm calmly dealt with the brutal blow, "I understand, thanks anyway, can we still be... Dinner is okay? Heh, hey! Let's go!" He jumped to his feet and gave himself a high-five, "Yeah!"

They got their things together and found some actual public showers. The existence of real public showers caused Malcolm to weep. After spending a few minutes in the beach restroom, Sharon returned and incredibly enough, her one-piece was transformed into an evening gown. Chicks get all the funky duds. It was doubtlessly some kind of Italian fashion trend. It looked great, and she definitely had some far out voodoo voguely style thing going on. Malcolm had a pair of socks in his back pack and they matched, so he was feeling pretty dapper himself.

They started their journey up a steep path to the restaurant that had been carved into the sandstone facade of the cliff by mules or cattle or seagulls or something. Spunky little gal that she was, Sharon was thoroughly enjoying the hike, but Malcolm nearly died navigating the trail. After she got to the top, she waited about five minutes then came back down to see how he was doing.

It's not that he wanted to appear macho or anything, he just thought that dying might spoil the evening completely, so he offered to carry her up the cliff just to slow her down a little. After a brief but civil argument, Sharon allowed him to carry her hand and they made their way to the top.

XXII

Gatti's Restaurant had a beachy ambiance. With the rough wood tables, checkered table clothes, and fishing nets hanging down the walls, the simple casual decor betrayed the international cuisine prepared by world renowned chefs. It was a place for people who were interested in a quiet evening, where the only unexpected distraction was a captivating panoramic sunset that spanned the Pacific and preceded a warm clear moonlit night. They entered the restaurant and Malcolm began to open the door for Sharon.

"Ahem," she said, to indicate that door opening was sexist and offensive.

Hmmm... When Malcolm opened doors for people, he did it as an act of friendship or respect knowing full well that the person he opened the door for was quite capable of opening their own doors. However, his action was interpreted as bigotry, so in order to balance the action, he grabbed his crotch, belched, and gave Sharon a quick shot in the arm. She let him go first.

"Good evening," said the maitre d'.

Malcolm thought, "Yeah, good evening to get dumped on."

Malcolm replied, "Hi."

The maitre d' asked, "Two for dinner?"

Malcolm was thinking, "No, fifty, stupid."

Malcolm said, "Yes, two please."

"The afternoon has been quite nice," the maitre d' said, "We expect to see a kaleidoscopic sunset over the ocean. Would the two of you enjoy verandah seating for dinner?"

Malcolm said, "No, throw us in the bathroom with a couple forks, we'll get by."

Malcolm thought, "Yes, plea... Oh, damn."

"Excuse me, sir?" asked the startled maitre d'.

Sharon and Malcolm quickly responded, "The verandah would be perfect."

Malcolm added, "I meant to say, I need to stop by the bathroom and I'll meet you at the table in a couple minutes."

"Very good, sir," said the maitre d'.

"You can grab a fork on your way past the kitchen, pinhead," the maitre d' thought.

The dashing maitre d' escorted Sharon to a small table and Malcolm found his way to the restroom where he hid out and flushed toilets for a few minutes then joined Sharon on the verandah.

As Malcolm sat down, Sharon shook her head and laughed, "You have an interesting way with words."

"I'm just a little nervous. I don't get out much," said Malcolm as he examined his fork.

Thoroughly enjoying the change of pace, Sharon smiled and looked at the menu. Coincidentally, Victor and Vanity were also dining at the romantic restaurant at a nearby table. In a rare attempt at cordiality, Malcolm waved to them and smiled like an idiot. They smiled back like they were smiling at an idiot then continued with their conversation.

The view was truly spectacular. The sky was changing from light blue to magenta as the sun gradually lowered on the horizon. Narrow lines formed by the silhouettes of seabirds sailed along the skyline as they slowly passed distant thunderheads.

A young waiter approached them and stood by the table, "Good evening, sir, madam. My name is Rex, and I'll be serving you this evening. May I go over the specials we have that aren't on the menu?"

Not accustomed to restaurant etiquette, Malcolm shrugged his shoulders, Sharon just stared and smiled, "Please Rex, tell us."

"Well, we have a grilled swordfish filet, basted with a light butter and garlic pepper dressing. The swordfish was brought in after lunch, and when it's that fresh, it practically melts in your mouth. We also have a baked Mahi Mahi dish that's stuffed with sundried tomatoes and red peppers and cooked in a very subtle Cajun sauce. It's highly recommended by the chefs and one of my favorites too," Rex explained.

"That's what I want," interjected Sharon who was more interested in the waiter than the menu.

"I think I'll have the broiled halibut," said Malcolm.

"Excellent choice, sir. The halibut is one of our five star entrees," said the waiter as he took their menus. He began to walk away but caught himself, "I'm sorry. I... can I get you anything to drink this evening?"

"What do you recommend?" asked Sharon.

The waiter lowered his eyes and smiled, "Well, I can't speak for the gentleman, but I'd suggest a nice bottle of Dom Perignon on an evening as romantic as this, for a couple as nice as you. Sir?"

"Yeah! ...Don Perry Jung, German, right?" asked Malcolm.

"European..." the waiter explained.

"Oh, yeah? Learn somethin' new every day. What the hell, bring out the whole bottle!" Malcolm said.

"Very good, sir. Thank you," said the waiter.

Sharon couldn't take her eyes off Rex as he left their table. He was a good looking guy, about 6'2", good build, tan complexion, straight teeth, no goiters. Malcolm wanted to hate him, but he couldn't. The guy actually seemed nice. Most guys would have had their eyes all over Sharon, but Rex was respectful, he probably wouldn't have even opened the door for her. Of course, Malcolm didn't know that the waiter was actually a multi-millionaire who was only working because he liked to meet people. Tall, dark, and handsome, with money and a genuine interest in people, and straight teeth. That guy had a lot of nerve.

Rather than dwell on his comparative weaknesses to Rex, Malcolm tried to make the most of his first and last evening with Sharon. It wasn't exactly a challenge. Sharon was perfect in every respect. Her conversations were sensitive yet practical, intelligent, but down to earth, provocative and steamy. So, Malcolm was looking into Sharon's eyes, thinking that they looked like big blue moons floating in milky white seas. She was truly a goddess.

As he thought about her, he overheard Victor speaking softly to Vanity, "I never noticed it before, but your eyes... In the candlelight, your eyes look like big blue moons floating in milky white seas. You truly are a goddess." Vanity smiled and looked out over the ocean.

Funny coincidence. Malcolm continued to muse over his friend, her hair flowed across her soft warm shoulders like waves of silk. It glistened like a moonlit ocean.

Reaching across the table to touch her hair, Victor said to Vanity, "Your hair is so beautiful. It flows across your soft warm shoulders like silken waves and as it cascades down it glistens like moonlight on the ocean."

Hum. Malcolm couldn't get over Sharon's smile. She had a smile that could light up the heavens, and warm the soul. When she laughed, she glowed and filled the room with happiness.

"Vanity, I must tell you, I love your smile. Your smile could light up the heavens and warm the soul. When you smile, you positively glow and fill the whole room with happiness," said Vic.

Malcolm noticed that the hangnails on Sharon's toes weren't as grody as they looked on the beach.

"Your hang..." Victor stopped and gave Malcolm a dirty look.

Malcolm smiled and touched Sharon's hand. He couldn't imagine a more perfect setting.

Victor looked into Vanity's eyes and reached across the table to take her hand. His powerful hand dwarfed Vanity's. Gently caressing her alabaster palm with his thumb, he spoke to her in a soft deep voice, "You seem unhappy this evening. You're not ready to stay with me?"

She lowered her big blue eyes as they suddenly filled with tears, "I know it sounds silly and old fashioned, but I wasn't brought up to live with a man out of wedlock. I know you love me, but it's just not right."

With a giant sigh of relief, Victor smiled and slowly lifted her chin with his fingertips. "This was going to be a special night. I didn't know that you had reservations about our arrangement, but I hope this helps ease your mind."

She watched with anticipation as her lover reached into his jacket pocket and brought out a small black velvet box. Vanity tried to hide her excitement and covered her mouth after letting out a short joyful laugh.

Victor looked deep into her eyes and said, "I do love you and we belong together. Vanity, please marry me."

Tears streamed from her glowing eyes. Opening the small black box, he revealed a full carat diamond ring set in the center of seven smaller diamonds. She wanted to leap into his arms, but her legs were too shaky to let her. She stood and balanced herself with the table. Victor jumped to his feet and put his arms around her. She hugged him back and squeezed with all her might. Looking into each other's eyes they didn't need to say another word. Their future of happiness was sealed.

Victor wanted Vanity. Vanity wanted Victor. Malcolm wanted Sharon. Sharon wanted to try the Caesar's salad. It was well known that their Caesar's salad was one of the best in the whole county. The waiter returned with the champagne.

Sharon stopped him, "Excuse me, would it be possible for me to order a small Caesar's salad?"

The waiter looked into Sharon's eyes, "Anything is possible, anything you like."

Sharon blinked.

"And you, sir. Can I get you anything else?"

Malcolm hiccupped, "No, nothing. Thanks."

"Your meal will be ready in about fifteen minutes and I'll bring your salad out right away."

Malcolm watched Sharon watch the waiter walk away. He couldn't blame her. The guy was like perfect and Malcolm was a complete failure. He needed to change the subject before Sharon left the table.

"So what's that you're wearing on your neck?"

Awkwardly touching the small object that she carried with her always, she lowered her eyes from Malcolm and explained, "Oh, it's a pendant. I have a picture of my son inside it."

"Your son? That's nice. How old is he?"

"He would have been four this year."

"I'm sorry. I didn't mean to pry."

"No, that's okay. It always comes up eventually. He died in a car wreck about a year ago. His father, too."

"That's terrible. I'm really sorry... I can't imagine how you must deal with it."

A hardened smile crossed Sharon's face. It wasn't angry or spiteful, it was just a conditioned reaction to a tough question. She tried not to think of her son as she explained, "It's hard, and I'm not sure I really do deal with it. It's just something I'll always carry with me. Would you like to see him?"

"Yeah. Yeah, I would."

Sharon took off her pendant and opened it for Malcolm. Her little boy carried a strong resemblance.

"Beautiful child," said Malcolm.

"He really was," said Sharon and her eyes began to well up. "Sometimes I wonder if it's worth falling in love, y'know? What's the point? It never lasts, anyway. Just go for what looks good and forget about love. Who needs the hassles? Men are good for a while, but they're gone before you know it. I'm just better off with short flings. You guys are all the same. Love and trust mean nothing to you."

Malcolm smiled and shook his head, "No. I don't much about love, but I think you have to let your heart make some of your decisions. I'm really sorry."

She paused and wiped her eyes. She closed her locket and wiped her eyes again, "It's okay. I'm the one who should apologize. You didn't ask for that."

"It meant a lot that you could share your son's picture with me."

Wiping her eyes once more, Sharon let out a little laugh, "Depression is my life."

Before he had a chance to give her his own long drawn out pathetic reflections on depression, Malcolm detected the familiar smell of wood burning. Smoke was billowing from vents above the windows and flames were building up inside. Fire quickly engulfed the doorway to the verandah and filled the indoor dining area. At that moment Malcolm felt something rising up inside him, something he'd never felt before. It was a deep passion for Sharon, something moving his soul. There was nothing on his mind except her. She looked helpless yet unfrightened. Then it dawned on him, what an idiot he'd been. The whole day he'd been infatuated with her physical qualities, obsessed with spending time with her. Everything he did with her, he did for himself. Not that he wanted to take advantage of her, it's just that he was trying to impress her or get her sympathy for his own reasons. It's hard to explain, but he just wasn't offering her anything she needed, and he really wasn't showing her his true self because he was afraid she'd reject him. Well, she rejected him anyway, and she did it for the wrong reasons. If she was going to care about him or dump him properly, she'd have to know who he was and she hadn't even met him.

The one thing he knew about her was that her beauty came from her heart. Seeing her strength in a new light, he finally realized how incredible she was. She spent time with someone like Malcolm just to be nice. Yet, there she was, on the verge of disaster as the fire began to move onto the balcony, all because Malcolm wanted to have dinner with her. He couldn't believe what he'd done. Suddenly, her safety became the only thing that mattered to him.

"Get back," he shouted at Sharon and pulled the table cloth from their table.

Before she knew what was happening, Sharon was wrapped in the table cloth and in Malcolm's arms. Holding her tightly, he threw his back against the door to the restaurant and burst through it. Blackened burning shards of the door frame fell all around them. The restaurant was filled with fire, but Malcolm ran straight to the entrance and out to the front of the establishment. Fire trucks were coming up the hill as Malcolm set her on her feet just outside the restaurant. For a moment he looked her up and down to make sure she hadn't caught any of the flames. No flames and she still looked great.

"Are you okay?" he asked.

Staring at him in disbelief, she nodded that she was alright.

With a deep sigh of relief he smiled, hugged her, and would you believe the selfish bastard wanted to give her a kiss? As kissable as she was, very kissable, he probably would have just puckered up and laid one on her, but he noticed that his shirt sleeve was burning, so he just gave her a quick handshake. He didn't want to give Sharon the impression that he was trying to wash his hands, but he did need to prevent his arm from burning up in front of his date, so he grabbed a nearby hose and doused the fire on his shirt.

The fire trucks were just pulling into the parking lot, but there were still people in the restaurant. Wallowing in chivalry, he boldly took the table cloth from Sharon and soaked it water, then blew her a kiss, like a selfish bastard, and ran back into restaurant. Through the flames he saw Rex, Victor, and Vanity standing on the balcony contemplating their chances of surviving the fall. Covering himself with the wet cloth, he ran to the balcony. When he got there, he pulled two more table clothes from the balcony tables and gave them to Victor and the waiter. Then he wrapped Vanity in the wet table cloth and picked her up.

"Follow me!" he yelled at the two men and ran back through the flames with Vanity in his arms. Once they were safely outside, he set Vanity down and made sure she was alright. The waiter followed soon after. Sharon was still watching the blaze, and she still looked good, but Vanity was in shock.

"Victor!" she shouted. "Victor!"

Malcolm stared at the door, but Victor didn't show up. There wasn't much time and Malcolm knew that if Victor tripped and fell in that inferno he was probably nearly dead. But suddenly he remembered something that compelled him to go back into the fire besides Victor. He draped the wet table cloth over his head and ran back into the restaurant. A beam had fallen, blocking the doorway to the balcony and Victor was at the far edge of the balcony looking down the cliff's steep face. Malcolm took a chair and threw it through the window and climbed out to the balcony.

"Hey!" he shouted at Victor, "Come on! This way!"

Victor ran to the window where Malcolm gave him the table cloth and helped him through the balcony window. Then Malcolm went to the table where he and Sharon had been sitting. He searched frantically as the fire began to eat away at the balcony supports. The air was filled with smoke and the sound of wood cracking became louder with every second. Beneath the table he found what he was looking for. He picked it up, held it tightly in his hand, and went back to the window, but it was too late. The entire dining room of the restaurant was filled with fire and Malcolm's only exit was covered in flames. As he searched for another way out, the balcony began to collapse. Slowly, the structure arched and began to separate from the restaurant's foundation, and Malcolm knew the jig was up. Damn it!

The entire balcony slipped away from the restaurant and tumbled against the cliff's wall, throwing long broken braces and chairs and tables as it rolled, finally crashing in a flaming heap of death on the beach below. Nothing stirred but fire, not even Malcolm Tent.

XXIII

No, not even Malcolm Tent could have survived that fall... the jagged rocks, the sheer distance, and of course, the fire itself were all too much. There was no life in that, that, that shambled pile of fire and cinders at the foot of the cliff. If Malcolm hadn't taken hold of a table umbrella, he surely would have been killed. Instead, he managed to float down to the water's edge by holding onto the umbrella and using it as a parachute. What a guy, eh?

From the beach below, the flames of the restaurant looked spectacular. There was a helicopter shining a light on the water coming from the fire hoses onto the blaze. It took Malcolm nearly an hour to climb back up the cliff. When he got to the top he saw Sharon sobbing in the Rex's arms. He wanted to go to her and ask her out on a second date, but wasn't sure how the whole dating protocol worked when the restaurant burns down on the first date. Anyway, she was in the arms of someone who could give her what she really needed. The locket that carried a picture of Sharon's son was still in his hand. Knowing too well that Sharon was better off with anyone but him, Malcolm threw the locket as hard as he could at the waiter's head. When it hit Rex in the ear and fell to the ground, Sharon heard it jingle and looked down to see what it was. She took it off the ground, looked at Rex, and held him tightly as she burst into tears. The waiter rubbed his ear and looked back towards the cliff, but Malcolm had already ducked out of sight.

At the edge of the cliff he sat and wondered how he managed to get so desperate and so far from home. The smell of burnt wood was all around him. Hundreds of yards below him, the glowing red embers gradually faded into blackness on the beach. For hours he watched each hot spot slowly disappear. Eventually exhaustion got the best of him and he dozed off.

Deep sleep took away the painful reality of his daily life and his dreams took him to the tropical beach that gave him so much comfort. His dream girl was sleeping next to him in his dream world. It was the first time he realized that the woman in his dreams was Sharon. As he watched her sleeping, he dreamt that he fell asleep. His dream sleep was interrupted and he woke up to find her leaning over him. Her cheeks were smudged with charcoal and her eyes were filled with tears of joy.

"Malcolm! You're okay! You're alive!" she said.

"No. I'm sleeping. I'm dead," he replied.

She laughed and sat back on the sand, "No! You're okay! We thought you got washed out to sea after the fire."

She looked across the ocean then fell on him and wrapped her arms around him. She tried to say something, but he couldn't understand her. Her words were muffled by the sound of a diesel engine. They both looked up to see the giant shovel of a back hoe quickly coming down on them. With an agonizing scream he woke up and felt a downpour of rain washing over him. He crawled under a large green sheet of charred corrugated fiberglass that had been used by the restaurant to shade the verandah. There he contemplated his worth.

It wasn't the worst thing in the world, losing the girl of his dreams to a perfect guy after saving both their lives, burning down his apartment, getting fired, living on the street, being rejected by gypsies, failing as a thief, surviving with no personality, dirty fingernails, and bad karma. It could have been much worse. Well, if the rain would have stopped falling, then things could have been worse. Golly and darn it! There was nothing funny about it. Malcolm was down in the dumps. The only way he knew to end the depression was to vanish into the Haze. Never so badly had he wanted to hide in the mists of alcoholic abandon, but he knew he would just come out of it and find himself in a worse situation.

Sitting on the edge of the high steep cliff, he seriously considered ending his pointless suffering with an act of suicide. He stood up on top of a jutting boulder and gazed down. The fall would be frightening and possibly very painful, but at least the pain would stop quickly ...unless, of course, he didn't die. If he didn't die he'd be in lots of pain, he would suffer. He might just end up lying in a heap of his own twisted broken bones for days screaming for morphine. What if some little kid found him down there dying or dead or advocating drug use? Terrible stuff! Malcolm didn't want anyone to find him or care about him, he didn't want to cause anyone else any pain.

In a gesture that was strangely symbolic of a new beginning, he turned around and began walking down the cliff. As he began the sharp descent, something hit him in the head causing him to trip and fall down twenty feet into a thorny patch of dusty dry chaparral. The object that hit him landed nearby ...and... It was a bottle of sleeping pills. He didn't give much thought to where the bottle came from, he just figured it must have been rolling around in the parking lot above him and the wind pushed it down the over the side.

Standing on the edge of the cliff with a full bottle of sleeping pills after losing the girl of dreams he again wondered if he should just end it all right then and there. Sleeping pills were generally painless and the only thing that would find his rotting carcass on the cliff's edge would be some kind of vulture or a coyote. No reason not to down the pills and croak. The only possible consideration was that he might not quite die. He might just end up in a coma for ninety years ...or wake up with brain damage and spend the rest of his life in a mental institution adamantly trying to explain to a brilliant team of psychologists that alligators don't have the gumption to make it as world class beekeepers.

He continued down the cliff's face. There was no trail, so he had to climb around large shrubs and weave his way between tenacious trees. Suddenly something hit him in the shins and he was tripped up again as he ducked under an acacia tree's limb. He stumbled and suddenly felt a rope tighten around his neck. It was some kind of noose. It pulled on his throat quickly as he fell and suddenly he was lifted off the ground. There was a quick snap and that was it. Malcolm's neck had broken a tree limb. As he loosened the rope, he thought it was very strange that someone would leave nooses (neese) just hanging around on high cliffs. Must have been some kind of suicide society that was working to help desperate people end their lives when cliff diving wasn't a reasonable option. All he had to do was find a stronger limb and hang himself. Then he'd be Dead-O. Easy as pie... but, Damn! Did you know that when people die they basically lose all sphincter control and subsequently poop in their pants (especially when the die by hanging). Malc didn't want his tombstone to say anything about dirty underwear so he pretty much gave up on the suicide thing completely.

The beach would have to wait. Climbing down the cliff was way more dangerous than he expected. He decided to go back to the top of the cliff and maybe hitchhike back into town. As he turned to walk back up the cliff, a shiny silver object whizzed past his ear. It was a Hari Kari knife, but it was also a sign from Destiny. He picked up the instrument of death, raised it over his head, looked at it with a final resolution, looked past it to the top of the cliff and saw two small heads looking down at him. One of those little heads had a white bandanna on it.

Slurp!

Gurgle!

Ooooo!

Malcolm was so mad at those guys. He ran up the cliff and saw the two brats driving away in his old Toyota. Those mechanically inclined little runts! They fixed it! Futile as it may have been, he chased them across the parking lot waving the Hari Kari knife like a vengeful Samurai.

"Malcolm!" shouted a voice.

He stopped.

"What did I tell you about running with knives!" yelled the familiar voice. "Now go back and walk before someone gets hurt." The voice belonged to Malcolm's self-proclaimed father.

"What are you doing here?" asked Malcolm.

His father replied cleverly, "Where there's smoke, there's my boy."

Calming down a little, Malcolm threw the knife at a passing rabbit and asked again, "No, really, what are you doing here?"

"Really! I heard about the fire last night and figured you were around here somewhere," said his phony father as he abruptly took the Hari Kari knife from an attacking bunny. "You need to settle down," he said to Malcolm and shook his head at the bunny.

"Well, those guys were trying to kill me," said Malcolm as he pointed to the distant little car that carried Slurp and Gurgle back down the road to Nowheresville.

"Looks like you were doing pretty good all by yourself," said his father. "Now I want you to go back to town and get yourself a job! Make me rich, damn it!"

"But..."

"No buts."

"Yes, sir. Do you want to come with me?"

The father walked towards the trail that traversed the cliff and replied to Malcolm, "No."

"Oh, okay," said Malcolm.

After watching his friend vanish over the side of the cliff, Malc started walking and hitchhiking down the long lonely road that led to a stupid city that hated him.

Six hours later, he made it back to Nowheresville.

XXIV

The temptation to drink was overwhelming and he met his ultimate downfall that afternoon when he found a ten dollar bill lying in the gutter. He went out and bought a case of cheap beer. Not many people could put away 24 beers in a single sitting, Malcolm was no exception, but he put a damn good dent in it. 24 cans of cheap beer on the wall, twenty four cans of cheap beer, you take one down, pound it and then you pound ten more. An hour later he wasn't feeling any pain. With his coat pockets filled with enough cans of beer to make plenty of new low-life friends, he wandered around downtown Nowheresville.

The streets carried an eerie warmth. People didn't stand under the streetlights, they floated in a Brownian motion. They wallowed in a hazy dim presence that intercepted their thoughts and actions and turned their intentions into vain muted attempts at injecting purpose into pointless existence. Finally, Malcolm was at home. He could admit that he was no better than anyone else on the street and no one was better than him. They all suffered from and shared the same destiny. At that moment his actions were as meaningless as any meaningless action had ever been.

He could do anything, and it would be meaningless. He believed he could be anyone. Alcohol was swirling and twisting his imagination, injecting omnipotence into its victim. With nothing left in life, victims love to feel superior and create their own little world where they are supreme, even if it's just for a short time.

Of course, the whole concept of omnipotence is a fantasy that no rational being could seriously entertain. Imagine two omnipotent people at a cocktail party.

"Can I get you a drink?" an omnipotent one would say.

"No, thanks, if I wanted you to get me a drink, you'd get me a drink," the other would reply.

"Not if I didn't want to get you a drink..."

"If that were the case, I'd already have a drink."

"But it wouldn't have been one that I gave you."

"Not if I didn't want you not to."
"What? I don't understand."
"Then you can't be omniscient! Ha!"

Consequently the monotheistic theories gain credence, but the drawback there is that a single god would never be caught dead a cocktail party. What would a god wear to a cocktail party? Would it be subject to criticism? And if a god can't figure out what to wear at a cocktail party without being criticized then the god cannot be omnipotent, and consequently can't be a god. It all boils down to the impossibility of omnipotence and shall hereforetonow be remembered as the Cocktail Party Theory on the Non-Likelihood of an Omnipotent Being, and Grill.

Metaphysics behind him, Malcolm was free to mingle with the street people and transcend the mediocrity of individual omnipotence by ascending into collective power. He wandered along the streets of Nowheresville as a powerful non-god. That's how he introduced himself to everyone he met. Not only to the people he met, but also to every animal, every lamppost, every building, and he finally fell asleep introducing himself to each star in the sky.

The next morning he woke up with a plan. There it was. Just standing there on the corner of Roost and Fragen. First Dibs Rural Metropolitan Bank. The tenth largest bank in the city. Every day, big men with expensive looking suits and unspeakable fetishes waltzed into the bank humming to the sounds of Wall Street ticker tape machines while they quietly conspired on how to steal the next guy's money. Aspiring business women with uncomfortably tight skirts and socially acceptable fetishes made appointments with other aspiring business women to discuss the shape of the world. Nothing ever got done, and lots of money was made ...more money perhaps than they knew what to do with, but Malcolm knew what to do with it, he had a plan.

The first step in successful bank robbery was to know the bank inside and out. A well trained crook would know all the tellers' schedules, all the entrances, where the cash was kept, everything down to the last intimate detail had to be deeply ingrained in the robber's head. Malcolm's head was an empty canvas. His first course in his underworld education of major bank heists was to figure out where the front door was.

Of course, as a criminal, he couldn't just walk into to the bank and ask for directions to the front door. For you amateurs, that would be considered a "suspicious tip-off." No, no. Much more practical is the covert surveillance that makes for so many overrated action movies. Malcolm Tent waited nonchalantly four blocks from the bank, thinking in code so as not to create a "suspicious tip-off." Then, when he least expected it, he dove into a storm drain and fell quietly, but painfully down below the street. It was a brilliantly executed maneuver that drew little or no suspicion from the crowd standing beside the subterranean entrance. Malcolm Tent was under the city streets, exactly where he wanted to be.

After several hours of feverishly bumping into walls and opening manholes all around town, he finally found the manhole in front of the bank. He peeked at the bank from under a manhole cover and caught glimpses of the front door as cars moved in and out of his line of vision. The possibility of a car hitting the manhole suddenly crossed his mind, so he dropped the cover above his head and sank down. The odds really weren't too good when you considered that the opening was in the center of the street. A car would have to swerve across the center dividing line to actually hit the manhole cover. Given the slim chance of disaster, Malcolm cautiously lifted the heavy metal plate again. He held it up for several minutes before peeking out. There were no problems. Lots of cars went by, but none were even coming close to the manhole. What dopes. Malcolm had a clear shot of the bank. There was a guard near the front door who held the door for people on their way out and there was a steady flow of customers. Suddenly he heard the rumbling of a diesel truck. He looked down the street and saw someone down the street looking at him from beneath another manhole cover. The voyeur looked startled and quickly dropped below the street. Malcolm realized the truck was coming up behind him and felt pretty confident that he was in serious danger as the manhole slammed into his head and launched him straight down to the bottom of the storm drain.

He woke up several hours later with a severe headache and an extraordinary lump on his head. It was very late in the day so Malcolm didn't see much point in scoping out the bank from such a dangerous vantage point any longer. He returned to the surface to find a nicer, gentler lookout.

The next 3 weeks were spent studying the bank, watching it for days on end from an abandoned outhouse in a vacant lot across the street. Finally, after figuring out the exact pattern of bank deliveries, employee schedules, and police patrols, Malcolm knew it was time to make his move. It was six o'clock on a Wednesday morning. The police stopped for doughnuts at the coffee shop next door to the bank at 5:30 every morning. That day was no different. By 5:50 a.m. about 13 coppers had finished their breakfast and were on their way back to their rigs (cop talk). One said to another, "See ya later," and the other laughed. It was cryptic, but not that cryptic. They wouldn't see each other again for quite a while. The bank wasn't going to open until 8:30 a.m. By Malcolm's calculations he had exactly five hours and twenty-two minutes to complete his criminal activity.

There it was, just waiting to be ripped off. The moment Malcolm had been dreaming of for nearly a month was close at hand. Casually, he walked towards the front of the bank, never letting on that he had a dangerous weapon in his pocket. The security lights in the bank were still on, and Malcolm had to wait for the right moment. It was close enough. He looked up and down the street, over his shoulder, and under his shoes. It was safe. He drew a heavy duty rubber band from his hip pocket, held it up to the headline of the bank's newspaper that was lying on the sidewalk on the bank's front steps, grabbed the paper and ran.

For twenty blocks he made a mad dash. He ran as fast as he could, faster than the wind, faster than humanly possible, never looking back. Well out of harm's way, he leaped into a door stoop and slowly looked back. As he turned, he found himself staring face to face with a four foot tall boy scout.

"Hey, mister, you dropped this pen when you picked up your paper," said the scout.

Looking away from the good deed doer dude, Malcolm muttered, "No, no. I think you must have confused me with someone else. I can't write. Illiterate, y'know."

The scout squared his shoulders and insisted, "It's yours. I saw you drop it."

Malcolm needed to get rid of the kid so he went along with it, "Okay..."

"Five bucks, mister." The child held out his sweaty little sugar coated hand. Malcolm gave him a five dollar bill and the little social squid skipped off, scouring the streets for other victims of insignificant misfortune. Finding none, the lad shoved an old lady into a crosswalk where she was nearly hit by a newspaper delivery truck.

Malcolm opened the pages, looked into his stolen paper and laughed maniacally. Finally, he had access to the information the rich guys had. Everything they needed to know about the world of high finance was in that paper. It was his opportunity to get into the rich man's head. He glanced through the daily and saw what he was looking for. First Dibs had free checking for one year with all new accounts. That's what he was after. He sat and thought about how he'd use the information to his advantage. Then he felt guilty and doubted his motives. He couldn't take it anymore. Wrought with regrets, he refolded the newspaper and tried to return it.

Outside the bank, a crowd of onlookers went back about their business as a sad young scout was escorted in handcuffs to a police car. Malcolm covered his mouth and pointed his pen at the boy, and the little scout snarled back before hitting his head on the door frame of the cop car. When the crowd finally vanished, Malcolm casually returned the folded newspaper to the front door of the bank.

That poor kid got hauled off for Malcolm's wrong doing. It was kind of funny, but it wasn't fair. If someone was going to be punished, then a serious crime needed to be committed. No more of these gag crimes. With a renewed sense of criminal justice, Malcolm decided to go ahead and open up a free checking account. He walked into the bank and pretended that he didn't know anything. He went to an information desk and sat down. Within twenty minutes a young lady sat down to assist him.

"Good morning, sir. How can I help you?" asked the polite assistant.

"I'd like to open a free checking account," said Malcolm.

The assistant smiled, "Certainly, and where did you hear about our offer?"

"Um, a, uh, guy in jail told me about it," said the quick thinker.

"Oh... Well, I guess he's still entitled to a commission. We'll get to that later. First we need some more information. Do you have any other accounts here?" she asked with a nauseating, yet tantalizing perkiness.

"Oh, no. I wouldn't dream of it," he said, overdoing the precautious thing a little.

"Okay. Could I see some identification, please?"

"Yeah, sure, here's my driver's license."

"Yes, and we need two forms of ID."

"I actually have 2 driver's licenses, and I have a gas card ...and I could probably steal a credit card, if I really need to have good credit."

"No sir, we need to be sure you are who you say you are. We need to see the name on your underwear," the assistant said as she licked her lips.

That was it. They were onto him. "My underwear? Oh. I, uh, I left them out in the car. I'll be right back." He just lied. The criminal element was hardening inside him by the second. Nervously, on tip toes, he tried to leave the bank, but he couldn't. He was petrified by fear and absurdity.

As he wobbled and groaned in his feeble escape, an attractive teller flashed him a knowing smile.

"Thank you for calling First Dibs," she said as she answered a phone call.

He'd seen her before, but as hard as he tried, he couldn't remember where or when. He thought, and thought, and... he thought. All that recollectin' rocked his noggin enough for him to figure out why he couldn't make a clean getaway. He was chewing bubble gum and walking at the same time. Yup, he spit out his gum so he could focus on walking and stepped effectively out of the bank. It was the first major phase of his master plan: casing the joint from the inside. That was truly the point of no return for Malcolm Tent. The fact that he had absolutely no sense of direction beyond that point didn't concern him in the least.

Then, as if by some divine intervention, Malcolm remembered where he'd seen the teller. She was the girl in the restaurant, the drug dealer's girlfriend, Matilda! It was a sign! The Eternal God of the Big Bank Heists was telling him that fate led him to First Dibs Rural Metropolitan Bank. Uncertain if the sign meant that he should rob the bank or avoid it, he walked across the street and sat at a corner bus stop where he waited for further instructions from the devious deity. On the bench was an abandoned newspaper with the emblazoned headline, "First Dibs Rural Metropolitan Bank to Replace Faulty Alarm System Pretty Soon." An old friend, Rob, came by and talked with him about the national collapse of banks and S&L's and how anyone could run our financial institutions more efficiently that the modern banker. Lightning struck the bank several times. Finally, he tossed a coin to make up his mind, but a passing condor swooped down and swallowed it. That did it. He had to rob the bank if only to get another dime.

XXV

During the next week, Malcolm went back into the bank several times to get into the hang of robbing it. He was working his way up to the big money by stealing deposit slips, credit card applications, spare paper clips, pens with chains, and a few brief attempts at taking pens with chains with desks attached. All his practice paid off. Not only had he gained the confidence he needed to enter the bank and steal things, but he also made about twenty bucks selling off used rubber bands.

Malcolm was finally ready to rob the bank. It was a Tuesday morning and the weather was nice, the streets were dry, and nobody suspected a thing. Oh, no they didn't. Heh heh heh. After pacing in front of the guard for two hours, inconspicuously, he went into the bank and casually approached Matilda's teller window. There was already a customer standing at her counter, so Malcolm waited in line, just like a pro. The other customer was Matilda's sleazy boyfriend, Jimmy Shwirl. Without attracting too much attention, Malcolm listened to their conversation.

"You gotta take off early. Just tell your boss your mother's sick," said the tacky drug dealer.

Matilda was angry, like a hungry parakeet, "Last time you wanted me to leave I had to tell them I was attending my mother's funeral. I don't think they'll buy the sick mother routine this time. I'm tired of this. You can't come in here and treat me like dirt and make me play all kinds of games with your money. It's not worth it. What are you running away from now?"

"Trust me. We gotta leave town for a few days... I promise this is the last time. We'll go some place nice. We'll go to the beach. We can stay at Rick's place. You like the beach. We just gotta get outta here now," the drug dealer looked back and saw Malcolm.

Matilda shook her head, "I can't. Tammy and Jill are out today. They'll never let me go."

Shwirl slammed his fist on the counter then rubbed his forehead. "I suckered some punks in the Marina. If they find me, they're gonna want their money or their merchandise and my throat, so I gotta get outta here. They're small time and they're leaving town on Sunday. They won't come back... They don't know the territory. They won't be back."

"So go!" said Matilda. She looked over her shoulder to make sure her overly interested employers weren't eavesdropping.

Holding back his anger, the drug dealer tapped his knuckles on the window. "I can't take my car. I got too many warrants and I'm holding. If I get pulled over it's gonna be for at least five years," he said and looked back at Malcolm again.

"You're holding?" she asked in disbelief. "You have drugs with you right now?"

The dealer opened his jacket to expose two large plastic packages of cocaine and smiled a cheesy smile.

"Are you high, too?"

Shwirl nodded his head and grinned.

Taking a step back, Matilda stared at the drug dealer with hatred. She spoke softly and firmly, "Get your ass out of here... and I don't want to see you ever again."

Laughing quietly, Shwirl turned around and told Malcolm, "This line is closed, dude, go stand in the next line."

"What!" Malcolm shouted, "The lines closed!? My goodness, the line's closed, and you're the last person to get any help in this line! This must be your lucky day! Hey, everybody!..."

"Dude, chill," he said as he gestured for Malcolm to keep it down.

"I'm sorry, sir," Matilda said to Malcolm, "I'll be with you in a moment."

The drug dealer looked at Matilda and said, "I'll be outside. If you're not out there in ten minutes I'm coming back in and I'm telling your little boss about all the assistance you've given me with my personal accounts." He looked at Matilda and pointed to his watch then walked past Malcolm giving him the old evil eye. "Penny ante job, penny ante bitch," he mumbled as he walked away.

As Malcolm proceeded to the counter, Matilda was rubbing her temples, her eyes were red.

"I'm sorry about the inconvenience, sir," she said, "How can I help you?"

Malcolm looked around briefly, "I'm sorry you're having a bad day. Do you remember me?"

She forced a smile, "Look, sir, I hate to sound rude, but if this is a come on, the timing couldn't be worse."

Malcolm dropped his head and put his hand on a gun his pocket, "Well, it's not a come on, it's a hold... hold... could you hold my place in line? I need to go back out to my car for a second."

"Oh yeah," Matilda perked up a little, "You're the guy from the restaurant! I'll hold your place. Just hurry back, okay?" she said with a smile and began organizing her counter.

Before Malcolm stepped away, the gravity of his plans finally dawned on him, "Look, I've actually got to get out of here. I've got some very important things to do, and I got to get started right now. I'm so sorry."

Slightly amused, Matilda asked, "What's so important?"

Malcolm was embarrassed but also a little relieved. He tried to explain, "I need to straighten out my life... I need to get a job and an apartment, and I need to stop looking for an easy way out. Then I'm going to open a great big checking account... at your window."

Matilda laughed, "You're serious?"

Malcolm smiled and nodded as he began to walk away.

"Well," she said, "I'm kind of in the same boat."

Malcolm stopped for a second. Matilda said, "I'm going to have dinner tonight at your restaurant. What are my chances of comparing notes on a new life with you over dessert?"

Stupid Malcolm was hesitant, "I don't think so, nope, not for me, thanks. No way. Unh uh... Oh, okay, but I need to get an apartment so I can I invite you over to have coffee and cheese."

Matilda smiled coyly, very very coyly, too coyly? She said, "Well, I have a spare room if you can't find anything suitable in the next three hours. I also run into a lot of local merchants and if you need a job I might be able to help out with some connections."

Something was very suspicious about the girl. Malcolm looked closely for a halo around her head, but saw only beautiful flowing blond hair.

"I'll see you tonight," he said as he walked towards the door.

Walked. He floated to the door, he glided to the door, he wafted to the door only to be barreled over by some maniac toting a sawed-off shotgun. It was the girl's drug dealing boyfriend. As Malcolm fell to the floor, his gun fell out of his jacket and slid out of reach.

"Nobody move!" shouted Shwirl.

Ashamed of his clumsiness, Malcolm crawled across the floor and picked his gun up to hide it. The drug dealer saw the gun, let out a shrill scream and ran out the door crying. Before anyone knew what was going on, Jimmy Shwirl was gone and Malcolm Tent was standing in the doorway holding a gun, looking somewhat unprepared for everything. The security guard, Clem, had been waiting years for this moment. It was a true bank robbery, with lots of guns and bad guys and awkward moments of bravery, confusion, and lust. Reaching into his holster (as he did every morning in front of his bathroom mirror), Clem drew his gun with the well honed skills of a Spaghetti Western gun slinging aficionado. And, like a true Spaghetti Western outtake, the gun flew out his hand, hit the floor, and fired a round at the vault wall before sliding to Malcolm's feet. The gunshot ricocheted off the lens cap of the security camera and nicked Malcolm's shoulder. Ye-ouch! His adopted father's magic charley horse was telling him to stop the robbery, but, no way!

Wounded, but tough, bleeding, but coagulating, punished, but deserving worse, he decided to make the best of a bad situation and continued his bank robbing odyssey. With a strange new conviction, he barked out, "All right, nobody move! We don't want me more not want to hurt! Iiii... I don't hurt not nobody, now, move!"

The customers stared at him with deep confusion.

Standing there, more posing, in his dirty jeans and rough shave, he looked pretty good for a bank robber. He saw his reflection in a mirrored wall and thought he looked good. Finally, for the first time in his life, he was starting to feel good about himself. There's something very satisfying about a first brush with self confidence. Suddenly self-empowered, he commanded, "I, I just want all the money in the vault, then I'm outta here. So no tricks! Now where's the vault?"

Everyone in the bank continued to stare. Everyone, except Matilda, she motioned with her eyes to a wall behind the teller aisle.

"I know exactly where it is!" he yelled to the general public. "You!" he pointed to Matilda, "Get me your emergency bank robbery procedure manual."

Timidly, she said, "It's just the standard bank robbery procedure manual, but I..."

"That'll do," said Malcolm with a patronizing air, like a jerk.

He calmly took the manual from Matilda and began to read. The manual was well written, better than most books. It had the appropriate blend of important information, useless information, and snottiness that eludes so many manuals of lower quality. The instructions clearly stated, *"Emergency alarm buttons are located on the underside of the teller counter directly in front of each teller window and under each desk on the right side below the center drawer."*

Malcolm shouted to the bank employees, "Back away from the counter and get away from your desks!"

The manual continued, *"Take in as many distinguishing details about the robber as possible; hair, weight, height, clothing, jewelry, tattoos, goiters, etc."*

Quickly surveying the bank personnel and patrons, Malcolm screamed, "All right, I want everybody to look at their shoes! Don't stop looking at your shoes! I'm just a short fat Chinese guy and I'm not wearing any clothes."

The customers looked at him, most of them were snickering.

"I said look at your shoes!" he demanded.

The snickers suddenly turned to chuckles (incredible metamorphosis). Bankers and bankees alike looked down at their shoes and generally began laughing.

"Stop laughing," he yelled and waved his weapon, accidentally discharging it at the ceiling. Then he went back to reading the manual, *"Above all, you must cooperate with the bank robber."*

Terrified, he yelled, "Everyone, stop cooperating! Nobody do what I say!"

Immediately, the customers went back about their normal business.

Malcolm pointed his gun at the guard and at Matilda, "Get in the vault, both of you."

They went, he followed.

Once in the vault, Malcolm decided to put together a plan. Examining the vault's contents, he saw stacks of money, bags of coins, coffee supplies, and Grandma Smith's secret lumpy turkey gravy recipe. He forced the guard and Matilda to stand in the corner of the vault. It went something like, "Stand in the corner, okay?" and they did. Probably not the most pivotal moment in criminal history, but only three people had to endure it.

Like a kangaroo with kleptomania, Malcolm began stuffing his shirt and pants with cash and coins. Matilda and Clem, the guard, watched him nervously. Malcolm looked uncomfortable. He was uncomfortable. Try walking around with 20 pounds of nickels in your underwear! It's really uncomfortable.

In his special secret holster, Clem packed a little derringer. His hand was poised and ready to retrieve his backup gun at the first opportunity. For a moment, Malcolm looked away. The guard grabbed for the gun, but to his embarrassment he found that the strap on his holster was fastened and he couldn't get it out. Malcolm didn't notice.

"How much do you think I got so far?" he asked Matilda.

"A lot," she said, feigning enthusiasm.

"Not enough," he said as he continued to stuff his pockets and socks with cash.

During all that crazy confusion, the guard loosened his holster's strap. Noticing the guard's actions, Matilda shook her head to persuade him not to do anything stupid. She asked Malcolm, "Do you have a plan here? ...or did you just blow in off the highway?"

Frothing maniacally, Malcolm replied, "I've got a plan all right, I've got a big plan!"

"You are the guy from the restaurant, right? You are who I think you are, aren't you?" Matilda asked.

It was one of those stupid mind reading questions, but he answered it anyway, "No, actually I'm from out of town."

Rolling her eyes, she answered herself, "Yeah, we met in that restaurant!"

Malc had the jitters, "No, I don't eat... in restaurants."

"You seemed like a really nice guy," she confided, "Why would you want to rob banks?"

"Hey, I'm no nice guy. If I was a nice guy would I be able to do this?" he said as he took off his broken wristwatch and smashed it against the floor.

"You might," she admitted.

"Okay, would I do this?" asked Malcolm as he took the guard's wristwatch and smashed it against the floor. The guard writhed in frustration.

Shrugging her shoulders, Matilda said, "You just might."

In a final act of desperation he took Matilda's watch from her wrist and raised it over his head. "There isn't a nice guy alive who'd do this!" he shouted as Matilda stepped back in fear. With all his might, Malcolm set the watch carefully on the floor and confessed, "I am a nice guy. I can't help it. I'm on a mission to wipe out poverty and social injustice in the Western hemisphere by invading the financial strongholds of the oppressors and distributing their holdings equally among the oppressed. It's a revolutionary concept that just might make me famous."

"You, and Karl Marx, and Robin Hood," said Matilda, nonchalantly.

Malcolm balked, "No, it's my idea. All mine."

"Where'd you get it?" she dared him to answer.

"I wanted to help a homeless man... So, I'm going to get a million dollars and give it to him so he can finally, um, retire?"

"You're robbing this bank for a bum?"

Malcolm grimaced, "Well, when you say it like that, it sounds stupid."

"Oh, you're helping a bum by robbing a bank," she rephrased more intelligently.

"I'm doing it for my father."

"Your father's a bum?"

"No," replied Malcolm, humbly.

"He's sick and insane? You're following in his footsteps?" she teased.

"I'm robbing the bank for an old black man who told me he was my father."

"Well, good, I was worried that this was just some crazy act of random violence."

"Look, I'm helping out..."

"That's enough, just rob the damn bank and get out of here."

"Hey. I was on my way out of here until your stupid boyfriend came into the bank and got in my way. He's the one who had a gun drawn. He started it."

Matilda rolled her eyes, "Right. I... oh, who cares? Just finish your robbery and go, please."

Watching the whole enchanting conversation, the guard snickered and almost completely forgot about shooting Malcolm.

"Actually," said Malcolm, "I'm kind of new at this. I was wondering if maybe you could give me some advice?"

"You expect me to help you rob my employer?"

"I assume you've been robbed before so I figured at least one of us has some know-how."

"Forget it. You're on your own."

"I've got a gun, y'know."

The guard, still quietly standing in the corner, moved his hand towards his pistol.

"And what? You need me to show you how to shoot it?" Matilda asked Malcolm.

The guard chuckled, "Heh heh heh."

"Look Bozo," said Malcolm as he aimed his gun towards the guard's head.

The guard grabbed his hidden gun and pulled it from his holster. It flew out of his hand, hit the roof, fired, fell to the floor, and fired again.

Outside the vault, the bank manager was relaying a conversation to the police via his secretary, "Marla! Tell them we just heard two shots go off in the vault."

"We just heard two shots go off in the vault," said the secretary. She listened for a second then spoke, "How many sausages are in the vault? ...What? Oh. How many *hostages*, are in the vault?"

"Just two," said the manager, Mr. Grimeldiano.

"Just two," she echoed to the cops then forwarded the next question, "...Who were they?"

"The guard and a teller," said the management man.

The secretary conveyed, "Our best teller, and our guard, Clem, who's an ass." She paused momentarily then spoke to the manager, "Can you? See, them!"

The manager gave her a sour expression as he said, "No, no, no, the vault's around the corner and they're in it. What do you think, I've got X-ray eyes?"

"Only X-Rayman has X-ray eyes," smiled the secretary, "He'd look at you and see your fuzzy underwear!"

"Just tell them the bank robber is out of sight," Mr. Grimeldiano said.

"The bank robber is out of sight... Yes... Yes, he's groovy," she giggled. "Huh? ...No. What's *your* name? ...Marla ...Uh huh," she looked over her shoulder, "I gotta go my boss is watching... Okay," she said and hung up the phone.

Her boss looked down at her disdainfully and the phone rang. "Thank you for calling First Dibs, how may I direct your call?" Marla answered, "...Oh, hi! It's the police! Is Ernie there? ...Oh, Hi! ...Okay. Just a second," she covered the mouthpiece with her hand and asked her boss, "Are you in?"

"Who is it?" the manager asked.

"It's the police," she whispered.

"I'm not in," he whispered back.

"He's not in right now, can I take a message? Hello? ...Oh, hi... Yes... Okay," she said and looked out the front window of the bank to see the police chief waving to her from behind his police car. She somehow gave the cops a backwards wave of her hand as she spoke into the phone, "Wow, you guy's are good," then turned to her boss, "I think you just got majorly busted."

He looked out the window and grimaced, "Oh, all right," and took the phone, "Well it looks like we've got a situation here. We've got at least one perk cornered in the vault and another perk got away before we could collar him... Yes, at least two perks... Perp? ...Yes, perpetrator... No, I said perp. And I'm just about to go in there and kick some perp butt! ...Hmm? ...Well, if you think so. But I want you to know that I'm not afraid of these punks. They're only lucky they've got you around to protect them... No... No... They haven't demanded anything... Well, I suppose I could do that... Yes, I'll be right at it... Well, could I have your phone number just in case...? Okay," he addressed secretary, "Marla, take down this number... Okay, go ahead... 5-5-5... Is that all? ...Oh, yes of course, we wouldn't want that to happen. All right, if anything goes wrong, we know how to get in touch. Mwuh!" And he hung up the phone.

"Marla, go ask the bank robbers what they want... And bring me back a cup of coffee."

Marla scurried off to the back room. The infamous Malcolm was standing outside the vault explaining to Matilda how one act of kindness can provoke multiple acts of kindness and progressively snowball into entire societies of selfless generous people and finally materialize in the form of international peace, happiness, and great deals on used military equipment.

Marla turned the corner, Matilda turned flush, Malcolm thought of the tern he'd seen on the beach and shouted, "Hey, what are you doing here?"

Marla stopped and smiled, "I'm getting some coffee. Do you guys want anything?"

Squinting his eyes and speaking with a gravely voice, Malcolm asked, "How do we know you're not a spy? I could easily take you hostage. How do you know we'll tell you what you want to know?"

"I think we have some decaff," peeped Marla.

Matilda grinned, "Ooo, Marla, can I have some of that French mocha?"

"Okay," Marla bubbled.

"I'll take mine black," said Malcolm.

"I'll be right back," said Marla as she happily skipped away and went back to her boss.

Mr. Grimeldiano was waiting, trying to make cowboy facial expressions, wondering if the cameras were getting his good side, then wondering if the cameras would make his butt look fat.

"Matilda wants mocha, the bank robber wants black, and Clem's an ass," Marla explained to the big boss.

The bank manager rubbed his chin, "So they wanna play hardball."

All observers witnessed an awesome dramatic pause.

"I'll show them hardball like they've never seen before. Get them both decaff," the manager said with frightful resolve.

Marla's jaw dropped, "But..."

"Okay, okay, don't do anything until we hear from the cops. And get me the cops on the phone."

Marla dutifully called the police and conveyed the bank robber's demands. The cops told her to cooperate with all their coffee requests, but to push back on any doughnut demands. It was touch and go during the whole conversation.

There was nothing Malcolm wouldn't do to get out of his potentially deadly predicament. He began to close the vault door so he could think without any more distractions.

"What are you doing?" shouted Matilda.

"We'll suffocate!" added the guard.

"Is suffocation worse than drowning?" asked Malcolm.

After a long arduous discussion on the differences between suffocating in a bank vault and drowning in a shallow puddle, the guard punched Malcolm in the stomach. Malcolm doubled over.

"Damn," shouted Malcolm.

The guard stepped back and looked down at Malcolm with a sense of great power. Malcolm reached into a bag below him and pulled out a roll of quarters, then used it to smack the guard in the jaw. The guard fell to the floor.

"He is evil," said Malcolm as he looked over to Matilda who wasn't quite sure what to make out of the unbridled macho expo. "I am good," concluded the lad with a big old smile.

Matilda stepped towards Malcolm with an expression of rage, Malcolm kissed her.

"Now what'd you do that for?" demanded the vixen.

"Dropped your guard," he replied, slyly.

Matilda squinted at Malcolm and laughed, "You must have been waiting to say that for a long time."

"Yeah, it's always been kind of a dream of mine."

"So are you done now, or are you still planning to rob the place?"

"Well, as long as I'm here..."

"You're kinda sick, aren't you?"

"No he is sick," said Malcolm, pointing to the guard. "I am healthy."

"If you're so healthy, why don't you just get a job and stop hassling people?"

"I had a job, once, nearly killed a man. That's when I promised myself I'd never work again. No, ma'am, I've seen the working world, I've seen the ugly side of it, the dirty side. It's way too yucky for me."

Matilda smirked, "I'm hungry."

She looked at Malcolm for a response or some sense of consciousness.

Focusing on a nail in the wall, Clem rubbed his jaw and cleverly produced a stick of beef jerky from his hip pocket without even looking. Clem's talent was Malcolm's shortcoming. Malcolm had no jerky in his hip pocket.

"Y'know? I'm hungry too," admitted Malcolm, "I'm kind of in the mood for pizza. Think they'll deliver?"

In a move that seemed a little overly rehearsed, Clem pulled his Elasto-Man lunchbox off the bottom shelf of a rack in the back of the vault. From the lunchbox, he removed a sandwich. From the sandwich, he removed a slice of bologna. Clem took the meat slice and flung it at the ceiling, where it stuck for a second, then fell to the floor with a soft slap. Then he sat on the floor and laughed like a little kid.

Malcolm and Matilda were astonished. The only food in the whole bank and he wasted it.

"How could you do that? We're in here starving and you're throwing around sandwich meat like there's no tomorrow!" yelled Malcolm.

Clem leaned back with his arms crossed over his chest and smiled, "I know you're holding the gun, but I want you to know who's holding the real power. There's more where that came from. If you don't play your cards right, all they'll find of you will be skin and bones. Work with me and I'll keep you both fat and happy."

Malcolm looked at the guard, then at the lunchbox. "Oh, that's just baloney!"

"So, Clem," Matilda prodded, "Why is it that a single guy like you has worked in this bank for over two years, surrounded by young eligible women..."

"Bachelorettes," interjected Malcolm.

"...and never made a pass at anyone," finished Matilda.

"He is gay. I am straight," said Malcolm as he raised his eyebrows repeatedly at Matilda.

Grabbing Malcolm's ear and twisting it, Matilda chastised him and made him apologize for judging anyone for anything. Malcolm apologized, then tried to kiss Matilda.

The guard sat up and leaned back against the vault door, "I'm not gay, you ninny. I just don't see any point in getting all worked up about someone who's got the same physical qualities as my mommy."

Malcolm's writhing brow seethed!

"It's not your mother you're looking at!" he exclaimed as he glanced over at Matilda's freshly shaven legs. "Besides, your mother shipped you off in cardboard carton with eleven of your unhatched siblings. You never even met her!"

Suddenly Clem's eyes welled up and he began speaking in a very soft voice, "My mommy loved me a lot. She never would 'o shipped me off in a carton. You better take it back." He searched frantically for his company issued zip gun.

In the light of dim wits, Malcolm too searched the premises for the elusive weapon but couldn't get his eyes past Matilda. She was the most dazzling vision of beauty and tension he had ever seen ...since Sharon. Regardless of her captivating presence, Malcolm Tent had to find that gun, he just had to. If the bumbling guard got a hold of it, Matilda would probably get shot and the guilt would be unbearable, just unbearable. With sweaty, catlike movements, he rolled around on the vault floor looking for the gun.

As she watched the two buffoons grapple for that long piece of steel machismo (easily obtained at the corner gun store by anyone with a little spare cash and a short ego), Matilda wondered what the world would be like if there were no guns, if there was no need to cheat and steal to acquire self esteem. She wondered about world peace and democracy at all costs. She wondered why the stars fell down from the sky every time, she walked by, then she looked over at Malcolm and noticed that he was moving closer to her with a goofy gangly look on his face. Her finger slowly caressed the trigger of the gun beneath her thigh.

That's right. She was sitting on the gun. She didn't care that the bank was being robbed. You might think that a bank teller's life is an exciting rewarding fun filled experience, while in reality it's just a job and the teller's day is mostly dictated by some stupid sadistic biscuit who's always in the process of getting a divorce and liposuction while her whiny anal retentive assistant runs around spreading stupid rumors about who's on who's you-know-what list. Deep down, Matilda was kind of disgruntled and secretly hoped that a bank robber would come in and shoot one of her nemeses in the foot.

Pulling the gun out as she stood up, Matilda quickly pointed it at the cop and the robber and said quietly, "If either one of you tries anything cute I'll turn you both into a cheap paint job for the vault."

Mesmerized by the spontaneity of her cliché, Malcolm gazed into Matilda's eyes and asked, "When you say cute..."

In an attempt to keep the goofball from getting overly mesmerized, Matilda fired a round just above Malcolm's head. "That's what I mean." Then, suddenly and without warning, Matilda held the zip gun to her chest and tilted her head and smiled. Then she put it near her mouth. "Which looks better?" she asked.

"I think both poses are provocative, yet they retain that... oh, how do you say, visceral and tasteful essence that's launched so many young ladies to stardom and, later, prison," Malcolm confided.

Clem whined, "My mommy would 'o never shipped me off."

Matilda smiled and nodded, then placed the barrel of the gun between her eyes and stumbled out of the vault.

"Matilda! What are you doing?" shouted her annoying boss.

Looking to Malcolm for a suggestion, Matilda got lucky as he shouted, "She's been hypnotized! I am a master hypnotist. All I have to do is say the magic word and she'll pull the trigger. So..."

Oglette interrupted, "I bet the magic word's 'abracadabra.' Right? It always is."

"No!" yelled Malcolm as Matilda gave Oglette a dirty look, "Now I want everybody to shut up for a minute."

"Hocus pocus? ...Shazam?" persisted Oglette.

Quickly, Matilda pointed the gun at Oglette. Oglette's panties were suddenly moist to the touch and she stopped talking.

"Now listen," said Malcolm, "I don't..."

"Alah kazam!", "Voila!", "Rumplestiltskin!" and several other popular magic words were volleyed out by various bank employees. As Oglette began shivering fiercely, Matilda rolled her eyes and smirked a little as she pointed the gun back to herself.

That was enough funny business for Malcolm. He took the gun from Matilda and shot a hole in the roof to get everyone's attention. "Now who's got a cellular phone?" he shouted.

One of the more sophisticated people in the bank raised her hand and pulled out a small portable phone.

"Cool," said Malcolm, "Can I borrow it?"

She smiled and held it out to him. He... took it!

"Okay, now who's the most important person in the bank?" he asked.

Everyone nodded and pointed at him with big phony smiles.

"No, no, no. Who signs your paychecks?" Everyone put on bigger phony smiles and pointed to a large man sitting behind his desk pointing to himself.

"What do you do?" Malcolm asked the big man.

"Why... I'm the manager," said Mr. Grimeldiano.

"Yeah, but what do you do?" asked one of the tellers.

Raising his bushy eyebrows with indignation, the manager thought for a moment and frowned, "Why... I wear real nice suits. I think you have to feel good about the way you look so that other people..."

Malcolm held up his hand and motioned for him to stop, "Okay, I want you to go back into the vault."

Grimeldiano protested, "But I'm negotiating with the police."

"You are? Really?" asked Malcolm, knowing that someone ought to be.

"Yes!" bellowed the big boss.

"Okay then, I'll take her as my new hostage," said Malcolm, pointing to Oglette.

Putting on the expression of a pregnant virgin, Oglette acted like the last person on earth who could pass for a hostage, but Malcolm directed her to the vault anyway.

"You too," said Malcolm to the guard. The guard made a sour face and walked to the vault. Matilda and Malcolm followed them.

Inside the vault, Malcolm stopped and thought for a minute, then he put the gun to the guard's head. "Kiss her," he said.

The guard looked at the gun, "What?"

"Kiss her!" Malcolm repeated.

The guard looked at Oglette then looked at Matilda, smiled, and moved towards Matilda.

"Not her!" said Malcolm, "Her!" as he pointed to Oglette.

Clem looked at the gun again, then went to Oglette and gave her a peck on the lips.

"Use your tongue!" Malcolm demanded.

Hesitantly, Clem kissed her again with a long meaningful smooch.

Oglette gagged, "You weren't very good."

"Shut up," said Clem.

"Well, you weren't," said Oglette.

"Shut up," whined Clemens.

"Both of you shut up!" yelled Matilda. "God, I hate you!"

Clem looked at Matilda, "Hey, you're not hypnotized. You're in a lot of trouble!"

"I don't think so," said Malcolm, "You just kissed that girl and it was a French kiss."

"And it was really sloppy," added the little Oglette, "and I'm secretly a professional extortionist!"

Matilda was amazed at Oggie's confession. Malcolm was suspicious (she didn't look like she could put her heels behind her ears). Clem immediately went from hiding his feelings of ecstasy, to hiding his feelings of criminal conspiracy.

"If you even think of telling anyone about Matilda, I'll find the mother that shipped you off and tell her what you just did to that girl," said Malcolm.

Clem went pale and Oglette smirked. Malcolm pointed to Oglette, "And you, young lady. I'll tell everyone in the bank that you asked Clem to go steady and he said yes because he luuuuuvs you!"

Oglette went pale and Malcolm laughed and added, "And if either one of you gives me anymore trouble, I'll tie you both together and steal your underwear and see what other rumors I can start up."

He laughed again, then took Matilda out of the vault and slammed the vault door shut.

Shaking her head in disbelief, Matilda said, "You just locked them in there for the night."

"I think we should get outta here," said Malcolm.

Matilda said softly, "I'll go with you."

"Why?"

Mati smiled and said, "Well, you're kind of funny to watch... and you're harmless!"

Comments like that are a real big turn-ons for funny looking, harmless guys and Malcolm was no exception. Quickly, cunningly, he leaned over, slipped his hand under the back of her blouse and nibbled on her ear. She giggled for a second, in, um, fake sensual pleasure, then took a healthy bite out of his arm.

Friskiness before five? Never! As diplomatically as possible, Malcolm untangled his fingers from the back of her bra and grumbled, "All right, all right, I've got a plan."

Using the cellular phone, he made a few quick calls. Twenty minutes later, drivers from fourteen local pizza companies were lined up at the back door of the bank. Pizza people sport some really happenin' duds. The colors and themes were incredibly imaginative, almost insane. Malcolm let them into the back room and gave them all $50 tips for staying inside. He gave a $500 pity tip to the girl dressed up like a giant pepperoni.

So, basically, Malcolm and Matilda were surrounded by 20 pizza deliverers, 80 lukewarm pizzas, 7000 packets of crushed red peppers, plenty of stale parmesan cheese, and 1 spent escape plan. That was all Malcolm could dream up on short notice. He had money, he was hungry. Pizza seemed like a reasonable course of action. Matilda expressed her disapproval by throwing a pile of anchovies at Malcolm. Malcolm told her to hold the anchovies. She did, but then hit him over the head with an extra large vegetarian combo. He spun a box of ham and pineapple at her, but it landed on the shirt of Son-of-Salami's best delivery driver. What followed was the most exciting pizza party food fight Nowheresville had ever seen. The pizza war raged on for almost nine minutes before a high school vice principal burst through the back door and demanded to know what the heck was going on. He had a pretty good idea who started it.

Camouflaged in tomato paste and unwanted anchovies, Malcolm snuck out the back door of the bank. Matilda, still clean, cute, and tidy, forced herself at gunpoint out the door and followed Malcolm. The pizza delivery people stayed behind and played spin-the-bottle with the vice principal and some of the more adventurous bank employees.

XXVI

None of the police expected anyone to escape out the back of the bank. And they certainly didn't imagine the bank robber was clever enough to disguise himself as a giant slice of pizza. In a random act of accidental brilliance Malcolm unknowingly outwitted the cops, and unwittingly outknowed them, he did. They still thought he was holding hostages somewhere inside the bank. The people in the bank also assumed that he was around there somewhere, possibly hiding under a big pile salami, or locked in the vault with Clem and his bologna. They were all so stupid.

It was truly the crime of the week, but it was far from a clean getaway for Malcolm. As he ran, he was constantly slipping around on the sidewalk until he tripped over a misplaced manhole cover and landed on his head. A small bevy of passing nuns saw the pizza sauce, and figured Malcolm was bleeding to death. Being good nuns, they offered him medical assistance, psychological counseling, and sanctuary at a local nun hangout. Matilda politely declined their offer, but Malcolm had often thought of entering a nunnery, so he started asking the nuns a bunch of embarrassing personal questions. The nuns were angered and beat Malcolm about the head and knuckles with wooden rulers. Matilda thanked them for disciplining Malcolm, and the two bank robbers continued in their escape. The nuns gave them their blessings, and went back to their regular nun work.

They were out of the bank. They were safe from their brief brush with death. Matilda was still under a little pressure because she could have been viewed as an accomplice, but she knew she could convince the authorities that she was just a hostage. In all the excitement, she forgot that she still had her car back at a garage near the bank. They went to the car and drove away. While they rode, Malcolm called the cops on the cellular phone.

"Okay, what's going on in there?" asked the cop.

"Everything's under control," replied Malcolm with his best bank robber voice.

"Who were all those people running around in pajamas?" the cop questioned.

"They were delivering pizzas."

"In their pajamas?"

"Sure, one time I shot an elephant in my pajamas. And I think one time an elephant took a shot at me while I was wearing his pajamas. Why do you ask?"

The cop's anger intensified as he yelled at his police crew and tapped his foot, "Didn't anyone secure the rear of the building? C'mon people! You're not listening here!" He clapped his hands twice and commanded, "Now get back there and make sure he doesn't order any more pizzas without my permission!"

"Listen, General," said Malcolm, "We've already eaten and it's been a really long day. We're just going to get some sleep. I'm a light sleeper, I've got hostages, and I wake up with an attitude, so don't try any stunts. Get some sleep and I'll talk to you in the morning. Don't enter the bank!"

There was a short pause before the cop said, "Okay. Night night. Sleep tight. Don't kill anyone."

Malcolm hung up the phone.

Into the night, Malcolm and Matilda drove. He was safe from the immediate threat of prosecution and she was still technically a hostage, but she wondered if the guard would tell the cops that she assisted Malcolm. She knew that eventually she'd be asked to divulge his whereabouts or testify against him or something. On the other hand, she kind of enjoyed being his partner in crime. She could marry him. The world of outlaws and in-laws had a certain appeal. Then again, it was kind of repulsive. She went over the options repeatedly. She was confused. Malcolm watched her and recognized all too well the face of confusion. He'd seen it in many mirrors over the years and knew that she'd be stuck with that expression until a janitor came along and asked her to move along. She pulled out of it when her car ran into the mailbox in front of her home.

As politely as possible, Matilda asked Malcolm to hose himself off before entering her apartment. No problem for Malcolm, it was a free meal and a free bath. After rolling around under a hose dib for about twenty minutes, he went up to her room. It was a small but cute apartment. Whimsical and pretentious, yet dainty in a tough way. The walls were decorated tastefully with nature photographs and still life paintings. She was just getting out of the shower as Malcolm entered the living room.

Rather than satisfy his erotic perverted voyeuristic desires by watching her get dressed, he checked out the living room. Nice digs!

Wrapped in old sweat duds and a red flannel shirt, she listened to her answering machine. Malcolm eavesdropped profusely as the machine played back a message from her boyfriend. "Hey Mati!" it began, "So did they get me on camera? Did you tell 'em who I am? Call me right away!"

The several remaining messages were all hang ups.

Biting her fingernail, Matilda looked at Malcolm and thought how nice it would be to spend the night with a guy who wasn't totally abusive.

She picked up the phone and dialed, "Hi, It's me... Yeah... I didn't tell 'em... Yeah, I know... There was an off duty cop in the bank and... Yeah. I think they went to the station to go through mug shots... Yeah... Yeah... I can't go with you... No! I've got too much going on here... I can't!... Well, call me when you get there... Yeah. I won't tell anyone... Okay. Bye."

Deductive reasoning got the best of Malcolm and he figured out that she was dumping her boyfriend. Was she leaving Shwirl because he was a jerk or did she actually want to be with Malcolm? Don't ask Malcolm, he'd only been in the apartments of about three single women in his life, and even then he was just collecting money for his newspaper route. She approached him and took his hand.

"Was there a cop in the bank?" he asked.

"No."

"So you're getting rid of him?" he asked.

Without a word she looked down and nodded.

"Mind if I ask why?" Malcolm ...asked.

Slowly raising her big blue eyes, she smiled sadly, "I've wanted to for a long time. This just works out. It's a clean break. I don't think he'll come back."

"So you want to marry me?"

"Not yet."

"Good. I sure don't need the headaches."

All her hostility and spite suddenly rose up inside her and she let Malcolm have it, "You guys are all alike. You don't give a damn about commitment. All you do is run around robbing banks, and stealing trains, and ordering pizzas."

It bothered Malcolm that she forgot to mention sex, but he didn't think it was the right time to correct her, "All I meant was that it's been a very long day and getting married tonight might be a hassle. Let's be reasonable! The botched robbery, the escape, the sudden break up with your boyfriend. A wedding would just complicate things. Let's talk about it tomorrow."

Well, she certainly couldn't argue with that. Then again she couldn't back down, "And sex! That's all you guys think about. Banks, trains, pizzas, and sex."

Damn! She had all the men in the world pegged. "Well, you're right, but look at it this way. We can kill spiders and women can't."

Damn! He had her pegged. Maybe they were wrong to judge each other by such shallow observations. Maybe there were more important things to consider in the whole male-female social scheme. Maybe they could get to the root of all the world's problems by coming to a common understanding about how men and women should co-exist peacefully. It could probably start with a single mutual agreement on a fundamental approach to civilized behavior.

Matilda decided to initiate the revolutionary dialogue, "And what the hell is it with guys and toilet seats!"

"That's it, I'm outta here." Malcolm stood up and expressed his deep-seated anger, and then he expressed a little humility, "Can I use your restroom before I go?"

She shrugged her shoulders and pointed down a hall. Malcolm went to the bathroom then left her apartment without saying a word.

Before he could get to the bottom of the stairs, she leaned over the railing above him and shouted, "Wait! Please don't go!"

Malcolm stopped and thought of all the possible implications of staying and going.

Again she shouted, "I want to talk to you some more! You're different! You don't go to the bathroom like other guys!"

Strange, but true. Malcolm didn't turn to other men for advice in the bathroom and coincidentally managed to get the toilet seat thing right. He felt bad about not remembering how he left the toilet seat, but still took a certain amount of pride in his ability to do something right. Up or down is still a mystery. Looking up at Matilda with a goofy, innocent, really annoying expression, he shouted back, "Can we order pizza?"

"That's fine!" she laughed.

Malcolm jumped up and kicked his heels together. Things just might work out... He fell and landed on his hip, then rolled on his wounded shoulder, but he was happy. After limping up three flights of stairs, he found her in the living room, smiling and laughing and ordering pizza. He sat on her couch and looked at her phone. He wondered what Veronica Marvel was doing, and Armadillo, the gypsies, and all the little people. Matilda returned and sat down beside him. She was looking melancholy, baby.

"So what do you do for a living besides rob banks?"

Malcolm frowned, "I don't rob banks that often. I used to work in a warehouse, but it burned down and some other stuff happened, so now I rob banks, I guess."

Holding back the tears from that emotional story, she smiled and asked, "You're not very good at it. Do you live around here?"

Scratching his head a little, he tried to think of a dignified way to reply, "Well, you know those apartments at the corner of Down and Out?"

"The ones that burned down?" she asked. Malcolm managed a sheepish grin. Matilda continued, "But they burned down last winter."

"So since then I've been wandering around looking for work and no rent housing," he admitted shamefully. The dog.

Years of experience told her that if she offered to let him stay the night she'd have a hard time getting rid of him. She didn't want that. The only way she could get rid of him was by provoking a painful argument on a deeply personal subject. Fickle, yet practical.

"So, who did you vote for in the last election?" she asked.

"They wouldn't let me vote because I wasn't registered," he replied with proud patriotism.

"Why not?"

"I had a bad experience in a voting booth. You can't just do whatever you want behind that curtain. Freedom to vote isn't as free as it sounds. I can't talk about it. Anyway, they revoked my registration."

"Well, who would you have voted for?"

"I usually vote incumbent."

"Incumbent! Those people are all crooks!" she said with feigned conviction.

"See! If people had voted incumbent before they were elected we wouldn't have crooks now."

It quickly became obvious that Matilda's argument wasn't going to happen. "So why do you keep treating me like this?" she asked.

"Treating you like what?"

"Oh! You always do this. How insensitive can you get?"

He hadn't contemplated it before, but he didn't think he was insensitive. To prove it, he said, "I don't think I'm insensitive."

"Of course not, that shows how insensitive you really are! When was the last time you sent me flowers?"

"But I just met you!"

"No, we met at that restaurant, Mr. Insensitive."

"But I didn't really know you then."

"So that makes it okay?"

"Yeah, actually I think I'd go broke trying to send flowers to everybody I don't know."

"You make me sick. Let's talk about religion."

"I like the new Pope."

"That's it! Get out!"

Rats! Again, he was getting dumped. This time he could rationalize it. Let's face it, any girl who can't handle a serious discussion about the important aspects of world religions can't be worth the effort. Hesitantly, he went to the door, but Matilda stopped him for no possible reason, "Malcolm! I don't want you to go!"

He paused, "I must have misunderstood what you meant by 'Get Out'!"

"It's just been a really rough day. I'm not sure what I want."

"You'll feel better once the pizza gets here."

Matilda smiled, "Let's go to bed."

Bed. To bed. Bed, bedding, bed-ded. To paraphrase: "Let's do some bedding," "Shall we bed?" Malcolm liked to bed. Coincidentally, Matilda had a room with a bed in it. Into that room she went. He followed. It was difficult, if not impossible, for a guy to establish a good foothold on the whole casual relationship thing. In the fifties, these wild trysts were unheard of. They happened all the time, they just weren't heard about. In the sixties these activities became a social establishment. In the seventies they became a series of games. In the eighties, sex was outlawed, except for politicians. In the nineties all previous rules and customs applied. In the future, there will be complete and absolute sexual anarchy. Keep your fingers crossed... for starters.

So Malcolm found Matilda attractive and she didn't puke on his shoes, so she must have felt something for him. He liked the whole concept of intimacy. He didn't really know how she felt about it. The invitation was there for at least a little lovin' romance, but still he needed a signal. Just then the doorbell rang. That wasn't the signal he was looking for. Matilda came out of the bathroom wearing a white lace negligee which set off her soft tan skin, but that wasn't enough. Malcolm offered to get the door and she took his hand. "Maybe later," she said as she sat on the edge of her bed. He decided to skip the signal.

"Do you have protection?" she asked.

"I can take care of myself," he replied.

"You want to try something new? I mean, it's not exactly respectable, but I've always wanted to try it. What do you think?"

Malcolm was about as excited as he could get, "Is it nasty?"

"Uh huh," said Matilda seductively.

Malcolm nodded his head and sat back against the pillows. Crawling slowly across the silk sheets on her four poster bed with a fiendish smile, Matilda reached over Malcolm's chest. With the tips of her fingers she lifted a phone from her night stand and made an obscene phone call to an all night plumber. Disgusted by her lack of maturity, Malcolm tackled her and wrestled her under the sheets. They told ghost stories for a while, then made love and fell asleep in each others arms.

At three in the morning Matilda's alarm went off sending Malcolm over the side of the bed. She noticed the extra body in her room and looked around for empty liquor bottles. None. He poked his head up from the floor and she recognized him.

"Stop laughing," he insisted.

"I'm sorry," she said, "Here, have a cracker," and she offered him a salted starch wafer.

"You eat crackers in bed?" he asked.

"Yeah, sometimes."

"You get your butt out of that bed this very minute, young lady," Malcolm demanded.

"You're not gonna spank me, are you?"

"I mean it!"

"This is my bed."

"Ha! Gotcha!"

"That is not funny! You guys think you can just treat women like slaves and institutionalize sexist humor and then pass it off as a joke... I won't take it," she said as she jumped off the bed.

"Mercurial? Mercurial," muttered Malcolm.

"I'm serious!"

"I know you are. Here!" Malcolm took the crackers, jumped onto the bed, and started eating. "You try it. Go ahead. Kick me out of bed for eating crackers. It'll be fun."

"No! You stay right where you are," she said, then ran out of the room and came back with a container of bread crumbs. Before Malcolm could think of anything stupid to say, she threw the crumbs at him, stepped back, and laughed. He'd never felt more like a pork chop in his life. He was just a piece of meat in her eyes.

"I hope this is the start of something special," he admitted.

"Now get dressed and get out of here!"

"Do you mind if I shower first?"

She replied by snatching his clothes off the floor, and hurling the whole wad at him. Bread crumbs flew everywhere!

"C'mon, Matilda. It's not even 4:00 a.m. Can I at least stay until sunrise?"

"You better go or I'll call the cops."

Was she bluffing? Was she sane? Was she performing one of those teasing rituals that drive so many young men to drink and watch football? Whatever it was, Malcolm didn't like it. "All right, I'm leaving, but I want you to know that I'm not gonna hold this little bread crumb incident against you. Call me sometime if you want to have lunch."

They both knew he didn't have a phone and what he just said was totally inappropriate. He got dressed without brushing the bread crumbs off his body. He didn't want to make a mess. Consequently his clothes were kind of itchy. When he stepped he made a distinct crunchy sound. He liked it very much and suddenly had a new appreciation for all the other crunchy itchy people he bumped into when he was younger. Deep in his heart he knew the crumby sensation wouldn't last. He walked down the apartment stairs relishing the sound of every step (it really had been a long day).

As he got to the bottom of the stairs he heard Matilda shout down to him, "Malcolm! Wait! Don't go! Most guys just brush the bread crumbs all over the carpet. You're different!"

Was she worth it? He briefly considered calling her a flake, but knew she'd have a quick comeback. At that point he was so curious about her he couldn't resist perpetuating a relationship destined for disaster. He ran up the stairs crunching vigorously.

"Listen," he said. "I really hate to impose on you after all this, but I've got bread crumbs all over my crunchy bod. Would you really mind if I took a quick shower?"

Matilda smiled, "Okay, I'll help."

It was one of those situations where Malcolm could have been in trouble if he spoke or stayed quiet or made any sudden movements. He walked slowly towards the shower undressing calmly, keeping all his bread crumbs under control. Matilda, already naked, dashed past him and met him in the shower. They washed together and sat down for some coffee afterwards. A scintillating conversation ensued.

"So what do you do for fun?" he asked.

"I like horseback riding," she answered.

Malcolm knew what horses were. He wondered, "Are you an equestrian or a jockey?"

She had to answer, "No... I like horseback riding and water-skiing and I'm a semi-professional table tennis player."

"Wow! There's a lot of money in table tennis!"

"Well, not really."

"Well," Malcolm admitted, "not really."

"But I'm pretty good. I was Northern California champion two years in a row."

"Wow, you must be rich!"

"Well, not really."

"Yeah, not really," he agreed.

"I still have to work to afford some of the luxuries like electricity, food, water, stuff like that."

"But without all that, you're still doing pretty good."

Matilda looked around at her trappings and shook her head, "You don't pay much attention to reality, do you?"

"I can't see that it makes any difference. I'm just glad we got out of the bank without getting shot or ridiculed."

"They're going to be looking for you."

"Well, I was thinking of turning myself in and hoping they'd be nice to me," Malcolm humbly explained.

"What if they're not? What if they decide to put you away?"

"Do you think they will?"

"Cops in Nowheresville can be pretty tough. I don't think I'd want to be in your shoes."

Malcolm thought of the bread crumbs in his shoes and agreed. "Well, I don't know what I'm going to do, but I know I can't drag you into this mess any further. I'm going to turn myself in this morning. I'm going to tell 'em that I forced you to take me to your apartment at gunpoint and you had nothing to do with the whole thing."

"But that's the truth," Matilda interjected.

"Well, yeah, except for the part about forcing you anywhere at gunpoint. You can tell 'em anything you want," he said as he examined the gold ping pong ball on her coffee table.

She cocked her head and smiled like a ninny, "You know? We could run away together."

"That was plan B," explained Malcolm.

"Where would we go?"

"Boston or Phoenix."

Her eyes lit up, "Excellent choices. I'd like to see Florida."

Suddenly petrified, he yelled, "Florida! That's part of the United States! That's the first place they'll look."

Not at all petrified, she shouted, "Okay! ...Phoenix!"

"Yeah," he exhaled, "Phoenix is good."

She stared at his head, looking for any protruding electrodes. "Are you really that stupid?" she was forced to ask.

He ignored her, "Sometimes I don't really care. Anyplace would be better than Nowheresville. I can change my identity. Did I ever tell you about my cousin Wally? He works for the county recorder's office over in Anyplace. He can help me get my name changed. And if I ever need to put up a sign, he can help me get a permit for that. Right now I think we should just focus on the name change, but somewhere down the road we might want to put up a sign together."

A blank expression crossed her face as she exclaimed, "Not so fast. I'm not even sure I want to go with you... All of a sudden you're talking signs! That's a little much for a girl, don't you think?"

"Well, okay."

"Think so? You think a girl would have more trouble coping with all these changes than a guy?"

"Hey, I don't want to argue."

"Yeah, because you'll lose."

"Fine, I lose."

"And you think I want to just go to Anyplace with a loser?"

"But if I won, you'd lose and..."

"Shut up!"

"Can I get some drugs around here?"

Matilda folded her arms across her chest, let out a sigh, and said, "All right, look, I know we've been through a lot today, but I think it's too much, too fast. Call me in a week when things have settled down and maybe we can start a serious relationship."

Malcolm knew she was right. He hated to admit it, but it was true, "Yeah, I understand. I... I just thought we were having a good time together."

"Well, I thought so too for a while, but look at this, this is crazy. Somebody's gonna get hurt or arrested, and I don't want it to be me and I don't want to be around if it happens to you."

"Look, I've got no way out and nothing to lose. If you don't want to follow through with this, I'm not going to force you, but maybe you're right anyway. I don't think I'll... I think it's best if I leave."

Matilda smiled softly, "Yeah, I think you're right. I hope everything works out for you. If the police ask, I'll tell 'em it was all a big mistake. You weren't going to rob anybody. You just got caught up in the wrong place at the wrong time."

"Yeah," he said as he reached out to touch her cheek.

Matilda backed up and said with a sad smile, "Take care of yourself."

"Oh, okay, you too," he said and went out the door.

As he got to the bottom of the stairs, he kind of hoped that she would yell down to him and invite him up again. After all, he didn't give her the old lines, "I'll call you, later," or "Trust me, you were great," or "I left 50 bucks on the nightstand." He deserved something for being different, right? But there was no call down the stairs and Malcolm kept walking.

XXVII

After a solid hour of pointless introspection waiting for his first real girlfriend to call him in from the cold, he gave up all hope. It was over. He wandered down to the wharf. Some of the gypsies were fishing on a small pier and they saw him moping around so they laughed real hard at him. He didn't care anymore, much, although he did have a bad hankerin' to chuck some dirt clods at those dirty rats.

The bank robbery, the fires, none of the garbage that happened over the previous months hurt him as much as that last good-bye, but he knew she was right. Somebody was going to get hurt or even killed and nothing was worth hurting Matilda. What Malcolm didn't know was that Matilda felt the same way about him. Her life wasn't much more stable than his. She hated her job, her apartment. She'd been dating a drug dealer for almost a year, but she wouldn't have cared if her boyfriend got shot or arrested, no real loss. Still, she knew Malcolm's life would only get worse. He had some problems and took the wrong way out. Eventually he'd pay for his mistakes. So she sat on her couch wrapped up in her favorite fuzzy pink robe, and sulked. She knew she'd get over him in a day or two.

Meanwhile, Malcolm walked down a silent dark path knowing it would get darker. Contemplating his rejection, he sat at the waterfront and watched the water roll against the shore. As the sunlight began to warm the morning air, he watched an older couple walk past holding hands and laughing. He saw a younger couple arguing about something. Young Romeo stopped bickering long enough to roll his eyes and Juliet went ballistic. Her ears turned bright red, her cheeks puffed up like little balloons, and her head spun around 3 times. That made her boyfriend crack-up. It was kinda cute… so they hugged and kissed and thought about going all the way. At a nearby trash can, Malcolm noticed a middle-aged bum dude combing his fingers through the hair of a homeless woman. Malcolm got very sick. Love is a funny thing.

Darn that Matilda! She was too good for Malcolm, he deserved worse. He should have met a girl who scraped gum off the sidewalk and offered it to strangers. But no, Malcolm had to fall head-over-heels, ga-ga, puke-at-the-bums, crazy-in-love. He was totally smitten by a super sex kitten. It was too much for anybody. He cracked. He needed to get drunk and he needed to get drunk fast.

He chased down an old bum and stole his whiskey. The poor victim yelled, "Not again."

Malc chugged the whiskey like it was going out of style. His stomach and head were as empty as a politician's promise. The booze hit him like a trainload of horse manure. His mind was spinning like the water in a flushed toilet. Worst of all, he was having a severe analogous reaction to the alcohol.

Then! Malcolm bumped into a young kid. The kid was waiting at a bus stop, probably waiting for a bus. The whiskey had assaulted Malcolm's reasoning skills, and he thought of a kid he knew in high school.

"Hey! You're Joey Bergely burguly gurgly der duh der duh der. Aren't ya!"

The young man looked at Malcolm and smiled, "No, but here's a dollar. Go buy a gun!"

Malcolm laughed, "You're right. You're not. Joey would of never given me my gun money. He was afraid I'd shoot him in the knee. How'd you know I was gonna shoot him in the knee?"

"Seemed like he deserved it, being afraid and all," explained the innocent bus patron.

"Yeah, he did. That guy just got on my nerves! You know how some people are compulsive about stuff? You know, like always checking their watch or fixing their hair, or sucking on an empty soda bottle to get the last drop. I wished I had enough rat poison so I could mix it so he'd only die if he sucked the last drop out of the bottle. That'd teach him. Man! I hated that. Y'know?"

The young man agreed quietly.

"I don't know. It's just that some guys just get on your nerves. I mean we all have our own idiosneakersneeze. We all do some pretty strange thingsly. I know there's people out there that don't count their toes when they get a chance, sometimes I forget, and I know it. Hey, nobody's perfect! I'm not perfect. You're not perfect. You're not perfect! It's just Joey always had to suck that last drop. Why! How much did that last drop cost him? How refreshing could it have been? That bastard!"

The bus rolled up. The young guy got on and rode away. Malcolm was left staring at him and the bus. Nothing left to do but think, so he thought as well as he could.

He thought of Matilda... Maybe it wasn't rejection, maybe it was a clean break, a fresh start, and a new beginning of a long drinking career. It didn't matter. The alcohol took away all his concerns, but it didn't take away his appetite that morning. His bank robbery left him with a couple rolls of twenty dollar bills, a few loose tens, and a powerful hunger for green eggs and ham, so he stopped at the first restaurant he could find and grabbed a booth.

Comfortable in his padded brown vinyl seat, Malcolm started talking to himself. Someone in the booth behind him was talking to herself. She was clucking and muttering about patio furniture, chimney sweeps, and all the thieves she'd known who'd stolen her heart. It was Matilda. Malcolm was just thinking about her. She was drunk too. They talked to themselves a little longer, then decided to talk to each other. Malc climbed over the booth and sat next to her at a small table near the window.

"Hi," said Malcolm.

"You Malcolm, y'know how I seemed like, all schizo bat ack my aparment? ...I was. I'm much bear now," she exprained.

"Drink much?" he asked, all smart-alecky-like.

"Ho, yes. Very much, today. You see? I was confused and scared. You didn't know what I wanted and I knew you didn't. But the funny thing is, you didn't either. See? So when I got mad at you for getting mad at me for eating craggers in bed, I wasn't really mad at you, therefore I just got mad."

Malcolm snuck another shot of whiskey, looked at the ceiling and started to ramble, "I know. It's terrible how these things happen. I tell you what. I'm going to buy you this restaurant. Then we can kiss. Waiter? How much for this restaurant? The whole deal. I'd like to know. I might buy it."

The waiter was nowhere in sight, but Malcolm continued to contemplate the purchase.

Matilda's unrelated overt thought process continued as well, "You see, the toilet seat things really torbs me off, but it's not so bad. It cou' be worse. What if there were no toilet seats? What then?"

"I think I can afford a cool million for this place. Maybe fix it up a little. Maybe put a patio back there and throw in one of those fry cook things where the guy cooks it all right in front of you. What do you think about maybe starting a restaurant?"

"Of course when you were talking about craggers in bed I sure thought you wanted to share one so I was a little disappointed. You know! Those were the good bread crumbz and I guess I wasted 'em, but you shoulda seen your face! You were so... funny! I've never seen anybody covered with bread crumbs look so funny. Order some bread crumbs when the waiter asks," Matilda whispered as she loosened the tops of the salt and pepper shakers.

"I've heard that restaurants don't do well unless they have a lot of financial backing. Oh, sure, they'll turn a profit, but until you put the trendy entrees on the menu, your name is duck soup. Maybe I'll just buy a massage parlor or a boat store."

"Bread crumbs!"

"Then... once that took off I could go back to teaching. I've never been a teacher before. I could go back to studenting. Finally! I could learn to talk... Oh, oh, oh! My father! He might not even be *my real* father. I wonder what that makes me?" said Malcolm as he checked his pockets for nothing at all.

"I don't even like bread crumbs. Unless I could have 'em on a salad... Not crumbs. Did you ever see that picjure?"

"Well, he's not going to get rich off me. If he wants me to be rich so bad, why doesn't he just get rich for me? I could go back into the band or something, but I didn't get too far with that. I'd go; massage parlor, band, band failure, school, art student, bum, living artist. That would do it. I'd learn to paint."

"That picjure with the four faces on it? Andy... Warwal! Andy Warhol! ...Painted it."

"Yeah, he probably had a massage parlor too. Then a New York band, then art school, then pop. Fame! Talk about amazing coincidences."

With a scrutinous air, she looked at Malcolm and waggled her finger, "I bet you he got that idea from a soda cragger!"

Smiling at her eyes, he replied, "I love soda crackers."

"I love art," said Matilda.

"Art Linkletter?" Malcolm asked.

"And just art," she clarified.

He raised his eyebrows and asked, "Salvador Dali?"

"Sure! Yves-Tanguy, Magritte, Picasso, Matisse... What about Jackson Pollock?"

"Yeah, all those guys are funny, but they haven't done much lately. I meant the painter, anyway."

"I know everything."

Astonished and amused, Malcolm could really hook into this, "You do? That's excellent."

"I do and it is," she grinned.

"What do you know about Haiku?"

"You mean where you stand in a park and pose like a stork?"

"Yeah!"

Matilda had to explain, "Well, that all started back in 1925 in San Francisco. There was lots of Asians who came over from Asia as cheap labor and got oppressed by anyone who wasn't already oppressing somebody else. They were kind of forced to live in one room apartments and in basements, and so on, so all possible space was used for sleeping. Well, when the earthquake hit, thousands of people were killed and lots of San Franciscan Asians were killed because they were crammed into big cheap buildings. So after the earthquake a bunch of Asians thought of a way to avoid being crushed was to stand up in parks, instead of sleeping so they could get out of the way faster. And they decided to stand on one leg because if for some reason they need to run, they don't need to waste any time raising a leg."

"That's amazing," said Malcolm as he balanced a pepper shaker on a salt cellar, "I'm gonna try it."

Mati nodded, "Yup, it's good for you too. Helps your socks last longer."

"Oh, wait, what's Tae Kwon Do?"

"That's a kind of bird."

He frowned, "Okay, Miss Know-it-All. Tell me a bird story."

Finishing off the last of the whiskey, Matilda rolled her eyes and said, "What story? There was an egg, it hatched, Tae Kwon Do. The egg came first if that's what you mean."

Malcolm was humbled, "You do know everything. I'm still trying to get into Harvard."

"You will. I was born smart so I don't need to worry about knowledge as much."

"Yeah? So what's the oldest school in the world?"

"Oxnard."

"No way!"

"Sure! Founded by the British in 1842, it's still the oldest school in the world. Some of its original teachers are still there."

Good stuff. Malcolm needed to know more, "What's I.R.S. stand for?"

"Truth, justice, and the American way. Go ahead, ask another."

"How many miles between here and Hawaii?"

"430. That's too easy. Ask me something challenging."

"What keeps those one piece bikinis in place?"

"Just your imagination."

Malcolm was delighted. He'd learned more by 6:30 a.m. than most people learn in a lifetime. The woman was a wealth of useless information and he was an untapped reservoir of stupid questions. Finally, he could see himself sharing a future with her.

"Y'know," said Malcolm. "This may sound totally nutty, but I think we can still pull it off. I think that we could go back into that bank, cop a million, maybe two, and get to Anyplace by tomorrow morning. What do you say?"

Matilda ignored his question and asked, "Does this place sell whiskey?"

"Waiter! Bring us a bottle of your cheapest whiskey and hold the cork," Malcolm demanded. He was getting good at being demanding.

For the first time since they'd been in the restaurant the waiter acknowledged their presence. It was one of those snooty prissy waiters that got bent out of shape if you asked for ketchup. He brought Malcolm a bottle of Darren Devil's Double Buck Bourbon and set it on the table. By the time he had the shot glasses on the table Malcolm was wiping his mouth and passing the bottle to Matilda. The waiter scurried off in a huff for no particular reason.

The callous inebriated Malcolm pounded his fist on the table and announced, "I say we talk about physics and religion and politics and the parallels between them"

The fluttery and pickled Matilda slammed the bourbon bottle down in front of her and replied, "Alright, but I want to hear some obvious naughty innuendoes and lots of swearing."

"Damn right, lady! You just bet your sugar sweet ass you will! And I'll bet mine... Winner takes all!" he shouted... and so began another one of the most earth shattering conversations of the century.

"I been with every man who ever stood on the deck of the U.S.S.S. Enterprise!" she bullied.

"And I been with every woman who's been with every man who's ever… did that, whatever you're talkin' about," Malcolm bragged.

Matilda winked and pointed at Malcolm, "and I don't even watch space shows."

"Well, not anymore. I'm sure."

After an hour of drunken dribbling dialog, the waiter approached.

"Excuse me sir, would you care for any dessert?" asked the dumb waiter.

"No, your All-you-can-eat-breakfast-waffle-bar really filled me up," said Malcolm.

Without looking at him, the waiter continued, "It's really good, I recommend the Mile High Coconut Pie."

"No, really, that last helping of pork fried grits and sour cream put me over the edge."

"Are you sure? You can take it home with you. It's very good."

"No thanks, just the check please."

"How about you, Miss?" asked the waiter, "A little dessert?"

Matilda shook her head, "No, I'm on a diet."

"Oh! We have a low-cal crepe suzette that is divine. One order? Two?"

"No, thanks. It sounds delicious, but we really have to be going," she said.

"I get a commission…"

"Sorry," she insisted.

"Coffee anyone?"

Malcolm was getting annoyed, "Coffee? No. Could you bring me another waiter?"

"Oh, very good, sir. I'll be right back with a check."

"Goodie," said Malcolm and then he, y'know, nodded.

The waiter returned promptly with a check. Malcolm looked at it and left some money on the table.

The waiter took the cash, started to walk away, but stopped suddenly after he examined at it for a moment. "Hey, this is bait money."

"No it isn't," Malcolm replied.

Matilda looked at the money and frowned, "Yes it is."

"Everybody! Grab him! I'll go get some cake!" shouted the waiter.

In a panic, Malcolm took out his gun and pointed it at the waiter. "Hold it. Nobody move!"

Matilda couldn't believe how quickly the scene became so chaotic. She didn't want to get involved, but some big greasy guy with disco chains grabbed her from behind and coincidentally began fondling her. Quick like a bunny, she had a steak knife pointing at his throat before he could say, "What's a babe like you doin' in a place like this?" He actually did say it immediately after she put the knife to his neck, so she cut him just enough to draw a little blood.

"Button your shirt, Scum Bucket, before I turn you into a sweaty bloody pukey mess," she said, nervously. "Everybody get back into the kitchen!"

A flurry of pertinent jabber came out of the crowd.

"What do you want from us?"

"They're organized crime!"

"They're terrorists!"

"They're crazy!"

"That's right," interrupted Malcolm, "We're crazy terrorist criminals and if you don't do exactly what I say, it's curtains for the whole pudgy lot of ya... Argh! We're with the Slobbervation Limeration Army, and we're gonna hold all of you as hostages until somebody orders Eggs Benedict from the waiter."

Some wiseguy in the back yelled, "But I don't have any ostriches!"

Malcolm wanted to shoot the guy, but couldn't be sure who said it, "Not ostriches! You idiot! Hostages!"

The crowd went silent. Nobody went for the Eggs Benedict.

"I didn't think so," Malcolm boasted, "Okay, everybody get into the kitchen and start eating. I don't want anyone to come out until all the food is gone! Then I want somebody to clean the dishes! Hurry up!"

Most of the restaurant patrons went into the kitchen and made faces at the cooks. The remaining patrons snuck out without paying as soon as the waiters and waitresses were out of sight.

"Come on," Malc said to Matilda.

She looked at him, smiled and grabbed the whiskey, "Let's go rob a bank."

He laughed, she took a swig and tossed the bottle to Malcolm. Together they ran back towards the bank, swigging and laughing... laughing and swigging. Unfortunately, neither of them had much stamina at 7:30 that morning and they nearly collapsed after running for two blocks. Fortunately, a taxi cab was parked nearby and the driver was happy to accept their bait money and take them anywhere on the planet.

When they got to the bank, they found that it was still surrounded by the police officers who'd been quietly staging an all night siege and poker game. It wouldn't be easy getting back into the bank, but they had to. Malcolm was determined to finish the job and Matilda needed an alibi if nothing else. The streets in front of the bank and the alley behind it had been barricaded to keep the freelancing pizza deliverers and the general public away from the volatile situation. The rooftops surrounding the bank were covered with sharpshooters and camera crews. There was a cop at each end of the back alley and one on each side of the bank's back door.

Malcolm tried to take in as many details as possible without being conspicuous, but he had a pretty good idea of what he had to do to get back inside. His plan went something like this: Matilda would distract the sharp shooters somehow. Malcolm wanted to suggest that she use her outrageous body, but didn't want to sound sexist, so he left that unspoken option up to her. Next, Malcolm would conk the closest cop on the head with a karate chop and steal the cop's gun and uniform and put it on real quick, then he'd go down the alley dressed like a cop and when the other cops guarding the bank door least expected it, he'd give them double karate chops and flip them on their backs and knock them out cold. By that time the cop at the far end of the alley would start running towards him shouting, "Hey! Stop, thief?" and so on, and Matilda would run to the bank door at the same time. That's when Malcolm would grab all the guns and start shooting and laughing and yelling, "You'll never take me alive, Copper!" Finally Matilda would go inside the bank and Malcolm would follow her, but not before taunting and mocking the oncoming police officer. Once inside, they'd live happily ever after. Done deal.

He was ready, he was amped. He spit on his hands, whispered to Matilda, "Distract the sharp shooters in a non-sexist way or somehow," and then turned the corner to give the cop a karate chop.

Matilda said, "What?"

Malcolm raised his lethal hand and saw three cops running down the alley towards him. Quickly, Malcolm slipped back out of sight and planted himself against the wall. The cops stopped at the end of the alley and spoke to the cop that Malcolm intended to clobber.

"Did you hear that?" asked one of the door cops.

"What?" replied the reprieved clobberee.

"There's another hostage situation. They're trapped at The Carpe Diem Buffet and Grill."

"No way!"

"Way."

"Somebody's holding restaurant patrons for ransom?" asked a nearby good cop.

A bad cop, a real smart ass, overheard and asked, "Lots of money pass hands at breakfast?"

"Look's that way," said the serious cop who was still trying to pass his sergeant's exam.

"Do we know who?" the good cop questioned.

The serious cop looked down at shoes, "Terrorists."

"Damn!" cursed the bad cop.

Using a management skill he learned back at the academy, the serious cop told both the good cop and the bad cop simultaneously, "We're getting pulled off this detail."

Whining like a rookie, the good cop asked, "Who's going to watch the door to the bank?"

"There's nothing happening here that the sharp shooters can't handle until back-up arrives," explained an eavesdropping snitch.

"Okay, men, let's skedaddle, pronto!" ordered the serious cop. With a bunch of quick jumps and shoulder shifting, all of them ran away.

The sharp shooters were on the rooftops laughing, apparently throwing food and flying saucers at each other and they didn't notice the covert activity taking place below them. Malcolm and Matilda snuck quietly through the back door of the bank.

XXVIII

Inside the bank, Matilda sat outside the door of the vault. At 9:00 the vault opened and the guard burst out enthusiastically.

"Not so fast dishonorable guard," demanded Malcolm, "Get back in there and shut up."

The guard's excitement was replaced with dejection as he went back inside muttering, "I need to call Mom."

Oglette was sitting in the back of the vault smiling, adjusting her girdle, and applying a fresh coat of lipstick.

It was time for some demands. Stuffing everything he could find into his duffel bag, Malcolm had gathered up about three million dollars and change and he was ready to go. Nobody at the bank suspected that Matilda was operating as an accomplice, including Matilda. The guard was imagining all the terrible perverted acts that Malcolm performed on Matilda during the night and he felt sad, angry, and envious. Yes, he and Oglette had smooched and cuddled, but Mati was his dream girl.

"Okay, Matilda I'm ready to go. Should we call a cab or do you think that's asking too much?" Malcolm asked.

Matilda wasn't sure how stupid he really was, so she played along with him, "You know they're not going to just let you walk away from here."

"Yeah, I guess not," admitted Malcolm, "Penalty for early withdrawal?"

"Well, that and the armed robbery kidnapping thing."

Malcolm was beginning to sense that she doubted his intelligence. "No duh!" he exclaimed and removed any doubt from her head. "So a taxi's no good. We'll use a helicopter?"

"Maybe, but I'd go for an airplane. One of those private jets and get some caviar and champagne and chocolate milk."

"Will you go with me?"

"Never!"

"Will you help me escape again?"

"Sure, it'll be fun, but I can only take you as far as the airport. I'd lose my job if I went all the way with you."

"Okay," said Malcolm, suppressing the incredible temptation to comment on going all the way, "Jet, champagne... what else?"

"You're going to need to get to the airport."

"Taxi!"

"No. The rates around here are ridiculous. Just get on the phone and tell the cops what you want."

Cautiously, the two of them left the vault and went to the bank manager's desk. Malcolm held the gun to Matilda's cheek, and gave her a back rub as they walked. The gun wasn't loaded but it still looked impressive. He went up to the moronic manager and started demanding bank robber demands, "Give me that phone."

Without giggling or wincing, the manager set down his crayons and told Malcolm to use a pay phone down the street. Since he was still a novice felon, Malcolm shot the phone on the manager's desk and apologized and gave him forty bucks for a new phone. Being a successful entrepreneur, Mr. Grimeldiano was able to get Malcolm to fork over an extra twenty dollars to cover the cost of any long distance calls that might have been screwed up as a result of his criminal action. All phone bills settled up, Malcolm proceeded with his robbery.

"Okay everyone, my name is Malcolm, and since we really didn't get a chance to know each other earlier, I'd like to take minute to introduce ourselves. Just say your name and tell us a little something that will help everyone get to know you better. I'll start. My name, again, is Malcolm. I'm a bank robber. I just started yesterday, and so far I really like it. You've all been very friendly. Some of my hobbies include shipbuilding and croquet. My favorite color's black," he said with a smile and pointed to a young clerk.

"Me? Okay, I'm Candy. I'm working here at First Dibs as a teller. The job sucks because all the managers are butt kissing idiots and Oglette, the girl who works next to me, is a compulsive anal retentive dweeby little witch. Um, I really enjoyed being robbed and I think you did a really good job on your first day. My favorite color's red and I like cheese."

"Thank you, Candy. You're very sweet."

Candy began to smile, but suddenly became depressed and left the room.

"Who's next?" asked Malcolm, "How 'bout you?"

"I'm Caitlan, and I'm a customer and I like to come in here and spill the free coffee on Oglette's counter because she gets totally frustrated and starts lapping the coffee up with her tongue and barks at me like a dog until I go away."

An anxious bystander began to introduce herself, "I'm Tessie."

"Oh, and my favorite color's blue, because that's the color of the sky," added Caitlan.

After rolling her eyes at Caitlan like a spiteful evil person, Tessie started over, "I'm Tessie."

"On a clear day," finished Caitlan.

Malcolm had to ask, "What?"

With a humble smile, Caitlan explained, "...blue skies on a clear day."

"Oh, okay. Tessie?" prompted Malc.

Tess shook her head at Cait and continued, "I'm Tessie and I don't know who you think you are, but you should be ashamed of yourself. How do you know I didn't leave my daughter out in the car? She could have suffocated or drove off and that's a new car!"

A guy in a blue and white flannel shirt jumped in, "Hi, um, I'm Greggg, with three g's and I like washing my car and it's green and I think it's great what you're doing. More people should rob banks and order pizza... I like fishing... Okay?"

Malcolm smiled and nodded with approval at Greggg.

After fidgeting and biting his nails for a minute, waiting for the opportunity to get involved, Mr. Grimeldiano stepped forward, "I'm Dave and I'm the manager here at First Dibs. I've been branch manager for six years and I've got twelve people under me; men and women of both genders. According to our accountant we're looking pretty good this quarter. We offer free savings accounts and coffee, which our employees bring in. It sounds expensive and maybe it is. We just want people to think that we've got souls and we're not just faceless robots. We're just like real people. I was at a Christmas party a couple of years ago, which was no cheap affair, and I met the mayor and a doctor.

"I haven't always been in my position. When I was younger, I often thought of getting into medicine and politics. I probably would have gone one of those routes if my older father, who was also a banker, hadn't forced me to go to a private college somewhere on the East Coast. You have to understand, all this was not just given to me. It was forced on me. I'll never forget the time I almost got thrown out of school. My attendance was down, as were my grades, but let's face it, if the classrooms were easy to find, they wouldn't need entrance exams to get into them. The home tutor really straightened me out. Boy, I tell ya," the manager wiped his brow and looked around hoping to find sympathy.

"I'm not saying a degree is the only way to succeed, but you earn it! It's no wonder so many kids go crazy in school. No home cooking, no polo ponies, no mothers to tuck you in. It's a rough life, and a hard life, and a very mean life. Mean! Now I'm happy, successful, and married, to a beautiful woman. You'd love my wife," he said with a rich kid's wink.

Malcolm smiled and nodded, "No doubt. I hope you're both happy. We should probably move on."

"Hi, I'm Oglette and I work at First Dibs also. I came in early yesterday because the power went out in my house during the night and I set the clock, but I didn't set the alarm. So the alarm went off, but it went off at the wrong time and so I thought, 'Well, I'm up, might as well go into work.' It was only about two hours early, but it was just the right amount of time. I'm always doing things like that," she tossed back her head back and laughed. A thoughtful woman standing behind her caught her head and put it back where it came from. "I'm sure paying for it today. I'm tired, but I'll keep working even if it kills me."

The other employees in the crowd looked at each other in disbelief. Grimeldiano looked at her with great pride.

The intros continued until everyone else in the bank had a chance to share some of their history. It was really a nice way to run a bank robbery. The only person who hadn't spoken was Matilda.

Malcolm wanted to know more about her, "How 'bout you? What's your story?"

Matilda wasn't sure how to respond, but she went along with it, "Outside of being held hostage at gun point all night in the back of the bank, I like taking long walks along the beach, tango dancing, body painting, ice skating, hula hooping, and snorkeling. My favorite color's grey."

Listening with great enthusiasm, Malcolm said cordially, "Grey is nice." It was the right thing to say, but pleasantries soon turned to formalities as Malcolm went back to the robbery. "Okay, I think we're all pretty well acquainted. Who wants to be taken hostage?"

All hands went up in the air, except for Mr. Grimeldiano's. Once he noticed that he was alone, he raised a hand, then another, then began shouting, "Oooo, oooo, me, me, pleeease! Me! Me!" The rest of the bank joined in. That Dave, he was just full of contagious charisma. Since Malcolm didn't want to hurt anyone's feeling, he picked everyone and there was a brief moment of gleeful chatter and short vertical leaps.

Malcolm got on the phone to the cops, "Okay, General, I think we're all ready to go. I want a helicopter, no, an airplane at the airport to take us to an undisclosed location. And I need five or six taxis... Make it a bus! A school bus for all my hostages."

The cop at the other end objected, "Look, I can help you, but you have to work with me. I'll give you an airplane, but you have to give me your hostages."

Immediately! Malcolm scratched his chin and complained, "That doesn't make much sense to me, coach. If I don't have any hostages, I can't bargain."

The sly cop replied coldly, "Hey, it's just like banking. If you want a five hundred dollar loan, you have to put down five hundred dollars before they'll give it to you."

Looking around the bank for some kind of affirmation, Malcolm saw all the bank employees nodding in agreement while the manager scratched his head and fumbled through some papers on his desk.

The cop continued, "It's just a security thing, standard procedure, nothing to worry about."

"Just how stupid do you think I am," Malcolm asked reluctantly, "If releasing hostages was standard procedure, all your jails would be empty."

There was an obvious logical way to deal with Malcolm's concern, but the cop knew it would take a while to explain. "Okay, you got me. Just keep your silly old hostages."

Silly old Mr. Grimeldiano felt secretly thrilled.

Cleverly, the cop explained, "We just have one problem, partner. We got an airplane lined up, but the only transportation we have to get you to the airport is an old Fiat that needs an oil change."

"Fiat's a nice car!" said Malcolm, eyebrows raised.

The cop further clarified, "Yeah, but see, it can't hold more than three people, eight tops and you've got all those hostages to move. I just don't see how we can do it."

"No problem, I once took a whole clan of gypsies to the polls in a Buick Wildcat," Malcolm proudly explained.

The cop snickered, "Avocados?"

"No, no, no. Avocados gave *me* a lift. I'm talking about Zarathustra's Family."

"Yeah, I heard he suckered some kid into… uh, well. Look, this is a Fiat and you're not going to be able to make that many trips. Besides, you'll have to go directly through the train yard to the airport. There's no other way."

Malcolm didn't like the sound of that, "So I can't have my hostages?"

The people in the bank overheard most of the conversation and felt terrible for Malcolm, "Look," said Candy, "I've got a mini-van! We can take forty people."

The bank manager was beginning to feel left out and dopey. "I can have my limo brought around to the front," he offered.

Malcolm went back to his phone conversation with the cop, "Look, chief, we've got our own transportation. You just make sure that plane's out on the runway and ready to go when we get there." And he hung up the phone (without saying good-bye).

Shortly thereafter, Malcolm called the cops and asked, "So, where exactly would we find this police airplane?"

"We're fueling up at the Fringe Air Force Base, on the west end of Nowheresville."

"That's a nice base."

"Yup."

"I've got one condition."

"Shoot."

"No guns."

"No guns?"

"Yeah, if I see one more gun, I'm gonna puke," warned Malcolm.

"Hey! Hey, come on now, Champ. Nobody wants to see this thing get ugly. Don't upchuck while the camera crews are out here. You keep your end of the deal and we'll keep ours. I'll have all the guns removed from the Air Force base by the time you get there. No problem."

"Okay. Later," he said and hung up the phone. "Later" and "Good-bye" are interchangeable and despite their positive psychological value, they were both totally useless in context of Malcolm's conversation.

He called back again, "One more thing, Commandant. How do I get to the Fringe Air Force Base?"

"You're going to have to follow one of our people."

"Okay. Have him wear a green hat with orange trim and red plaid pants."

The cop had to think for a minute, "No can do. We need to use one of our undercover agents."

"Plastic nose and mustache glasses or the deal's off."

The cop had taken all the bullying he could stand, "All right you, you, you puddinghead! You'll get your plastic nose and mustache glasses, but you better hope I never meet you in a dark alley with two machetes, a bullet proof vest, and a can of aerosol cheese spray."

"Yeah? Why not?"

"Do I have to spell it out for you?"

"Ha! Don't bother. I think I'm doing pretty well considering your French accent."

"Always one step ahead of me, aren't ya, punk? I don't have a French accent and I never did. One of these days you'll slip and I'll be there and I'll be all over you like cheap syrup on a microwave pancake."

Aah! Malcolm was ready for that one, "Oh. Okay! And I'll be there like a boo-boo under a bandage. Anyway, talk is cheap and time is money so get off my back and save your breath."

Damn! Malcolm did a pretty good job of intimidating the cop and the cop didn't like it. The phone on the other end hit something and then there was silence. Confused and angry, Malcolm hung up the phone vengefully and went back to rapping with the bank people.

XXIX

A short time later the phone rang again, Malcolm picked it up and listened.

"This is Sergeant Nelson. I'm going to be working with you to make sure you don't get hurt and nobody else in the bank gets hurt. Can you assure me that everybody's okay?"

Untangling the yarn from the ends of his fingers, Malcolm replied, "Yeah, we're all fine. What happened to the other guy?"

"He went out to find a cliché that would shut you up for good. I don't think we'll be hearing from him soon."

"Okay, did he tell you our demands?"

"No, he, uh, just stormed out of the war room muttering something about boo-boos and bandages. I think he's serious. Look, all I want to do is make sure no one gets hurt. Can we do that?"

"Will it make me seem wimpy?"

"No! No, not at all. I'll have one of the sharpshooters take your ear off if you want some battle scars," the cop suggested congenially.

Tempting, but, "Maybe later. What I want right now is a plane that can take me out of the country and some transportation to the airport."

"All right, it looks like we got a... Wait a minute!" The cop balked, "Just a darned minute. It looks like he was trying to put one over on you. Assuming you're the suspect, he had you sitting in coach over a wing in a smoking section."

Malcolm was amazed, "There must be some kind of mistake. That's a terrible seat! What's the entree?"

"Turkey and gravy, with mixed vegetables."

"Damn it! I wanted the sirloin steak... with apple crumb cake!"

"Well, we'll have to see about that. How would you like some prime rib with mashed potatoes and chocolate pudding?"

"Uh huh. Yeah," Malcolm was drooling, "And pizza and throw in a bottle of Darren Devil's Double Back Bourbon."

"You got it, bud. Hey, I never got your name."

"Well, if you had my name..."

"Okay, I don't need to hear it. Let's just go over the plan. What are we going to do now?" asked the police negotiator.

"I'm all for getting out of the bank. It's totally stuffy in here. I think we just need a ride to the airport, a plane and we'll be set. I can drive and one of the hostages offered to let us use her minivan..."

The police dude at the other end sounded calm, professional, yet pensive as he spoke, "The plane's all lined up, but we just have one or two logistical problems with the transportation to the airport. You're really not supposed to drive unless you sign an insurance waiver. I forgot to bring all the right forms. Sorry about that. Harry was trying to make rental car reservations for you, but I can't understand the notes he left behind. They start off okay and then they become very illegible, scratchy, with doodles of nuclear bombs and daggers. We're sending them to our handwriting experts at Quantico for evaluation. Anyway, I need some more details. How many hostages do you have now?"

Smirking, Malcolm said, "All of 'em."

"I need a number."

"Is it seven?"

"Come on! Work with me!" shouted the copperoo.

"Okay, I've got twenty people in here, including myself."

"Thank you. Now let's think about this. How many hostages do you need? We're not going to try anything as long as you've got just one person at risk, so, if you want, you can let just about everybody go," the cop said diplomatically.

"Hey, I don't want to play that game again. I'm taking everybody. They're my friends. They're *all* my friends. I can't just say something like, 'Dave is an indecisive nitwit with a wonderful wife, so he's outta here.' That wouldn't be fair. If one goes, we all go." A contemplative pause, "And I'm not going to stay. So if all of us can't go, nobody goes?"

Grimeldiano quietly wiggled his toes and smiled.

There was no understanding or arguing with Malcolm's foolproof logic and the cop at the other end knew it, "Okay, stay calm. We're going to need a bus and that's going to take a little longer. We'll work this out. As long as you don't hurt anybody, we'll cooperate with you. Is that a deal?"

Bus takes longer, Malcolm doesn't hurt anybody, cops work with him. It sounded good. Maybe too good. Maybe he had them right where he wanted them. Maybe, just maybe, he could take the opportunity to do something he'd always wanted to do. He had to try, "All right. I like the plan, but I've got one request and if it's out of line, say so. Is there any possible way we can ride to the airport on that Partridge Family bus?"

The cop was quick, "I don't think so. That bus is being used to unload the planeload of passengers hijacked from Cuba. They won't be done with it for a while. I can get you something covered with obscene graffiti if you'd like."

"Close enough! Let me know when the bus is ready to go... I'll be here. Don't call me until the bus is ready," he said and hung up the phone in a pre-emptive disconnection.

Then he perused the bank, and asked sincerely, "Okay, how's everybody doing? Can I get anyone a pizza?"

The bank was quiet. It was an unusual situation. Everyone's life was in imminent danger, yet nobody seemed to care. Maybe they'd come to the conclusion that it didn't matter whether they lived or died. Perhaps they wanted the cops to storm the building with tear gas and assault rifles and discount coupons to the annual Nowheresville Policeman's Barbeque and Dance. Or maybe they didn't understand the gravity of the situation. Possibly they knew that Malcolm couldn't hurt a fly and there was absolutely no threat to their safety.

Malcolm considered all the possibilities and came to the only possible conclusion, "Hey! I might not look dangerous, but I really am. I've done some pretty dangerous things in my life and no one is safe when I'm in the room. Grrr."

The entire bank broke out in laughter.

Malcolm shouted, "Hey! Come on! I'm robbing a bank here. I think I'm being pretty menacing and I would really appreciate some cowering or even quaking."

After a couple more snickers and a few pats on the back, he was assured that he was adequately terrifying and shouldn't have any doubt about his intimidating qualities.

Feeling a little more comfortable, he felt confident enough to ask, "Okay, does anybody have any objections to being taken hostage? Seriously, I want to be threatening, not mean. So if you don't want to be taken hostage, please let me know right now."

The bank remained quiet for a moment until the bank manager stood up and said, "I think I speak for everyone when I say that you're doing a bang up job of robbing us and we'd all be honored to take part in the successful progress of this heist as official hostages. We also want you to know that we're open on Saturdays to meet all your armed robbery needs and ensure that grand larceny is a pleasant and convenient experience for you."

Malcolm was very happy, "I've really enjoyed stealing all the money in the vault and meeting everyone. I never knew it would be so much fun. And you're open on Saturdays! That is great!" He looked around the bank and saw nothing but smiling faces. "Okay, so let me tell you my plan so far. When the bus gets here, we'll get on it and go to the airport. Once we're at the airport, we'll get on the plane and fly away. It's so simple I can't believe it."

Matilda was a little concerned about the sparsity of the plan, but she didn't want to seem inordinately helpful. "Not that it's any of my business," she started.

Mr. Grimeldiano nodded to assure her that she could speak openly.

"Do you think you've covered all the details? I mean sometimes they put cops under the seats and in the luggage compartments. We could be ambushed or something," she cautioned.

Malcolm thought about her concerns, "Maybe you're right. Maybe I should revise the plan. I still like the taxi idea."

"No," she exclaimed, "I'm just saying that you need to be aware of all the possible problems. The bus is the only way you'll be able to get this many people to the airport in one trip."

"But the airplane could have booby traps too. There could be screaming children and obnoxious flight attendants. We might get sloppy baggage handlers. Anything could happen. Maybe I should just turn myself in," said Malcolm as he hung his head down low.

A short outburst of no's from the bank quickly followed.

"Quiet, Matilda, you're going to upset him!" said Candy.

Matilda knew the whole thing was absurd, but she couldn't resist getting involved, "I'm just trying to get him to consider all the possibilities. The only thing worse than being robbed by a violent criminal, is being robbed by an inexperienced thief. Nobody needs to be injured."

After listening carefully to the conversation, Malcolm was once again filled with self doubt and loathing. He went to the window and saw all the cops and guns and contemplated the danger he was imposing on all the innocent people. Calmly, he set the gun down and went to the bank manager, "Look, I'm sorry. I know I got everybody's hopes up, and I know you were looking forward to an exciting plane ride to some exotic destination, but those guys have guns and dogs and bad attitudes and I know somebody's gonna get hurt if I don't put an end to this."

The manager grabbed Malcolm's shoulders and looked him squarely in the eyes, "Now you listen to me. You're talking nonsense. You started this thing and you're going to finish it. Nobody walks out of First Dibs without a smile on their face and a cheap pen in their pocket. I assume you've picked up one of our pens."

"Yeah, thanks."

"Well, then, all you need is a smile. Young man, you go pick up that gun, rob this bank, and cheer up for once, darn ya," Grimeldiano said.

When Malcolm lowered his head, the manager picked up the gun and placed it firmly in Malcolm's hand.

Again, Malcolm had regained enough self confidence to finish the robbery. He jumped up on a desk and shouted, "Okay then, here's the deal. When the cop calls back, I'm gonna send three of you to check out the bus. I want you to look at the roof, under the seats, and anywhere else you think a heavily armed law enforcement person might hide. I'm going to have the cops open the luggage compartments so you can look real quickly and see if anybody's inside. Then we're all going to get on the bus. I'll need to aim the gun at somebody, but it won't be loaded so nobody needs to worry about getting shot accidentally. We'll get on the bus together and go to the airport. When we're at the airport we'll do something similar before we get on the plane. Okay? Above all let's try to have a good time! Sound like fun?"

Everyone clapped and Malcolm felt pretty damn good.

Within minutes, the bus showed up at the bank. The phone rang and Malcolm picked up the handset.

"Okay, we're ready to go," said the voice on the other end.

Malcolm replied, "Not yet. I want you to open all the baggage compartments so I can see if you're trying to sneak anyone past me."

"Hey, come on," said the cop with a forced chuckle, "That's not really necessary, is it? I mean, I think you can trust me. Have I done anything to make you think otherwise? I got you the bus, I got you a plane. Can I send in some aerosol cans of spray-on cheese as a sign of good faith?"

"That cheese won't cut it with me, chump. Just open the luggage compartments."

The voice of the hostage negotiator cracked as he said, "Okay, look. If for some strange reason there just happens to be a cop or two stored in one of the compartments, it's not because I was trying to deceive you. That bus just came back from a police convention in Barstow and some of the extra personnel might have been stored in those luggage compartments. It's a bus rule, I'm pretty sure."

"I understand. Just open 'em up."

There was no phone discussion as the luggage compartments were opened and a small army of uniformed militia rolled out of the lower half of the bus. Not just street cops. There were SWAT team members, national guards, navy SEALS, three smiling politicians, a couple boy scouts, and a cute little white lion. Malcolm didn't get angry. He knew they were all just doing their jobs.

He picked up the phone and spoke to his counterpart, "Okay. I hope everybody's out now. Here's the next step. I'm going to send three hostages out to the bus. They're going to close the luggage compartments. They're going to board the bus. They're going to make sure nobody else is hiding inside. Then one of them is going to come back and get the rest of us. I don't want you to stop any of them or interfere with 'em in any way. You can see for yourself that they're all in good shape." The bank manager stood up straight and smiled. Malcolm shook his head and finished, "And when I get on the bus I'll tell you what I want to do next."

"Look, friend, just to make sure we're all absolutely clear on this. There were a lot of cops at that convention and there was a lot of drinking. It's just possible that one or two police officers overindulged and passed out on the bus and maybe got stuffed under some of the seats. Nothing to worry about, just some good clean fun. An honest oversight at worst. You're not going to go berserk and start shooting people or ask for frequent flyer miles or anything, are you?"

"One or two cops are understandable. But if I see forty commandos step out the door, I'm going to start doubting your integrity."

"Okay, okay, let me be square with you. There are probably more than two people on that bus. Give me a chance to check the bus real quick and we'll get on with it."

"I'll give you five minutes to clear out any stray cops."

Seconds later, a police dude ran out to the bus and jumped inside. A parade of law enforcement personnel began stumbling off the bus. They all looked disappointed and dejected. The group included about a dozen marines, a frogman, and a bunch of celebrity crime stoppers, including Charlie's Angels. Malcolm knew he was ruining a perfectly good action sequence for the super heroes and he felt a little shameful. They all looked so good. He thought about sending the Angels back on board, but knew that he couldn't let his sensitive side take control of his reasoning. He had to forge ahead.

"Is that everybody?" he asked.

"Yeah, really," answered the cop.

"Okay, I'm sending those three hostages to the bus and one more hostage out to get some autographs. Remember, no police interference."

"Gotcha."

Malcolm made good on his word. The hostages went to the bus and closed the luggage compartment doors, then took a quick, but thorough look inside the bus. After they stepped off the vehicle, one of them broke away and ran to the crowd to get Cheryl Ladd's autograph. Tired of being outdone by his co-worker, another hostage ran over to get the frogman's autograph. Barely controlling his excitement, Malcolm shouted to the angel's admirer, "Hey! Ask her if she eats crackers in bed."

The autograph hound conveyed the question and was quickly leveled with a beautiful right hook. The lovely angel shook her fist at Malcolm and blew a kiss to the crowd. Damn. Meanwhile there was a brief commotion on the bus. A red and blue object fell from the ceiling to the floor of the bus. Seconds later, a depressed Captain Spidercop lumbered off the bus and walked into the comforting arms of Wonderful Girl. The third hostage returned to the bank and told Malcolm that everything was okay.

"Everybody line up and walk in front of me," Malcolm told the remaining hostages.

Matilda took his arm and whispered in his ear.

"Wait," Malcolm said thoughtfully to the group, "Let's form a tight circle and I'll walk in the center."

A brief argument followed and ended with the general understanding that all the hostages would take turns walking in the center during future bank robberies. Everyone made it safely to the bus.

The driver assigned to drive the bus seemed slightly suspicious to Malcolm, so Malc asked, "Hey, pal, are you a cop?"

The driver looked straight ahead, "No talking to the driver."

Malcolm wasn't satisfied with that answer. "Look, I'm just trying to make sure that everybody's gonna be safe and that all my demands are met."

"This bus goes to the airport with no stops. Express to the Airport," the driver responded coldly.

"That's it, you're outta here. Get off the bus, fat man."

The driver took out his bus driver manual, "I don't think you can do that."

Malcolm called the sergeant on a cellular phone, "Hey, I want this driver off the bus."

"Okay, put him on the line."

Malcolm passed the phone to the driver.

"Look, Simpson," said the officer, "You need to get off the bus now."

The driver held the phone to his ear and stared straight ahead, "No talking to the driver."

The cop became a little irritated, "Simpson, you get off that bus immediately or you're fired."

The driver took out his manual again, "I don't think you can do that." Then he whispered, "Besides, I'm undercover. If you keep giving me orders and firing me, you'll blow it for me."

"If you don't get off that bus right now, I'm going to get on and shoot you in the foot."

Examining the manual once again, the driver looked up at Malcolm and said, "My physical well-being or that of my passengers may be in serious danger. I'm going to deboard and call the police." He got off the bus and left Malcolm scratching his head.

As much as he wanted to get rid of that driver, he still needed someone who could drive a bus and get him to the airport. A quick survey of the other riders established that none of them had the right stuff. He looked out the bus window for some kind of assistance. It's true that no two bus drivers in the world look alike, but all bus drivers have a certain air of confidence about them. It's a look that comes only from wielding the fate of dozens of people with a steering wheel and a four million horse power engine. It's a look that says, "I've endangered civilian vehicles on a regular basis with my menacing power, but I controlled it and nobody was seriously hurt. I've sat behind the wheel of one of the stupidest looking motor powered contraptions ever made and held up to the ridicule. I have no fear." It's an impressive look. You should see it sometime. As Malcolm's tired eyes passed over the observers on the other side of the police barricade, and after a bum driving a big bulldozer pushed a stack of shopping carts out of the way, he saw a guy who carried that look. Wearing a sweaty, grease stained baseball cap and spitting tobacco, the guy had exactly the kind of do-it-yourself rebel appearance that Malcolm was looking for.

He phoned the police, "Hey. There's a guy behind that barricade next to Caesar's Salads and Grill in a red baseball cap. Send him over here."

"Look pal, I can't. There's absolutely no way I can give you any more hostages. Look at it from my perspective. There's a possibility that nineteen people could get killed or injured. If that number was increased to twenty and I could have prevented it, his blood would be on my hands."

"How would his blood get... Oh. All right, I'll give you two hostages if you send him over."

"Make it seven."

"Seven? No way, fritter face. Five! Final offer!"

"You're meaner than you look. Five it is, but don't ever call me a fritter face in front of my men."

"Sorry, I'm just a rookie bank robber."

"Ah, don't worry about it. One time a rookie hooker called me a caterpillar cop. You get used to the harsh language quickly in this business."

With a sigh of relief, Malcolm said, "Okay, go talk to the guy in the red hat. Let me know if he'll do it."

"Fair enough, I'll give you a signal and you send out the five hostages, then I'll send him over."

"Okey dokey," said Malcolm as a guy with dark glasses and a suit approached the potential bus driver. The potential bus driver shrugged his shoulders. The suit man gave Malcolm a cheerful thumbs-up.

It was up to Malcolm to release some of his hostages, a painful duty. "Sorry everyone, but I've got to let five of you go," he said solemnly to the passengers.

They all ran to the back of the bus and hid behind the seats.

"Oglette, get off the bus, you buttwipe, and hurry up about it. Tessie, you're sanctimonious and pretentious, I never liked you. Good bye," said Malcolm resolutely, yet somehow mournfully.

The two feebs whined and sniffed and smelled as they walked past Malcolm. That was the easy part. Now he had to excuse three more people, and he liked them all, so it was no easy task. He had to weed out the incompatible hostages.

"How many of you like ballet?" he asked the crowd.

No hands.

"How many of you like opera?" he drilled.

One hand hesitantly rose from the back of the bus.

Sometimes the hardest things to say are really for the better, "I'm sorry, we'll have to ask you to leave."

The woman was sad, obviously guilt ridden. She looked back tearfully as she stepped off the bus and waved bye-bye. Her departure was followed by sporadic sobs and deep breaths.

Malcolm continued with his duty, "Anybody doesn't like Dragnet?"

No hands.

"Any beer drinkers?"

All hands went up enthusiastically, as did Malcolm's.

"Any smokers?"

A ghastly pall covered the bus. Two hands went up and the entire bus gasped.

Malcolm sensed the tension and knew that violence could break out at any moment. "Okay, I want all the smokers to calmly get off the bus."

The remaining hostages quickly moved away from the aisle and began hissing and cussing and spitting. That crowd was a powder keg that could ignite from a single spark. You can only imagine how horrible it must have been to be trapped on a bus with two people who actually smoked cigarettes. In the dark ages that's how they tortured blasphemes when the iron maiden was out of WAC. At any rate, the evil smokers made their way down the aisle. They were decrepit, awful people, a man and a woman. The woman looked like a tramp with her gorgeous figure, nice eyes, pleasant smile, and positive outlook. One had to wonder how she could live with herself. The man was an older guy with a wedding ring and a tie that looked like it must have been a Father's Day gift. That's right, the awful evil smoking man subjected his wife and children to his vices. If the crowd suspected that he was a secondhand smoke victimizer they would have torn him to shreds. The tobacco-heads managed to get off the bus unscathed, and by some miracle they looked remarkably relaxed. Probably their diet.

Once the five hostages were all off the bus and tackled by the police, the man behind the barricade stepped over the police line and walked slowly towards the bus. He seemed indifferent, nonchalant, believe it or not, the guy was bored. Malcolm wasn't sure if he could handle that kind of rugged individual, but he was going to try.

The young man stepped up to the door and looked at Malcolm, "They said you all got some pork rinds in there."

Malcolm was caught off guard. The police had lied to the guy. "No pal. I'm sorry, we have potato chips, but that's it."

"That'll do," he said unflinchingly. "Ain't never gonna listen to no cops again."

"Tell me something," Malcolm demanded, nicely, "Can you drive a bus?"

"Yup. I can drive near most anything."

"Would you drive this bus to the airport?"

"Can we stop off and get us some pork rinds?"

"Sure," said Malcolm. What did he care? Big deal! So what?

"Well, sir, you got yourself a driver. I'm Bud," said …Bud as he stepped onto the bus, shook Malcolm's hand, got in the driver seat, closed the doors, adjusted the mirrors, started the engine, and yelled, "Dag nab it! Where to?"

"West end of town."

Bud popped the clutch and stepped on the gas. They were mobile. As the bus rolled away, the police on the scene went nuts. Dozens of unmarked police cars took off in all directions. Militia stormed the bank with dogs, metal detectors, Geiger counters, and divining rods. Peanut vendors followed on their heels with warm bags of overpriced goober peas. It was total mayhem. The crowd dispersed into the atmosphere.

"So, Bud, what do you do for a living?"

"Ah, hell, I can do most anything, I s'pose. I fix cars and boats. I paint some, I worked as a welder, merchant marine, drove a cab, a helicopter, worked as head chef at Jacques d' Rue sans Greel. I do believe I could do anything I put my mind to."

"Well, what do you do right now?"

"I'm unemployed right now, but I got a few good leads. You won't be needin' a bus driver tomorrow, will you?"

"No, I think this is just a temporary job. Besides, I'm a lousy employer."

"I work real cheap. A bag of pork rinds ever' so often and I'm set."

"Oh, that's right. We were going to stop and pick up some food. Pull into a convenience store and I'll get something for you," said Malcolm.

"I know a good place up the road a spell. It's got the best rinds in town and the cheapest beer t'boot."

"We'll get some roasted pig skin and some brews and we'll be rollin'. But we can't spend too much time at it. I've got a plane to catch," Malcolm said with a smile.

"Yee hah!" said Bud as he stepped on the gas and got the bus moving down the main drag at a lazy eighty miles per hour.

XXX

After performing several daring high speed bus stunts, the getaway vehicle pulled into a large convenience store. Bud's eyes lit up as he walked down the aisles towards the pork rind section of the store.

"Man," he said as he stood in front of a glow in the dark Wham-O Frisbee display. "I could sure go for one of those things. They look like a flying saucer I saw once."

Malcolm smiled, "Well, they're saucers and they fly. You can make a movie. Go ahead and take one. I'm paying."

Bud drooled and took a Wham-O Frisbee. "Don't worry about it," said Bud as he lifted his shirt and put the Wham-O Frisbee underneath it. "I can get one at a great discount."

"Seriously," Malcolm said, seriously, "I can afford it. You don't need to steal anything."

Bud looked at him with great concern. "You just robbed yourself a whole bank. Let me have some fun for a while." Then he started pocketing combs and cigarettes and candy.

Malcolm wasn't up to causing any more trouble for anyone, "Bud, I can afford all this stuff. Just let me pay for it."

"Well, let's see if you can or not," Bud said as he took a dozen cigarette lighters and put them in his pants pocket. "I guess you don't need to pay for those." He put a couple boxes of animal crackers up his shirt sleeves. "We can both afford those, I reckon." He continued stealing things, but he was moving into high end merchandise; bags of charcoal, cases of beer, basketball hoops, poultry! He didn't care anymore! He was a man on a mission and loving every minute of it.

There was no way Malcolm could stop him so he went directly to the store clerk, "Hi, I know this is going to sound strange, but I need your help."

The clerk nodded relentlessly.

"My insane brother is a compulsive thief and the only way to cure him is by taking the thrill out of shoplifting. He's going to come through here in about five minutes with all kinds of junk hidden all over his body. Here's two hundred dollars. It should cover the cost."

The idiot clerk kept nodding and smiling.

After fifteen minutes of solid pillaging, Bud rolled through the check-out stand bulging in every direction. Strings and wrappers were hanging out of his shirt and pockets, and popcorn crackled beneath his cap. To avoid suspicion he went ahead and purchased a bag of pork rinds. He handed the clerk the rinds and two bucks. Nodding and smiling furiously, the clerk gave him back some change. Stumbling out of the store with his rinds and an enormous smile, Bud was beaming.

"That guy was so dumb," he said to Malcolm, "He gave me about seventeen bucks in change. Not bad for a dishonest day's work, I'd say."

Malcolm laughed, "Well, we better get going."

Then they got on the bus. Bud revved it up and they sped off. The store was immediately trashed by the authorities and nosy neighbors. There were film crews, fingerprinters, bomb sniffing dogs, dog sniffing dogs, forensic specialists, and juggling clowns.

Meanwhile, back on the bus, Malcolm, Bud, and the hostages rode towards the airport.

Suddenly, "Nothing. Nada. Zip," said Bud for the fun of it.

"Why'd you say that?" Malcolm asked.

"Oh, I don't know, guess cuz it makes me sound smart. I ain't sure about you, but I gotta get out of town pretty soon. I got busted a while ago for aiding and abetting a fugitive, I'd say you qualify as a fugitive. If my parole officer finds out about this he'll throw me back in the can faster 'en you can say greased pig."

"But you were picked at random. The police even told you to do it."

"Yup, same as last time. You're leaving the country aren't you? What do you say you take me with you?"

Malcolm looked at Matilda knowing that she couldn't go with him, and while Bud certainly wasn't as good looking as Matilda, he was kind of a kick to have around, "By any chance do you know how to fly a plane?"

"Sure. Flew a bomber in the service, trained on some little prop jobs back on the farm. And I built a hell of a lot of plastic airplanes when I was a kid. I'd say I can do near most anything."

"Okay, you're going with me. The other hostages are going to stay behind but they don't know it yet. Don't let on, okay?"

"Done deal," said Bud as he pulled down the brim of his cap.

They continued on to the airport. Nothing spectacular happened. It was just a bus ride.

As the airport got closer, Bud became agitated. "That's a military airport," he said.

"Yeah," said Malcolm, "It's a small one, but it'll work."

"No," said Bud, "No, it won't. Won't work at all."

"What do you mean?" asked Malcolm, expecting another pork rind request.

"I can't operate a vehicle on a military base."

"Oh, come on! You said you could do anything."

"Well, I won't operate anything that would kill another human being."

Malcolm was shocked, "Why not!"

"I'm a conscientious objector now."

"You're not going to kill anyone! Might even save my life!"

"Don't matter. By operating a vehicle on a military base, I could indirectly cause the death of another human being."

"Not likely."

"Don't matter."

"Will you at least go along for the ride?"

"Hell, yeah! If somebody gets shot, I don't want to miss it."

They drove down a two lane road surrounded by a chain linked fence and there was a kill zone on each side of the fence. The barren landscape gave Malcolm some serious shivers. Bud pulled up to the guard post at the front gate, then got out of the driver's seat, and went to the back of the bus.

A guard in green garb stepped up to the driver's window, knocked on it, and asked, "Bank robber?"

Malcolm got into the driver's seat and opened the window. The guard put his hand on the window and asked again, "Bank robber?"

"Yup," said Malcolm.

The guard stepped back and motioned them through.

Malcolm looked at him for a minute and the guard stepped back up to the window again, "Bank robber?"

"Uh, yeah," said Malcolm.

The guard took a step back and again motioned them through the gate.

Malcolm said, "We have a little problem."

The guard stared at him with absolutely no expression. None.

"We need a driver," Malcolm explained.

The guard stepped away, looked at the back of the bus, and went into his little guard station. He came back out with another military dude.

The new dude looked into the window, "Bank robber?"

"Yes! We need a new driver."

The guard looked at Malcolm for a second then said, "I can drive near most anything."

"Great, get in here and take us to the getaway plane."

The guard nodded once, got on board, and drove those people to the airfield.

The getaway plane was waiting at the Fringe Air Force base runway number 9. It was a Quadrofluge Winky Dink with turbo thrusting heliopods. Malcolm had all but given up on driving the bus to East Berlin, but if he thought the gas would last, he would have snatched up the opportunity like a big old porcupine on a pincushion. He knew damn well that the coppers would track his plane until the hostages were freed and then blow him clear to Kingdom Kong.

Another minor oversight in Malcolm's diabolical robbery scheme was the actual hostage release process. Malcolm remembered a film where the hostage thing almost worked except that one of the bad guys didn't count on the pistol hiding in the sun visor that the FBI agent could pull out and quickly blow a small hole in the perpetrator's head. In an effort to outwit his adversaries, he tore off the sun visor and spit on the floor. Malcolm didn't actually need the cops except for getting directions. In most of the "bad guy" movies Malcolm had seen, the hostages were huddled around the kidnappers like secret service agents, but in the long run the bad guys always got shot, or ended up staring into the muzzle of an impressive gun while thinking, "Well, was it five shots or six? Must have been six because why else would the guy ask? I thought I counted eight... damn cops." Then they got shot anyway. That wasn't the way Malcolm wanted to go out. For one thing, he wasn't wearing clean underwear (if he'd known the bank robbery was going to take two days he would have packed extra). For another thing he didn't like the thought of being a kidnapper. Furthermore, what the hell was Malcolm Tent gonna do with 14 whining bank customers? The answers to those questions were far beyond his grasp. Still within his grasp, the grasp of his right hand, was a 9 mm semi-automatic hunting rifle (generally used after a bull moose makes a wisecrack about a hunter's wife).

He needed another unexpected plan of attacked.

As the bus approached the Quadrofluge, Malcolm noticed something interesting in a nearby hangar. Putting two and two together (four), Malcolm came up with perhaps the cleverest idea of his life. "Stop the bus!" he shouted at the military driver. The driver kept going. Malcolm put the gun to his head (the driver's head) and shouted, "There's two ways I can get you stop this vehicle. I'm giving you one more chance to do it the easy way."

The driver stopped the bus and swore at Malcolm, "Poop! You'll never get away this, you doughnut-head!"

Ignoring the driver's harsh insult, Malcolm ordered, "Everybody out of the bus! No funny stuff! No magic tricks! And no singing! Follow me!"

Training his weapon on the crowd of hostages, Malcolm guided the group into the open hangar. He knew that there were probably dozens of sharp shooters set up around the Quadrofluge and the change of plans would doubtlessly cause them some problems, possibly even some consternation. They'd have to restructure, reposition, and get new orders before they could quickly blow a small hole in his head. Inside the hangar was an airplane that had rarely been seen by the average American. Malcolm took Matilda by her arm and pulled her aside. She tossed her hair back coquettishly.

"I want you to go on the plane first and let me know if there's anybody on board," he demanded.

Matilda was sharp enough to know the right questions to ask, "Did you know that's a Stealth bomber?"

"Sure, I read the papers, I know all about it. It flies below radar and goes fast and stuff," Malcolm correctly responded.

"Did you know that it also carries an arsenal of weapons, possibly nuclear weapons?"

"So I'll watch out for speed bumps."

"You're not thinking about trying to fly it!"

"Give me a break, I've played video games. I'm up to level 8 in Death Flight Glider."

"Well I'm out. This is suicide."

"No! This is the only way I'm going to get out of here alive. Look, if I can't get it off the ground, I'm busted, you're safe. If I can fly it, you and I are set for life. Hell, we'll have 3 million dollars in cash and our own jet. I think you're doing all right."

"Damn it," Matilda muttered, "this really isn't in my job description."

Malcolm smiled, "Consider it a career change."

Matilda shrugged her shoulders and spit on Malcolm's shoes, "I expect my new employer to tolerate physical and verbal abuse and I get to work my own hours."

"Good enough, when can you start?"

"Well, I'm leaving the country in a few minutes, so, maybe when I get back."

With a short laugh, Malcolm said, "Well, it's been a real treat, but my butt's on the line here, so if you don't mind, would you go onto the plane and let me know if anybody's working up there?"

Matilda spit on his shoes again, called him a tyrant and then walked cautiously up the ladder into the plane. Malcolm watched her and drooled a little. She disappeared briefly into the cockpit, then stuck her head out wearing a World War I pilot helmet, gave Malcolm a wink, and wiggled her fingers at him.

He ran back to the bus to get his money. The bus driving military man looked up at the Matilda, then at Malcolm. "She in on this?" he asked Malcolm, trying to obtain some confidentiality.

Putting on a cold sinister expression that he learned in his childhood by reading monster comic books, Malcolm looked into the driver's eyes and said, "If she tries anything, she's dead, and between you and me, once we get out over international waters, I'm going to eject her with a life raft. Do these planes have homing signals?"

"No, but they've got several short range radio transmitters. If you've got an ounce of decency, you'll send one with the girl."

"We'll see."

"Come on, buddy, this'll never work. You don't want to hurt anybody. Things just got out hand, and you just got a little crazy. They'll let you off easy if you give it up right now."

"Thanks pal, but I've gotta go. I've got nothing to lose. Tell the press I didn't start this thing, Jimmy Shwirl started it and somewhere out there he's got a car full of drugs. I don't give a damn if you believe me or not. As far as the cops are concerned, I'm a bank robber and a kidnapper, or at least an accessory. No way they'll let me walk away from this."

The driver shook his head in disappointment.

Malcolm responded, "You want to catch a bank robber? Check that guy's car and ask the witnesses. Jimmy Shwirl. Maybe the cameras picked him up, but the way that bank operates, I doubt they had any film. Show the witnesses some mugshots of Shwirl. And the money? People were shooting at me, I earned it."

With that, Malcolm jumped out of the bus and ran to the plane surrounded by his small group of dedicated hostages. Hidden under the dashboard was another 9 mm semi-automatic hunting weapon that the driver was supposed to use on Malcolm if he had the chance. There's a balance between following orders and taking chances, the driver took a chance and chose not to follow orders. Malcolm was allowed to escape.

As the team of disorganized criminals and victims stumbled to the jet, Malcolm explained that they'd done a great job. He told them that the jet couldn't hold so many passengers and it was time for them to go back home. Some of them didn't want to go, but he argued that they couldn't be hostages forever, and they knew this day would come eventually. He gave them a big group hug, saluted them, and got on the plane. Matilda climbed in with the excuse that Malcolm dropped his wallet and a bag with $3,000,000. The bankers joked that he didn't want to forget that! Bud ran after Malcolm and jumped on the plane behind him. The remaining hostages ran back to the bus to tell the driver what a nice guy Malcolm was.

On the plane, Malcolm sat down in the cockpit and looked at the controls. There were lots of controls. Malcolm couldn't spit without hitting some kind of button. Carefully avoiding spit gobs, he began to throw switches like a professional switchman and pressing buttons like a boutonniere. He asked himself repeatedly, "What would a sane person do here?" Then he yelled out the window, "Clear to take off!" Nothing happened.

Matilda tried to find out what the problem was, "What's the problem," she asked ironically.

"I can't figure out what's wrong!" he explained, "I yelled, 'Clear to take off', and threw all kinds of switches. And nothing's happening! ...This sucks."

Bud snickered.

Matilda scratched her head and said, "It sounds pretty quiet."

"Baby must have a smooth ride," said Malcolm.

Matilda sighed, "Yeah, but you're probably going to have to start it before you go anywhere."

Malcolm shrugged his shoulders and Matilda motioned for him to get out of the way. He did, she sat down, looked around, turned on the ignition, pulled back on the throttle, and that big black bird started rolling.

As the door of the Stealth bomber closed, a confused ground crewman appeared from a neighboring hangar. His confusion increased as the jet began to lurch towards the runway. "Hey!" he shouted. "Hey! Heyyyy!" He ran after the jet. He shouted "hey" about fifty more times and threw his official flight cap down on the tarmac. "Rats!" he exclaimed finally. The plane was well out of earshot and the mechanic was out of a job.

While Matilda navigated the big bomber off the base with amazing skill, Malcolm was bowled over with admiration. With a gooberly smile, he asked, "Where'd you learn to do that? Huh?"

"Well, it's no crop duster," replied Matilda, "but it's still an airplane." She flipped on the auto pilot and within minutes the plane was gliding over the Pacific at Mach 2! Fast, man!

It was exciting, but not exciting enough. Malcolm wanted more. He told her to turn the plane around and head east. They went back across the continent at a low altitude to avoid radar and changed direction regularly to avoid predictable positions from ground sightings. After a brief argument about where to find the world's best uncharted islands, Matilda convinced Malcolm that she should turn around and head west. They did.

Back on the Fringe runway, a small propeller plane sat in the sights of twenty hidden snipers. An assassin posed as a pilot and another waited in the cargo bay. The ground crew continued to load the Quadrofluge with stale peanuts and K-rations in the event that the flight lasted more than two hours. The supervising lieutenant was a little confused to see one his Stealth bombers flying overhead a second time.

The lieutenant barked, "That bomber scheduled for a test flight, McGillicutty?"

"No, sir!" responded a dutiful subordinate human.

"I... can't... hear... you!"

"Oh. I said, No sirree, sir. Nuh uh."

"Well, for crying out loud, I want you to get on the radio and find out what the heck is going on with that bird. Jiminy crickets! If that plane gets out of U.S. airspace there'll be 'H' 'E' double toothpicks to pay. Do you follow me, mister?"

"You can bet your fanny pack I do, sirper dirper!"

"Well, get to it!"

Before the obsequious sergeant was out of earshot, a bus carrying several former hostages came rolling toward the observation deck.

"Open fire!" ordered the lieutenant.

A barrage of bullets pelted the bus. The driver, thinking quickly, pulled a tin can from under his seat and tossed it in the air. His diversion worked, those snipers kept that can up in the air a good fifteen, twenty minutes. That gave the driver an opportunity to debrief the lieutenant. "Hey, you moron, what are you shooting at?"

"You know anything about that Stealth bomber that just flew by?" the lieutenant asked, "And don't try any of that double talk, buster."

"I'm Finnegan, FBI. That plane's carrying an alleged bank robber and two hostages," the bus driver said.

"That's all I need to know. McGillicutty, terminate that flight!" shouted the lieutenant to an officer at the control panel.

"I said there are hostages on that plane. You can't just blow it up."

"Just watch me, G-Man!"

Finnegan pulled a miniature microphone from under his lapel and spoke into it, "Johnson, I've got a constipated C.O. here just itching to pull the plug on the suspect's jet. I'd like to exercise some federal powers over this clown. He's a Lieutenant Michelson. Transfer him to Anchorage as of yesterday."

He looked up at Michelson, "You're AWOL, cornball, go pick up your orders or I'll have you arrested."

The lieutenant took on a new shade of white.

"Move it!" Finnegan yelled and started issuing orders into his microphone. "I want four F-15's in the air and on that plane's ass immediately. Let's move 'em out. Do not attempt to alter the plane's path. I want our fighters to maintain visual contact with the suspect and radio contact with us at all times. I repeat, do not fire on or attempt to force that bomber down."

The fighters were deployed within seconds but couldn't pick up the aircraft on radar. They put out orders to any freighter, fishing boat, and row boat in the Pacific to contact the Coast Guard immediately if they spotted a big black top secret military weapon flying around over the ocean. They were also instructed not to yell too loud as the pilot was reported to have been drinking earlier that morning and probably had a major hangover.

Meanwhile on the runway, two small figures approached the getaway Winky Dink. They climbed into the plane. Moments afterwards, two military commandos in combat gear were ejected from the plane's door. The plane started up and flew off into the wild blue, yonder. The two hijackers could barely see out of the cockpit, but the bright white bandanna of one young hoodlum was clearly visible from the ground.

Several hours passed with no radio contact from the bomber or the Coast Guard. There were tons of crank calls from a variety of fishing boats. Reports of big blue footed boobies, flying ninja warriors, leaping lizards, and magic dragons began pouring in, but no one had seen the bomber. Things on the base were getting pretty tense. The agent who drove the bus was interrogated at length by his superiors about Malcolm's plan and why Malcolm wasn't shot. There was a lot of yelling, and shouting, and maybe some things were said that shouldn't have been said. Maybe there could have been just a little more emotional bonding instead of so much pulling apart. There were some apologies, some hugs, a few tears. Real nice moment in military history. After everyone was feeling a little better, they all agreed that the Stealth bomber should be blown up. The remote self-destruct mechanism was activated and they all went back to business as usual.

XXXI

Once the bomber was triggered to destroy itself, there would be a ten minute delay before the explosion. The plane builders threw that feature in to give passengers a chance to cancel any return flight reservations.

From the speeding plane, the sky looked like a blue canvas mottled with white splotches of condensed hydrogen floating slowing across the horizon. Really, and maybe that's what it was. The ocean passed below them at, like, two thousand miles an hour. The bomber stayed relatively close to the water to avoid radar just in case the secret cloaking mechanism was on the fritz (which happens to almost all space fighting machines from time to time). Malcolm stared at the water hoping to catch a glimpse of a sunken pirate ship or something, but saw only an expansive blur.

He found some stale peanuts in the glove compartment and offered them to Matilda, "Here. Take these and pinch my butt."

"Why?" she asked.

"I always wanted to know how a stewardess feels," he grinned.

Matilda punched him right in his magic charley horse shoulder.

Bud was sitting behind the cockpit when the self-destruct light came on. "So it's got one of those," he said.

"Got one of those what?" asked Malcolm.

Bud pointed to the light, "A red light for the self-destruct."

Noticeably disturbed, Matilda tried to clarify, "You mean the light itself turns red before it burns out."

"Turns red before the plane blows up," explained Bud.

"So this bomber's going to explode pretty soon, eh?" asked Malcolm.

"Ten, fifteen minutes," Bud said calmly, "We don't have a return flight reservation do we?"

"Ten minutes?" Malcolm echoed, "I think we can work something out. Everybody check and see if these seats can be used as floatation devices! Oh, and damn it... Where are those emergency exits? Why didn't anyone point 'em out! Next time, we're flying Mahalo Airlines."

Bud grimaced, "These seats don't float. Besides, there wouldn't be 'nuff left over to hang on to. There's a life raft in the back you could use, but that's going to blow up with the rest of us."

Meanwhile, Matilda was trying to figure out a way to survive after the explosion as she took the plane to an altitude of 10,000 feet. "Okay," she said, "Find all the parachutes."

"There's three on top of the life raft," said Bud, like an idiot.

"Okay, everybody put one on!" yelled Mati, and they did. "Okay, Bud, grab the life raft." He did. "Malcolm, sit in the pilot's seat!" He did! She was sure spunky! "Bud! Sit in the co-pilot's seat!" Of course, he did. "Malcolm! I'm gonna sit in your lap!" And she did! Naturally she had the good sense to hold the money. "Get ready to eject!" They all did, all of 'em. Matilda reached up to a switch in the cockpit and flipped the lever.

"Pwooosh!" is what it sounded like as the windshield flew up and off the jet. "Psheee!" was the sound of the seats ejecting from the cockpit. "Yeeeoooow!" was the noise Malcolm made as he flew straight up into the air traveling at about 1600 miles per hour. Talk about a rush!

The three of them floated through the sky for a minute then pulled the rip cords on their chutes.

"Splash!" said Malcolm when he landed in the water.

The hijackers landed in fairly close proximity to each other. Bud inflated the raft and they all eventually got in. The explosion got their attention and they looked up to see an enormous ball of red and yellow fire fall into the ocean. All ties to their past were destroyed in that instant. None of them could ever go back to Nowheresville and they all knew it.

After about a day and a half of drifting and self doubt, Malcolm was about ready for Matilda to stop yelling at him. How was he supposed to know that they'd end up baking in a life raft in the middle of the Pacific Ocean surrounded by great white sharks? He tried to convey that sentiment to Matilda, but her only response came from the end of an aluminum oar.

Then it happened! The miracle they'd been dying for suddenly appeared in the distance. Land ho, baby! That's right, a small bump on the horizon that looked like heaven on water. They paddled feverishly and the bump gradually became larger. There was greenery on the island, which meant life! Maybe coconuts!

More feverish paddling revealed a small but demanding foothold of vitality. It had a beach and cliffs and tall tropical trees.

The sun was fading quickly off the edge of the world and by the time they made it to the breaking waves of the island, they were navigating by starlight. As they came closer to the beach, the night waves capsized the raft. The waves didn't just knock it over, they capsized it. After swimming to shore, the soggy passengers crawled up to the beach, collapsed on the sand, and fell asleep within minutes.

The next morning met Malcolm with a brief tropical rain. He awoke with Matilda curled up at his side. There was no sign of Bud except for his footprints which led up the beach into the jungle. Matilda looked so vulnerable while she slept, too vulnerable. Once again, Malcolm had met someone he cared about and thrown her into the jaws of death for his own selfish purposes. He looked across the sand and over the water and saw shellfish and porpoises. They were angry and they too had jaws of death. Malcolm couldn't win. It became clear to him that he wasn't hopelessly romantic, he was just hopeless. He'd never be able to give anyone his undivided love as long as he gained pleasure from giving for his own good.

Things had become too preposterous even for Malcolm Tent. He was lying on a beach next to a beautiful woman who looked so damn good after jumping out of an airplane, spending two days in a lift raft, washing up on shore, and sleeping in the sand. Even with all the coconuts and his own shellfish and porpoises, he still wanted to feel sorry for himself. Something had to change. If nothing else, he needed to lighten up. He gave Matilda a kiss to wake her up.

She opened her eyes and said, "EEEEEEYOOOOW!"

Apparently he didn't look as good as she did in the morning.

"Fine," he said, "I'll be in the tub." He ran into the ocean.

"I wasn't screaming at you!" Matilda screamed. "I was having a bad dream! I think you look good with your hair pointing straight out in five different directions. I like guys with lopsided heads!"

Malcolm didn't hear a word she said, and he really didn't care. He'd spent his whole life trying to make people happy or rich or pregnant, and he wasn't doing a very good job at it. The time had come for Malcolm to live for himself. If you're going to live for yourself, swimming in 85 degree water off the beach of a tropical island with a gorgeous date, and three million dollars in a duffel bag is a highly advisable starting point.

For several hours Malcolm played around in the waves, splashing Matilda like a jerk and trying to kick himself in the forehead. That kind of activity doesn't come without a price, dude got hella hungry. The two castaways entered the jungle looking for food. Beautiful Matilda envisioned dining on bananas, papayas, and wild berries. Malcolm imagined they'd have to survive on grubs and salamanders and eventually end up eating his hands.

Before getting too deep in the jungle, they came across a waterfall. Crystal clear shimmering water cascaded down from a high river into a serene blue pool. As they came closer to the falls, they heard laughing. A group of people was bathing under the spill rock. Judging from their dark skin and calm countenance, Malcolm decided they were native islanders. He approached them cautiously and attempted to communicate. He ascertained that they were a woman, a man, and a child, possibly cannibals. He named them Monday, Tuesday, and Wednesday respectively. Cannibals or not, he had to let them know that he meant them no harm.

When he and Matilda approached them, the natives became quiet and watched anxiously. Malcolm held up his right hand and spoke, "Me Malcolm. You..."

"Jim," said ...Tuesday.

"Oh," reacted Malcolm. Without letting on that he was a fugitive, he attempted to cleverly determine his whereabouts. "It's sure a nice day on this island of... Island of..."

"Islands," Jim explained.

"I fell from the sky and I have great magical powers," exclaimed Malcolm.

Looking at Monday's and Wednesday's expressions of disbelief, Jim thought it best to humor Malcolm and said, "Really! That is extraordinary. Your parents must be very proud of you."

"What tribe are you from?"

Jim grinned, "I'm just a tourist. I don't believe that the indigenous people here distinguish themselves through tribal affiliations, but I could be wrong. You might ask the mayor."

Malcolm smiled, "Mayor! Mayor of... Mayor of..."

"Mayors... You sure have a funny way speaking. Where are you really from?"

"We're locals."

"Oh. How nice. That explains the language barriers."

"Where are you from?" asked Malcolm.

"New York. We're staying through Sunday."

"Then you're not cannibals?"

"I can't tell you that," said Jim after his wife shook her head at him.

"Are you bank robbers?" Malcolm inquired.

"I'm a commodities broker," Jim replied and confused Malcolm to new levels.

"What do you do?" Jim asked.

Malcolm muttered, "I'm, uh, broker..."

"Really? What do you trade?"

Malcolm was just trying to confess that he was broker than anyone he ever knew, but the question threw him off. "I trade, everything, and again, nothing."

"Ah ha! Yes, I've heard that can be quite lucrative. And where are you staying?"

"Hmm?" Malcolm squeaked.

"On the island..." Jim clarified. "Where are you staying?"

"Oh, we just have a little place on the beach."

"Private?"

"Yes, very."

"That's nice. We're up at the King's Inn."

"Oh! How do you like it?"

"Well, the accommodations are marvelous, but the natural scenery here is truly incredible. It's no wonder the island is so exclusive," Jim said with a smile.

"No, duh!"

"I never thought anything could be worth four thousand dollars a day, but seeing is believing," Jim said as he looked at the surrounding wildlife.

Four grand a day? Malcolm knew what to say, "Yeah, it's worth it alright. I'll say!"

"Well, it was nice meeting you. We have to get back to the hotel for brunch. It's highly recommended back home. Banana pancakes that melt in your mouth," Jim said cordially.

"Maybe we'll check it out later."

"Okay, well, maybe we'll see you 'round. Have fun."

The family left and Matilda stood staring at Malcolm, "Four thousand dollars a day!" she said.

"Come on," said Malcolm, "He was either joking or high. Or else he really was a local. What a great sense of humor."

"Well," said Matilda scratching her head, "What's so funny about four thousand dollars a day?"

"It's not what he said, it's the way he said it."

"Oh, hm hm hm," she laughed with a phony annoying ...non-laugh.

"At least we know we're not stranded here alone," said Malcolm, a little irritated.

"So what are you saying?" asked Matilda, angry about some damn thing.

Malcolm knew he had to find the right words and only the right words to avoid an argument. He also knew that the right words didn't exist. It seemed wise to stay quiet. Silence, of course, would also create some friction, but it would limit the bloodshed. He started walking away. That's right, he was doing that typical male-avoiding-bloodshed-by-walking-away-from-a-direct-question thing. He had no choice.

"You always do this!" shouted Matilda, "Where are you going?"

"Just looking for a high cliff, dear," Malcolm mumbled.

Damn it. Malcolm began his ascent up the hill past the source of the waterfalls. The path was mostly jungle stuff; vines, trees, tarantulas, mongeese, civilization deprivation teams. Malcolm wished he had a machete but he had only his dull wit to combat the primitive treacheries. Fortunately, his dull wit was sufficient and he managed to make his way to the top of a pinnacle that overlooked most of the island.

He could see the beach where they spent the night and he also saw the tops of some very impressive hotels peeking out of the trees on the other side of the island.

"Mati! Mati!" he yelled, "Matimatimati!"

She walked up to him hoping for the opportunity to shove him off the edge of the cliff, but saw the hotels and thought there still might be hope.

"What are they?" she asked.

"Big ol' concrete huts," Malcolm quickly responded.

"No, what city?" she clarified.

Malcolm scratched his unshaven chin even though he knew it wouldn't get him anywhere, "I do not know what city they are in, but I know they are not in Nowheresville."

"Should we go down and find out where we are, you jerk?"

"Yup," said Malc, and they were off. They happened to find a trail that led them past a heliport and straight to the hotels. There were three sets of resorts, each more elaborate than the next.

On the water were about twenty thatched roof huts sitting on stilts. Each bungalow rested above a crystalline palette of powder blue water. Below the rooms were myriads of colorful tropical fish. Waiters and waitresses delivered drinks and gourmet dishes through the cove to the huts in small canoes.

Beautiful people dangled their feet off the edges of the decks in front of their lanais. Some of them jumped into the warm blue water sending ripples across the tranquil bay. Waves formed perfect curls on the barrier reef at the edge of island.

Malcolm sat down on the beach and soaked up the peaceful sounds of small waves breaking on the soft white sand. Matilda sat down beside him, "This must be heaven."

It was too good to be true, he couldn't accept it. Something was just wrong. Suddenly he saw someone and he knew he must be dreaming. It was Sharon. Sharon from the warehouse fire, and the restaurant fire, and the big ol' fire in his heart. He closed his eyes for a minute and tried to convince himself that he was just imagining the whole thing. When he opened them again, she was gone. Closing his eyes was usually a pretty safe option. Damn.

The delusions amounted to sensory overload for Malcolm. Imagine breathing in the warm tropical wind, the sand in your toes, the endless expanse of clear blue water before your eyes, all topped off with the love of your life there and gone with a blink of the eye. It was too much for him, he ran off into the jungle. It wasn't a wimpy getaway, he really ran like a tough guy. Matilda didn't follow. He wandered through the jungle just trying to understand what was happening to him. He wasn't sure if he was dreaming or insane.

He was asking himself that very question when a strange voice spoke to him, "You okay, pal?"

He looked up and saw a nice old man sitting on a rock staring at him.

"I don't know. Where am I?" Malcolm asked.

The old man chuckled, "Hard to believe, isn't it? Did you ever know such colors existed? The air, the life! It's all here. The island doesn't have an official name, but we have many names for it here. Serenity, Bellissimo, Bonita, I like 'Island of Dreams'. When did you arrive?"

"Last night."

"Last night? No... The chopper comes in at 10:00 a.m. and leaves at 5:00 p.m. No one arrives at night."

Malcolm didn't want to argue, "Yeah, 10:00 a.m. this morning. I just traveled all night, so it seemed like I got here last night."

It was only 9:00 a.m. but the old guy didn't let on. "Where are you staying?" he asked.

"At the King's Inn. They've got an excellent breakfast."

"Oh, yeah... Steak and eggs, the whole deal," said the friendly man.

"Best steak I ever had," said Malcolm.

The old man shook his head, "The last time we had steak on this island was 1945."

Malcolm sensed doubt of his credibility, "I like it well aged."

"Yeah? What's your story, pal? You didn't get here by boat, did you?"

"Yeah, actually, Olympic rowing team. Just rowed in. Whoo! Pooped!"

"Uh huh? You a friend of Bud?"

"Bud? You know Bud?"

"Oh, yeah. Hired him this morning. My last driver took off for the mainland last week and I needed a replacement."

"Well, Bud can do just about anything," said Malcolm.

"How 'bout you?" asked the old man, "What can you do?"

"I've got money."

"Everybody on this island has money. Except for the locals."

"Maybe I can help out," Malcolm said.

"Help out? With money? When you got paradise, you don't need money, but the offer's nice."

"You have a bank here?"

"Yeah, we have a couple local offices that have a few basic services."

"Can I make a deposit?"

"Sure. You can even buy an old man a beer. Mind you though, I don't drink before ten."

Malcolm laughed, "Well, it's after ten somewhere."

The two gentlemen spent a few hours sipping beers, munching fried papayas, and swapping tales of dirty deeds. In that relaxed peaceful setting, Malcolm was beginning to shed the bonds of civilization and felt with his heart once again. His heart... it was pumping more than just blood for the first time in years. The strength of his youthful heart was returning with the ability to feel and express passion. He had to share it with someone. He needed to go back to find Matilda.

"Well, sir," said Malcolm, "It was an honor and a pleasure. You remind me of a guy I knew back home. It's funny, because he was an old homeless man, but, it sounds ridiculous, but he motivated me to keep moving."

"You'll meet a few people like that from time to time. The really funny thing is, they're always there, but they don't jump in until they have to. Once in a while you might want to offer them something of yourself in return."

Malcolm gave that one some thought.

His new friend smiled, "Son, you look you have someone on your mind, and she sure ain't no old man."

The conversation slipped into Malcolm's head between thoughts of the women he'd met and he smiled back at the old man, shook his hand, and got to back on his feet. He ran to the beach near the hotels looking for his future soulmate. When he found her, his heart stopped beating completely. Matilda was walking hand in hand with a guy wearing some of those skin tight swimmy butt duds and a gold ankle bracelet on his, well, on his ankle.

Malcolm tried not to let it bother him. Matilda didn't owe him anything, he didn't deserve her... Still, it was rough, he was crushed. He sat down in the sand and looked out across the ocean. In the whole world, he finally had everything he thought he'd ever need and yet he had nothing. He was stuck with himself and he couldn't decide if it was heaven or hell.

"Malcolm?"

He laughed. He remembered that voice. It was heaven. Looking up from the sands he saw the most beautiful woman he could ever imagine. It was Sharon.

"Malcolm!" she smiled. "You look great for a dead guy."

"Thanks. A little fresh air does wonders," he said.

"How did you get here?" Sharon asked, "I mean, I really thought you were dead."

Looking into her eyes, he wondered if she would have shed a tear at his funeral. His memories of her beauty came back to him. "I hope I'm not disappointing you," he said.

"Oh, God, no! This is good!" Her eyes were filling as she spoke, "You saved me! And I never got a chance to thank you."

"Yeah, actually you did," said Malcolm.

Sitting down beside him, she asked, "What do you mean? How?"

"Well, I saw you with that waiter after the fire, and I saw you watching him at dinner. I wanted to see you happy and I think you met a good guy."

"Rex?" she asked, "He's okay, kind of self absorbed. He brought me out here to impress me or something."

"A waiter brought you here? I'd be impressed."

"Oh... His family has money. I think they sent him to charm school or something, but he's really pretty shallow."

"So why'd you come here with him?"

"I kind of owe it to him... He saved the only picture I have of my baby," Sharon said sadly.

"He saved your locket?"

"Yeah, after you fell off the balcony he saw it and grabbed it and brought it back to me. He tried to save you Malcolm, he really did."

Malcolm shook his head and looked down at the sand. "I saw the two of you standing in the parking lot and I threw the locket at your feet. I think I probably hit him in the head, though. Sorry about that. It was kind of mean and I shouldn't have laughed, or thrown it so hard," he explained.

"You? He told me..." she looked into Malcolm's eyes and knew he was telling the truth. "Men!" she yelled.

"I'm sorry," he said.

"Not you."

"Oh. All the other men on the planet?"

"How could I be so stupid? I should have known that rich brat would never do anything for anyone but himself."

"You want to dump him?"

"Yeah!" she said, without giving it much thought.

"Cool."

"We're leaving tonight and after we get home, I'll never talk to him again."

"I just got here. Why don't you stay here with me for a few weeks?"

Her face was red with anger as she insisted, "Well, I'd like to shoot him, but that would be wrong." She shook her head and looked for weapon, "I have to shoot him!"

With a calming smile, Malcolm suggested, "No, let's just go to the other side of the island until his chopper takes off. He'll go nuts trying to find you."

Sharon laughed, "A few weeks, huh?"

"If you want to leave sooner, I won't try to force you to stay, but if you think about the odds against me meeting you here, you gotta believe Fate's involved one way or another."

Sharon smiled, "Well, I guess I could call my boss. She'd probably understand."

Malcolm was ecstatic, "Look, I'm ecstatic!"

Taking her hand, he looked into her eyes and tried pulling her towards the water.

"Wait!" she said with a seductive grin. "How did you get here? ...The last time I saw you, you couldn't even afford bus fare to the beach."

Malcolm blushed, "You knew?"

"Yeah, but I didn't want to say anything because you were doing so well without any money. I remember wondering how you were going to pay for dinner. Assuming you were going to pay for dinner." Suddenly she turned pale, "You didn't start that fire to get out of paying..."

"No! No, no, no," Malcolm laughed, "But... No, I would never do anything like that, somebody could have been hurt."

Gradually, Sharon began to relax and started walking towards the water with Malcolm. She looked at him, then at the sand and said, "Well, I'm glad you're okay. But, I still want to know how you ended up on the Island of Dreams."

"What kind of an idiot names a place 'Island of Dreams' is what I want to know," Malcolm replied.

"It's a popular name among idiots. How'd you get here?" she snapped back with feigned anger.

"You really want to know?"

Looking back towards the hotels, Sharon said with a hint of genuine frustration, "If you're not going to talk, I can still ride back home with Rex."

"No! Listen, it's, it's just kind of hard to believe, but it's true," he said like maybe she'd let him off without an explanation. Instead, she raised her eyebrows to frightening new heights.

"Okay, I'll explain it to you," he continued, "But the weather here really is fantastic."

She stopped in her tracks and yelled, "Malcolm! Tell me!"

"Well, I stole a plane and flew here."

"You stole a plane?"

"Yeah."

"Um hmm. Okay, and say I believe you stole a plane, how are you going to stay here for three weeks without any money?" she asked, still smiling curiously.

"I, uh, the weather sure is nice. What kind of flower is that? Is that a dandelion? It's beautiful!"

Sharon stopped and began to walk away.

He took her hand and said, "Okay! What's the rush, you'll find out eventually. I just really want you to know that I'm a pretty nice guy, even if I did rob a bank."

"Alright, alright. Fine. Don't tell me. You've obviously got something going on, but I don't think you can prove that you robbed a bank."

He thought briefly and consequently created something to say, "You're probably right. I hope you're right. The army isn't going to tell anybody that they lost a Stealth bomber, and the people at the bank don't want to get me in trouble. I can show you the money!"

"How much money?" she asked to keep the conversation interesting.

"I've got so much money that you and I can fly to Paris and New York and New Zealand and back here to see any kind of art you want," he admitted enthusiastically.

Her eyes sparkled, "That's definitely going to take money."

"I got so much money! What if I could buy you a mansion on the Florida keys and in Denver?"

She laughed and clapped her hands together, "Go for it, cowboy!"

"I can to do it! You like diamonds?"

"Better than coal," she said as she sifted a handful of sand.

"I can buy both! You want to..."

She looked into his eyes and interrupted him, "You know what I really want?"

Looking back into her eyes, he held her shoulders and answered her, "Cash."

"No. Stupe. I want to meet a guy who really loves me, somebody that I can love."

A feeling stirred in Malcolm that he hadn't felt in a long time. He looked at Sharon and said, "That night at the restaurant... I know this doesn't mean much, but that night at the restaurant, I think I fell in love with you. I haven't had that many relationships, so maybe it's just a common feeling for most people. That night I felt like you were a part of me, and that was the only part of me that I cared about. I feel that way now. I don't know if love's got anything to do with it, but I do want to find out. I know I'll never hurt you, or lie to you, or use you, or kick you out of bed for eating crackers. I just know that I want to be with you. And as far as you loving me... You don't feel like puking, do you?"

She wasn't sure if he was serious but she covered her mouth and laughed, "No, not right now. I just want an honest answer. How did you get here?"

"I robbed a bank and stole a plane."

"I'm serious!"

"So am I! I just don't know if I can prove it," he said beginning to doubt his own story.

"Look... Okay... Here's the deal..." she shook her head, "You robbed a bank?"

"I tried to back out, but I got shot and I guess I was a little angry. Still I was nice about it. Honest, I was the only one who got hurt," he said as he rubbed the wound on his shoulder and thought about the magic charley horse his volunteer father gave him. A coin toss would decide whether the bum would get a million bucks in the mail.

She looked into Malcolm's eyes and said softly, "I don't know why I trust you."

"It must be my great body!" he shouted.

Before she could disagree, he flexed, and turned, and he ran down to the water. After a short hesitation, she chased him down and took his hand. She rubbed the deep cut on his magical charley horse shoulder and gave his shoulder a gentle kiss.

They walked together across the soft white sand towards the other side of the island. As they strolled, Malcolm explained all the details of the robbery and the restaurant fire. She wasn't convinced that he was telling the truth, but it was a good story and she actually began to enjoy his company. Gradually, she even began to forget where she was and what she was doing. She was forgetting herself.

They arrived at the beach and kicked back on the sand. Either she was dizzy from the tropics or Malcolm's sense of humor was improving because she was laughing at just about everything he said. They relaxed and talked for a while then Sharon rolled over and closed her eyes. Big blue, beautiful eyes. Malcolm started to doze off himself when he was startled by the sound of a diesel engine. Damn! Damn! Damn! He closed his eyes. If it was a dream, he didn't want to wake up, and if it was some kind of giant steam roller that was about to crush him, he couldn't think of a better time to go. The sound came closer, got louder. He could smell the exhaust.

It wasn't a dream, and he was going to die. The last image that he had in his mind was Sharon's beautiful smile, her eyes, and her warmth. He smiled and waited. And waited, and waited, and frowned. Suddenly, the motor stopped. Malcolm opened his eyes and saw Sharon looking at him with a pleasant smile.

"Drink?" she asked.

Malcolm was confused, she motioned for him to look over his shoulder. It was Bud and he was driving a small tractor pulling a portable beverage bar. "Bud?" Malcolm asked.

"Yup. Where's Matilda?"

Looking back towards the hotels, Malcolm answered, "She went on to a better life."

Bud eyeballed the couple and thought about the man with the ankle bracelet and Matilda in the hotel. He smiled and said, "Looks like you did too. I'm celebrating the first permanent job I had in two years. Sounds like my new boss and your old dad are good friends."

Bud paused for a second, then raised his index finger, "Your momma musta been a white woman! Well, your Dad will be glad to know that you landed on your feet. He told me to deliver a couple of these Piña Coladas to you. Oh, and he said to tell you that he's got more money than Moses, so you can keep your piddly 3 mil and find out how much good it does you. 'A little is all you need,' he says."

Malcolm was piecing it all together, as well as he could.

"I, on the other hand, have to work for a livin', so if you feel like giving me a tip..." Bud paused, "Ah, Hell with it. Keep the tips. I'm happy to be working. I owe *you* for helping me land work."

"Well, congratulations, Bud. This is Sharon."

"Howdy!" said Bud as he handed them the drinks.

"Howdy, Bud!" replied Sharon.

"Well, I'll be gittin' on and let you two continue with your time together. See ya 'round. Just gimme a holler if you need anything."

Bud drove off leaving Malcolm and Sharon sitting quietly together on the beach. Their silence was interrupted as a helicopter flew overhead. Blowing a good bye kiss to one of its wealthy passengers, Sharon gave up her search for the perfect man. At least she had Malcolm. Malcolm had some extra wealth of his own that he needed to send back to his home town charities. He'd tackle that challenge after a little relaxation.

The copter slowly vanished on the horizon as the sun began to set. Entranced by the peace and beauty that surrounded him, Malcolm didn't notice a small life raft slowly approaching the island carrying two young denizens. If he had noticed, he wouldn't have cared. Malcolm Tent was in love.

Sharon sat and thought about her new friend. He was different, interesting, he wasn't too bright, but he was truly in love with her. Only time would tell if they were a match, but at that moment, they were sitting together on a beautiful Pacific island. Maybe he wasn't the guy she imagined or promised her friends, but he was one in a million, and she really warmed up around him. Smiling, laughing to herself, she made a decision. She decided she'd give him a chance.

They sat through the panoramic tropical sunset surrounded by the sounds of ocean waves breaking on soft clean sand as exotic brilliantly colored birds sailed through the gentle swaying coconut trees. Cool evening winds caressed their bodies as they thought only of each other. The sun slipped down below a rainbow of thin clouds. Time passed while new light filled the skies, new dreams filled their hearts and minds, and they fell asleep together on the warm island sand beneath a blanket of endless stars.

www.ingramcontent.com/pod-product-compliance
Lightning Source LLC
Chambersburg PA
CBHW022353040426
42450CB00005B/166